the Irish Heritage Cookbook

the Irish Heritage Cookbook

Margaret M. Johnson

CHRONICLE BOOKS

SAN FRANCISCO

Library of Congress Cataloging-in-Publication Data:
Johnson, Margaret M., 1944–
    The Irish heritage cookbook / by Margaret M. Johnson.
    304 p.   20.2 x 23.4 cm.
    Includes index.
    ISBN 0-8118-1992-2 (pb)
    1. Cookery, Irish.   I. Title.
TX717.5.J64 1999
641.59417—dc21   98-4283
                                      CIP

Printed in the United States of America.

Designed by Poulson/Gluck Design

Distributed in Canada by Raincoast Books
9050 Shaughnessy Street
Vancouver, British Columbia V6P 6E5

10 9 8 7 6 5 4 3

Chronicle Books LLC
85 Second Street
San Francisco, California 94105

www.chroniclebooks.com

Acknowledgments

Thanks to the chefs, chef-proprietors, hoteliers, and good old-fashioned Irish cooks who contributed recipes and advice to this book; to Joe Lynam, publicity officer, Bord Fáilte, Dublin, who introduced me to *Bon Appétit*; to Karen Kaplan, senior editor, *Bon Appétit,* who introduced me to my agent, Madeleine Morel; to Madeleine, who guided me through the proposal; to Bill LeBlond, senior editor, Chronicle Books, for his nurturing hand; to Phil McGauran, An Bord Bia, New York; Georgina O'Sullivan and Hylda Adams, Bord Bia, Dublin; Aine McDonogh and Annette Mahon, Belvedere Communications; Fitzpatrick's Manhattan Hotel; Maebeth Fenton, the Northern Ireland Tourist Board; Fionnuala Jay-O'Boyle, A Taste of Ulster; to Carl Hawker for his continued computer wizardry; to Sandy Andreoli and Connie McGlew, for their recipe testing; and to my family—Carl, Mark, and Kate—who helped sample recipes for dishes like pureed parsnips, paupiettes of sole, and pheasant with kale when all they really wanted for dinner was pizza.

For my parents
and grandparents

⫯⫯

the McGlews,
Barrys, Sullivans,
and Crowleys

⫯⫯

thanks for my Irish heritage

Contents

6 ⇶ From the Wild 174

Introduction

The food of Ireland is like the Irish people: unpretentious and homely.
Simple and succulent dishes have been a tradition for centuries and are still
an important part of Irish life. What Gernow, Second Justice of the Province
of Munster, said in 1620 could still be quoted with truth today:

"What feeds on earth, or flies in the air,

or swimmeth in the water,

lo, Ireland hath it of her own."

THEODORA FITZGIBBON, *A TASTE OF IRELAND*

I grew up in an Irish-American household in a town heavily populated by families with surnames like Murphy and Lynch, McLaughlin and O'Brien. All of my friends had at least one set of grandparents who came from the "old country," and most of us could recite the place names of parishes, villages, and counties they emigrated from as easily as the times table. There were two Catholic churches in town, familiarly known as the Irish Church and the French Church, although each had an official name and parish school to go with it.

We worshipped at the Irish Church, of course, and went to the Irish school. We celebrated Saint Patrick's Day as if it were a holy day and national holiday rolled into one, had the day off from school, and performed some kind of pageant or Irish show the night before. When March 17 fell on a Friday during Lent, we were automatically exempt from fast or abstinence on that day, which meant we were able to eat what I thought was surely the most revered Irish meal in the world: corned beef and cabbage. Imagine eating meat on Friday! And during Lent! We interpreted this as a sign that the meal was heavenly endorsed.

Aside from the traditional Saint Patrick's Day meal, we never thought much about Irish food. We ate wonderful food like the kind Theodora FitzGibbon, the first to acknowledge Irish food as a culinary entity, called "unpretentious and homely, simple and succulent." We didn't eat food like German sauerkraut, Italian cacciatore, or French cassoulet. We were meat and potatoes people and made no excuses for it.

When my grandmother Minnie O'Sullivan came over from the village of Bounard, in the town of Rathmore, County Kerry, in 1898, she arrived not with a trunk full of recipes, but with a tradition of cooking that was based on the availability of ingredients rather than on techniques of preparation. Potatoes were boiled and mashed, meats roasted or stewed. Fish was grilled or cured, fruits baked in crust or mixed with cream. My grandmother's food was simple and unpretentious.

My mother's cooking was the same. She baked apple and blueberry pies, made custards and bread and butter pudding. She made gingersnaps, oatmeal cookies, and white cake that she covered with boiled frosting. She made cranberry sauce, orange marmalade, and mustard pickle. On Fridays, she made fish chowder, and on winter nights, chicken pie with shortcrust pastry. She cooked a roast for Sunday dinner—chicken, lamb, beef, or pork—with a proper potato—baked, mashed, souffléed, or new—to accompany it.

We had a milkman who delivered milk and cream three times a week from Webster's Dairy, and an egg man named Mr. Garand who brought fresh eggs and chickens weekly from his farm, and for special holidays we had fresh-killed turkey from Molloy's Farm. We bought bacon and butter at Kennedy's Butter Store, vegetables in season from Knight's or Pettingill's farmstands, and fish at Goodwin's Fish Market. My mother prepared all these fresh foods simply and unpretentiously. She was cooking Irish.

When I first visited Ireland in 1984, one of my first meals was a toasted cheese and tomato sandwich at a seaside pub in Lahinch, County Clare. I felt at home immediately! For dinner that night, I ate overly fried fillets of plaice with chips at an Eyre Square restaurant in Galway, where the waitress told me to sprinkle malt vinegar over the lot. "That's the way we do it here," she said, and thanks to my Catholic school training in obedience, I doused the fish and French fries with the vinegar as instructed.

When I returned to Ireland in 1991, and a dozen times more since then, I was pleasantly surprised at the turn Irish food had taken. Like the growing flock of visitors who head for the Emerald Isle today, I found that Irish cuisine had been undergoing a quiet revolution, a culinary renaissance of sorts, since those soggy fish-and-chips days of the 1980s.

Bright young Irish chefs, trained at world-class cooking schools and apprenticed with master French chefs, began to return to Ireland to work magic with their country's rich and natural native bounty: fresh produce, succulent meats, handmade cheeses, and fresh-caught fish from the Atlantic Ocean, the Irish Sea, and Ireland's pristine loughs and rivers.

Though cabbage, potatoes, fish, and stews are still important threads in the tapestry of Irish cuisine, Irish fare today is much more than soda bread and corned beef and cabbage washed down with a pint. Contemporary Irish food sparkles with a delightful combination of Continental sophistication and country charm.

The Irish Heritage Cookbook offers a new perspective on what Irish cooking is all about, along with a new appreciation of the foods that fed our ancestors, and more than two hundred recipes for simple foods reinvented for modern tastes. Best of all, as the rest of the world is beginning to discover, you'll be happy to learn that there is indeed an Irish cuisine. *The Irish Heritage Cookbook* will affirm its place among the great foods of the world.

Bain taitneamh as do bhéile! Bon appétit.

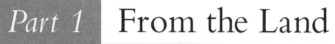

Part 1　From the Land

It's the Land. It is our wisdom,

It's the Land that shines us through,

It's the Land. It feeds our children.

It's the Land. You cannot own the Land.

The Land owns you.

DOUGIE MACLEAN, "SOLID GROUND"

⬦⬥

Food, we know, is essential to life, and of all the factors that influence a country's food, the most fundamental is the land itself. For the Irish, from the early Celts who first cultivated it to the millions who had to flee it, the land has been both a blessing and a curse.

Once potatoes were introduced at the end of the sixteenth century, the country's mild, moist climate and rich soil made them a natural crop and one that was easily cultivated year-round on even the smallest piece of land. Millions of Irish "cottiers," farmers huddling as renters on the tiny strips of land they tilled, subsisted almost exclusively on potatoes. It has been estimated that the average peasant family consumed ten pounds of potatoes a day and sometimes managed for an entire year on a one-acre yield. The Irish eventually became totally dependent on the potato, which provided a remarkably healthy and economical diet when supplemented by oatmeal and dairy products.

It was this dependency that would eventually lead to disaster when the potato blight struck in 1845. One million Irish died from the ravages of the famine, and another million left the country in one of Europe's greatest waves of immigration. By 1900, Ireland had fewer citizens than it had one hundred years earlier.

Although potatoes are the food most frequently associated with Ireland and its people, many other vegetables date from earlier times. Leeks, for example, are one of the country's oldest foods, and carrots, watercress, nettles, and garlic have been eaten since prehistoric times.

"The Irish feed much upon parsnip," a historian wrote in 1673, and most Irish households ate cabbage, onions, and cauliflower as well, with turnips thrown in for good measure. As with most foods that have a national identity, root vegetables, in particular, which were easy to grow and have excellent keeping qualities, are Irish favorites.

Today, there are millions of people around the world who claim Irish ancestry, and countless others who simply have fallen in love with the people, the land, and now the food. Add any of these traditional and contemporary potato and vegetable dishes to a meal, close your eyes, and you'll think you're there!

Colcannon

〰〰 In the old country, many traditional dishes are associated with festivals and feast days from both the Celtic calendar of the Druids and the newer Christian calendar. Colcannon (from the Irish *cal ceann fhionn,* or "white-headed cabbage"), a mashed-potato dish flavored with kale or cabbage, is the main dish of the Halloween (All Hallows' Eve) dinner. Its origins may lie in the need to use up the last leafy vegetables in the fall garden. In keeping with tradition, a carefully wrapped gold ring is placed in one of the bowls, and the diner who finds it is thought likely to marry within the coming year. Colcannon is turning up more and more on menus on both sides of the Atlantic, and like many Irish dishes, it is celebrated in song.

*Did you ever eat colcannon
When 'twas made with
 yellow cream
And the kale and praties
 blended
Like the picture in a dream?*

*Did you ever take a forkful
And dip it in the lake
Of heather-flavored butter
That your mother used
 to make?*

*Oh, you did, yes you did!
So did he and so did I,
And the more I think about it
Sure, the more I want to cry.*

*God be with the happy times
When trouble we had not,
And our mothers made
 colcannon
In the little three-legged pot.*

I pound cabbage, cored, quartered, and shredded
2 pounds boiling potatoes, peeled and cut into 2-inch pieces
2 small leeks (white and pale green parts only), washed and sliced
I cup milk
Salt and freshly ground pepper to taste
1/2 teaspoon ground mace
8 tablespoons (I stick) plus 2 tablespoons butter

In separate saucepans, cook the cabbage and potatoes in boiling salted water until tender, 12 to 15 minutes. Drain the cabbage and chop. Drain the potatoes and mash.

Meanwhile, in a large saucepan, combine the leeks and milk and cook over medium heat until the leeks are tender, 8 to 10 minutes.

Add the potatoes, salt, pepper, and mace to the leeks and milk and stir over low heat until well blended. Add the cabbage and 8 tablespoons butter and stir again to the consistency of mashed potatoes. Dot with remaining 2 tablespoons butter cut into small pieces. Serve at once.

Champp

Champ, a mixture of mashed potatoes and scallions that is sometimes called poundies, is served in a mound with a well of melted butter in the center. Traditionally, it's eaten with a spoon, starting from the outside of the mound and dipping each spoonful into the butter. In the old days, the tool used for mashing potatoes was a pestle-shaped wooden implement called a beetle. Thus the old Irish poem.

Serves 4 as a side dish

2 pounds boiling potatoes, peeled and cut into 2-inch pieces
1/2 cup milk, light cream, or half-and-half
6 tablespoons butter
1 1/3 cups chopped fresh chives or scallions
Salt and freshly ground pepper to taste

Cook the potatoes in boiling salted water until tender, 12 to 15 minutes. Drain and mash.

Meanwhile, in a medium saucepan, combine the milk and 4 tablespoons of butter. Heat over medium heat until the butter is melted. Add the chives or scallions, reduce heat to a simmer, and cook until the chives or scallions are soft, 2 to 4 minutes.

Add the potatoes, salt, and pepper to the milk mixture and stir until blended. To serve, spoon the champ into a deep bowl, make a well in the center, and top with the remaining butter. Serve at once.

*There was an old woman
that lived in a lamp;
she had no room
to beetle her champ.
She's up'd with her beetle
and broke the lamp,
and now she has room
to beetle her champ.*

Boxty

Makes about 16 pancakes

⇵⇵ Coming from County Kerry, my grandmother probably wouldn't have been familiar with boxty, a potato dish popular in Counties Leitrim, Mayo, Fermanagh, and Donegal. The word is derived from the Irish *bacstaí,* relating to the traditional cooking of potatoes on the hob (*bac* in Irish) over an open fire (*staí*). My mother never made boxty, and it wasn't until 1992 when I was wandering around Dublin's Temple Bar area that I came across Gallagher's Boxty House (20–21 Temple Bar), a restaurant specializing in traditional Irish food. Ever since Gallagher's started serving a contemporary rendition of this potato pancake (left) stuffed with a variety of fillings—beef, lamb, chicken, even bacon and cabbage—the old-fashioned dish has gained a new legion of fans. This version is more traditional.

Gallagher's Boxty:

To make a version of Gallagher's boxty, which has an almost crêpe-like consistency, grate all the potatoes into a blender or food processor and process until smooth. Add the remaining ingredients and blend to the consistency of pancake batter. Cook as for Boxty, then stuff with diced Beef and Guinness Casserole (page 65) or diced Bacon and Cabbage (page 39) and roll like a crêpe. Makes 4 large pancakes.

I pound boiling potatoes, peeled
3/4 cup all-purpose flour
I teaspoon baking soda
1/2 teaspoon salt
1/2 cup buttermilk
2 tablespoons vegetable oil for cooking

Cut half the potatoes into 2-inch pieces. Cook the cut-up potatoes in boiling salted water until tender, 12 to 15 minutes. Drain and mash. Transfer to a bowl.

Using the large holes of a box grater, grate the remaining potatoes into a small bowl lined with cheesecloth. Squeeze the cloth to extract as much of the starchy liquid as possible, catching it in the bowl. Add the grated potatoes to the mashed potatoes, then sift the flour, baking soda, and salt together over them. Add the potato starch liquid and buttermilk. Mix well. →

Brush a large nonstick skillet with vegetable oil and heat it over medium-high heat. Drop the potato mixture, a tablespoon at a time, onto the skillet; do not crowd the pan. Flatten each cake with the back of a spatula, then cook on each side until browned and slightly raised, about 3 to 4 minutes per side. Repeat until all the mixture is used. Serve immediately, or transfer the cakes to a baking sheet and keep warm in a preheated 200°F oven.

Esther Dunne's Potato Cakes

At Dublin's Oliver St. John Gogarty Restaurant, across the street from Gallagher's at 58–59 Fleet Street, the anecdotes on the menu are as entertaining as the choices. While deciding whether to have Seafood Molly Malone or Sackville Street Casserole, you can read about the famous Irish surgeon/poet/politician/imbiber/raconteur for whom the restaurant is named, and learn about Temple Bar history as well. Esther Dunne, for whom these potato cakes are named, was a nineteenth-century provision dealer with a shop next door at No. 57. Using Esther's original recipe from 1850, the current chef at Gogarty's serves these as a first drizzled with warm cranberry sauce, but they are also delicious as a side dish with meat or fish.

Serves 4 as a first course or side dish

8 ounces boiling potatoes, peeled and cut into 2-inch pieces

3 tablespoons butter

2 tablespoons warm milk

3 tablespoons mixed minced fresh herbs such as tarragon, thyme, or marjoram, or 1 tablespoon dried

3 tablespoons minced fresh parsley or 1 tablespoon dried

1/2 tablespoon ground nutmeg

Salt and freshly ground pepper to taste

1 slice bacon, finely chopped

2 cabbage leaves, finely chopped

Flour for dredging

1 egg mixed with 2 tablespoons water

1/2 cup dried bread crumbs for dredging

2 tablespoons vegetable oil

1/2 cup whole-berry cranberry sauce, warmed (optional)

Lettuce, tomato, and cucumber for garnish (optional)

Cook the potatoes in boiling salted water until tender, 12 to 15 minutes. Drain and mash. Re-cover and return to low heat to dry out the potatoes, 2 to 3 minutes more. Remove from heat, add the butter and milk, and stir until smooth. Stir in the herbs, nutmeg, salt, and pepper. Let cool slightly, 5 to 8 minutes.

Meanwhile, in a small skillet, cook the bacon over medium heat until crisp. Stir in the cabbage and cook until wilted, 4 to 5 minutes. Add to the potato mixture and blend well.

Shape the potato mixture into 4 evenly sized cakes. Lightly dredge in flour, then coat with the egg mixture, then the bread crumbs. In a large skillet over medium-high heat, heat the oil, add the cakes, and cook until browned, 3 to 5 minutes per side. Serve immediately, or transfer to a baking sheet and keep warm in a 200°F oven.

To serve as a first course, warm the cranberry sauce in a saucepan over low heat until slightly runny, 3 to 5 minutes. Place 1 potato cake in the center of each plate, drizzle with cranberry sauce, and garnish with lettuce, tomatoes, and cucumber.

Joe Friel's Fadge

Fadge, a potato pancake, is the Northern Ireland specialty that makes a traditional Irish breakfast (eggs, bacon, black and white pudding, sausage, grilled tomatoes, and mushrooms) an Ulster Fry. Donegal native Joe Friel, who emigrated to the United States from Gweedore in 1974, is now executive banquet chef at New York's Plaza Hotel and is often called upon to prepare Irish dishes like this one for visiting dignitaries and Irish social and cultural events.

Serves 4 as a side dish

1½ pounds boiling potatoes, peeled and cut into 2-inch pieces
¼ cup milk
3 tablespoons unsalted butter
¼ cup all-purpose flour
Salt and freshly ground pepper to taste
2 tablespoons vegetable oil for frying

Cook the potatoes in boiling salted water until tender, 12 to 15 minutes. Drain and mash.

In a small saucepan, heat the milk and butter over medium-low heat until the butter is melted. Add this mixture to the potatoes, then stir in flour, salt, and pepper until well blended. Turn out onto a lightly floured board and either pat or roll the mixture into a 1/2-inch-thick circle. Using a 3-inch biscuit cutter, cut into 8 cakes.

In a large skillet over medium-high heat, heat the oil and cook the cakes until golden brown, 3 to 5 minutes per side. Serve immediately, or transfer to a baking sheet and keep warm in a 200°F oven.

Potato Soufflé

Serves 6 to 8 as a side dish

While the simplest and most popular way to cook potatoes in most Irish households is to boil them in their jackets, mashing them is a close second. My mother's mashed potatoes were virtually lump-free. Her secret: She mashed them, then took the potatoes to the back door which she'd hold slightly open with her foot, while whipping them with a wooden spoon for a minute or two. She said the air "fluffed" them, and they went directly from door to plate. They were perfect potatoes, especially good for potato soufflé, which she served for Sunday dinner and for special-occasion meals.

> 2 pounds boiling potatoes, peeled and cut into 2-inch pieces
> 3 tablespoons butter
> 1 small onion, finely chopped
> 2 tablespoons sour cream
> 2 eggs, separated
> 1/4 cup heavy (whipping) cream
> Salt and freshly ground pepper to taste
> 3 tablespoons minced fresh parsley, thyme, or tarragon or 1 tablespoon dried
> 1 cup shredded Parmesan cheese

Cook the potatoes in boiling salted water until tender, 12 to 15 minutes. Drain and mash.

Preheat the oven to 350°F. Liberally butter a 6-cup soufflé dish.

In a small pan, cook the butter and onions over medium heat until the onions are soft, 4 to 5 minutes. Add the onion to the mashed potatoes, then stir in the sour cream, egg yolks, and cream. Season with salt and pepper. Add the herbs and shredded cheese and stir until smooth.   →

In a medium bowl, beat the egg whites until stiff, glossy peaks form. Stir 2 tablespoons of the egg whites into the potato mixture to loosen it, then fold in the rest. Pour into the prepared dish and bake until golden brown, 20 to 25 minutes (check after 15 minutes).

Duchess Potatoes

⌇⌇ Duchess potatoes are great for special occasions, and are especially impressive when piped around dishes like Fillets of Sole Bonne Femme (page 155), Chef Sean Dempsey's signature dish at Fitzpatrick's Castle Hotel (Killiney, County Dublin). Duchess potatoes are also a nice accompaniment to heartier fare like roast beef or lamb.

Serves 8 as a side dish

> 2 pounds boiling potatoes, peeled and cut into 2-inch pieces
>
> 3 tablespoons butter
>
> 2 whole eggs, beaten
>
> 2 egg yolks, beaten
>
> 1/4 cup shredded Parmesan cheese
>
> Salt and freshly ground pepper to taste

In a large saucepan, cook the potatoes in boiling salted water until tender, 12 to 15 minutes. Drain. Using a food mill or ricer, process the potatoes. Add the butter, eggs, egg yolks, cheese, salt, and pepper to the potatoes and beat with a wooden spoon until well blended.

Preheat the oven to 425°F. Lightly grease a baking sheet.

Using a pastry bag fitted with a 1/2-inch tube, pipe potato mixture into 8 mounds on the prepared pan. (To make ahead, lightly brush with melted butter and refrigerate for up to 2 hours.) Bake until lightly browned, 10 to 15 minutes.

Baked Parsnips

⇔⇔ For centuries, parsnips have been enjoyed in rural Ireland, where they provided variety in winter. While most cooks think of them as an ingredient to flavor soups and stews, on recent trips to Ireland I've found chefs serving them almost as frequently as potatoes and carrots. They can be baked, fried, or pureed, and their sweet flavor combines well with other vegetables.

2$\frac{1}{2}$ pounds parsnips, peeled and sliced

3 tablespoons homemade chicken stock or canned low-salt chicken broth

Salt and freshly ground pepper to taste

Pinch of ground nutmeg

4 tablespoons butter

Cook the parsnips in gently boiling water until just tender, about 15 minutes. Drain.

In an ovenproof casserole dish, combine the parsnips and stock or broth. Sprinkle with salt, pepper, and nutmeg. Dot with butter and bake until browned and tender, 30 to 35 minutes.

Pureed Parsnips

Parsnips combine deliciously with root vegetables like carrots and potatoes, and as I recently discovered to my surprise, apples. Cooked together in stock and pureed, this mixture is a flavorful alternative to plain mashed potatoes and especially good with roasted duck.

I pound parsnips, peeled and sliced

I carrot, peeled and sliced

I large russet potato, peeled and cut into 2-inch pieces

I Granny Smith apple, peeled, cored, and chopped

I cup homemade chicken stock or canned low-salt chicken broth

1/2 teaspoon ground allspice

2 tablespoons butter

Salt and freshly ground pepper to taste

In a large saucepan, combine the parsnips, carrot, potato, apple, and stock or broth. Bring to a boil, cover, reduce heat, and simmer until tender, 15 to 20 minutes, stirring once or twice. Drain and let cool.

Transfer the mixture to a blender or food processor. Add the allspice, butter, salt, and pepper and puree until smooth.

Parsnip Cakes

Serves 4 as a side dish

⇕⇕ I've always loved potato cakes, so when I was served parsnip cakes at a friend's country kitchen in Cork I wondered why I hadn't thought of this delicious idea myself.

1 pound parsnips, peeled and sliced

2 tablespoons all-purpose flour

2 tablespoons butter, melted

Pinch of ground mace

1/4 teaspoon salt

1/4 teaspoon freshly ground pepper

Flour for dredging

1 egg mixed with 2 tablespoons water

1/2 cup dried bread crumbs

2 tablespoons vegetable oil

Cook the parsnips in boiling salted water until tender, 12 to 15 minutes. Remove from heat and let sit for 5 minutes. Drain and mash.

Add the flour, melted butter, mace, salt, and pepper to the parsnips and blend well. Shape the mixture into 4 evenly sized cakes. Lightly dredge in the flour. Coat evenly in the egg mixture, then the bread crumbs. In a large skillet over medium-high heat, heat the oil and cook the cakes until golden brown, 3 to 5 minutes per side. Serve immediately, or transfer to a baking sheet and keep warm in a 200°F oven.

Note:

The Pureed Parsnips on page 16 can also be made into parsnip cakes. Prepare as directed, then shape into cakes and cook as above.

The Potato Famine and Irish Emigration

§§

The fungal disease that hit the Irish potato crop, the only staple food of the majority of the population, was first reported on September 6, 1845, in the *Waterford Freeman* and the *Dublin Evening Post*. The autumn arrival of the disease and its irregular spread during 1845 meant that the loss of foodstuff was relatively small, the main loss coming from the rotting of tubers before and after harvest.

Famine conditions were not noted until the beginning of 1846. The disease arrived full-blown early that year, and the shortage of seed tubers also resulted in a reduction of the area planted, so that the whole potato crop was destroyed by August, wiping out the nation's food source. "The Great Hunger" had begun. Mass emigration followed, and "coffin ships" began to sail.

For those who remained in Ireland, it was evictions, workhouses, soup kitchens, and death. The failure of the 1846 crop led to only about 25 percent of the land's being planted for the next year. Seed shortages, a snowy winter, and a cold spring, plus the arrival of the blight again in mid-July, set the stage for "Black '47," the year of the worst devastation. Emigration to America, Canada, England, and other parts of the world continued.

The Famine Museum at Strokestown Park

To memorialize the great Irish famine in a way that does justice to the tragedy, the Famine Museum has been created in the stable yards of Strokestown Park, County Roscommon, an estate that gained international notoriety during some of the worst months of the famine. Strokestown's landlord, Major Dennis Mahon, was responsible for clearing his land of thousands of destitute tenants to make way for larger farms. It was less expensive to send the poor to North America than to evict them and keep them in local workhouses, so Mahon continued his "assisted emigration" until November 1847, when he was ambushed and shot dead. His estate remained in the family until 1979, when the last Mahon sold it and the new owners began the restoration project that includes both the house and walled gardens as well as the museum.

The extensive Strokestown estate papers, now regarded as the best "big house" archive in Ireland, are used to explain the cultural significance of the famine, and museum exhibits offer visitors a chance to reflect on the ongoing tragedy of global poverty and hunger. The house, garden, and museum are open Tuesday through Sunday from Easter to October 31.

Annie Moore, Cobh, and Ellis Island

The most significant effect of the potato famine was that during the period of 1845 to 1850, the Irish population was reduced by more than 2 million people (one quarter of the population) through death or emigration, and even after the blight lifted, huge numbers continued to leave. An estimated 873,000 more Irish arrived in the United States between 1860 and 1880, and a million more followed during the next twenty years.

One of them was fifteen-year-old Annie Moore, the first immigrant to pass through the new Ellis Island immigration station in New York. With two young brothers in tow, Annie Moore left Cobh (formerly Queenstown), County Cork, on December 20, 1891, aboard the SS *Nevada*. After a ten-day voyage, she stepped ashore at Ellis Island and has since become a symbol of the 12 million immigrants from all over the world who followed in her footsteps.

To commemorate the young Irish girl's journey, a life-sized bronze statue of Annie was erected on Ellis Island in 1992. A matching statue stands at the Emigrant Museum and Heritage Centre in Cobh, where millions of emigrants set sail for a new life. Both are by renowned Cork sculptor Jeanne Rynhart. *Cobh: The Queenstown Story* is a permanent exhibit at the Emigrant Museum and Heritage Center, open year-round.

Turnip and Potato Casserole

**Serves 10 to 12
as a side dish**

≋ Like cabbage, turnips and rutabagas frequently turn up on an Irish table, but when I was young and palate-deprived, I frequently said "no, thanks" to my mother when she served turnips. "I'll just have the carrots, or the peas, or the potatoes," I'd tell her, despite the fact that turnips were, and still are, among the most inexpensive and flavorful of vegetables. My mother finally eased me into liking turnips by combining them with potatoes and topping them with bread crumbs.

1¼ cups dried bread crumbs

2 cups milk

1 cup sour cream

1 pound turnips or rutabagas, peeled

2 large boiling potatoes, peeled

½ cup chopped fresh chives

¾ cup minced fresh parsley

1½ teaspoons salt

½ teaspoon ground pepper

Sprinkle 1 cup of the bread crumbs in a baking pan and bake until lightly browned, 6 to 8 minutes. Stir halfway through. Let cool.

Preheat the oven to 375°F. Lightly oil a shallow 3-quart casserole dish and dust with the remaining bread crumbs. In a large bowl, whisk the milk and sour cream together. Using the large holes of a box grater, grate the turnips or rutabagas and potatoes into the milk mixture. Add the chives, parsley, salt, and pepper and mix until blended.

Spoon the mixture into the prepared dish and scatter the toasted bread crumbs over the top. Bake until the vegetables are tender and the top lightly browned, about 1 hour.

Turnip and Carrot Puree

Serves 8 as a side dish

⇸⇷ Like parsnips, turnips are perfect for pureeing, and when cooked with poultry or duck, the drippings can be used for added flavor. Here, I've added carrots for additional sweetness and sour cream for smoothness.

2 pounds turnips, peeled and cut into 2-inch pieces

2 large carrots, peeled and sliced

1 onion, chopped

3/4 cup sour cream

1/4 teaspoon ground ginger

1 teaspoon salt

1/4 teaspoon ground white pepper

4 tablespoons butter

In a large saucepan, cook the turnips, carrots, and onions in boiling salted water for 5 minutes, then cover, reduce heat to medium, and cook until tender, 20 to 25 minutes. Drain and mash.

Transfer the mixture to a food processor or blender and process until smooth. Return to the same saucepan. Stir in the sour cream, ginger, salt, pepper, and butter and blend well. Cook over low heat until heated through.

Buttered Green Cabbage

Serves 4 as a side dish

≫≪ Cabbage is second only to potatoes in Irish popularity. Boiled, it is a perfect partner to meats like ham, corned beef, and chicken, while raw cabbage, shredded in salads, is a mainstay of the cold lunch. This flavorful combination of buttered cabbage topped with crisp bacon can be served with any number of cooked meats or fish, and its neat little shape makes for easy serving.

I head cabbage

4 cups homemade chicken stock or low-salt canned broth

4 slices bacon, preferably Irish (see Resources, page 277),
   finely chopped

2 tablespoons butter, melted

Freshly ground pepper to taste

1/4 teaspoon ground mace

Cut the cabbage into quarters, cutting through to about 1/2 inch of the stem. Tie the quarters together with cotton string to reshape into a head. In a large saucepan, bring the stock or broth to a boil, add the cabbage, then cover and reduce heat to low. Cook until tender, 15 to 20 minutes. Using 2 slotted spoons, gently lift the cabbage out and drain.

Meanwhile, in a small skillet, cook the bacon over medium-high heat until crisp. Using a slotted spoon, transfer to paper towels to drain.

Preheat the broiler. Untie the cabbage quarters and place them in an ovenproof casserole dish. Drizzle with the melted butter and sprinkle the bacon pieces, pepper, and mace over top. Place under the broiler for a few minutes to lightly brown the top.

Red Cabbage Braised in Mead

Serves 10 to 12 as a side dish

The distinctive flavor and color of red cabbage teams up with the tang of apples and cranberries in this one-pot dish from Nancy Larkin Rau, who traces her Irish roots to County Longford. The addition of mead, the honey beverage favored by the ancient high chiefs of Ireland, adds a touch of sweetness to this traditional dish, which is delicious with all cuts of pork.

1 large head red cabbage, cored and shredded

2 onions, chopped

3 cups fresh or frozen cranberries

1 Granny Smith apple, peeled, cored, and sliced

1¼ cups homemade chicken stock or canned low-salt chicken broth

½ cup mead, preferably Bunratty Meade (see Resources, page 277)

¼ cup raspberry vinegar

¾ cup firmly packed brown sugar

In a large saucepan, combine all the ingredients and bring to a boil. Cover, reduce heat to low, and cook, stirring frequently, until cabbage is tender, 45 to 60 minutes.

Potato and Leek Soup

〰〰 *Brotchán foltchep* (from the Irish words meaning "broth" and "leeks") is a traditional leek and oatmeal soup that has been served in Ireland for generations. Most cooks now prefer to combine leeks with potatoes, however, to make that perennial favorite, potato and leek soup.

Serves 8

4 tablespoons butter

2 pounds boiling potatoes, peeled and sliced

1 pound leeks (white and pale green parts only), washed and sliced

1 onion, chopped

1 celery stalk, sliced

5 cups homemade chicken stock or canned low-salt chicken broth

2 1/2 cups milk

1 bay leaf

2 tablespoons minced fresh parsley

Salt and ground white pepper to taste

1/2 cup half-and-half

1/4 cup chopped fresh chives

In a large saucepan, melt the butter over medium heat. Add the vegetables, cover, and cook for 5 to 7 minutes, stirring frequently. Add the stock or broth, 1/2 cup of the milk, the bay leaf, parsley, salt, and pepper. Reduce heat to low, cover, and cook until the vegetables are tender, 25 to 30 minutes.

Discard the bay leaf, and let the soup cool for 10 to 15 minutes. Transfer to a blender or food processor in batches and process until smooth. (To make ahead, cover and refrigerate for up to 12 hours.)

To serve immediately, heat the puree in a saucepan over medium heat and stir in the remaining 2 cups milk. Heat through, ladle the soup into bowls, and swirl in 1 tablespoon half-and-half into each serving. Sprinkle with the chives. To serve later, return to heat and repeat as above.

Colcannon Soup

⇟⇟ The potato-cabbage combination known as colcannon translates beautifully to a creamy soup, like this one from 1996 Guinness Irish Chef of the Year Gerry Galvin, chef-proprietor of Drimcong House in Moycullen (County Galway). Since the 1970s, when his restaurant, the Vintage, did so much to establish the culinary reputation of the Cork village of Kinsale, Galvin has been both innovative and dedicated to the development of original Irish cuisine, a standard that has earned him the unofficial title of "the father of modern Irish cuisine." Serve this with brown soda bread (see pages 217, 220).

> 4 tablespoons butter
>
> 2 cups shredded cabbage
>
> 1½ pounds boiling potatoes, peeled and cut into 1-inch pieces
>
> 1 pound leeks (white and pale green parts only), washed and chopped
>
> 5 cups homemade chicken stock or canned low-salt chicken broth
>
> Salt and ground white pepper to taste
>
> Pinch of ground nutmeg
>
> 1¼ cups half-and-half
>
> 3 tablespoons minced fresh parsley, or 1 tablespoon dried

In a large saucepan, melt the butter over medium heat. Stir in the cabbage, potatoes, and leeks, cover, and cook over medium heat until slightly tender, 10 to 12 minutes.

Add the stock or broth and bring to a boil. Cover, reduce heat to a simmer, and cook until the vegetables are soft, 15 to 20 minutes. Season with the salt, pepper, and nutmeg. Transfer to a blender or food processor in batches and process until smooth. (To make ahead, cover and refrigerate for up to 12 hours.) →

Return the puree to the same saucepan over medium heat and whisk in the half-and-half. Heat through over medium heat. Ladle soup into bowls and sprinkle with the parsley.

Armagh Apple and Parsnip Soup

The apples from County Armagh are legendary for their quality and variety and best known as ingredients in cinnamon-laden desserts. Many contemporary Irish cooks are combining apples with sweet vegetables like carrots and parsnips, too, as in this soup that's been enlivened with an interesting combination of aromatic spices: cardamom, coriander, cumin, and curry.

Serves 6 as a first course

1 tablespoon butter

1 pound parsnips, peeled and sliced

1 pound apples, peeled, cored, and sliced

1 onion, chopped

2 teaspoons curry powder

1 teaspoon ground cumin

1 teaspoon ground coriander

1/2 teaspoon ground cardamom

1 garlic clove, crushed

Salt and freshly ground pepper to taste

5 cups homemade chicken stock or canned low-salt chicken broth

2/3 cup light cream or half-and-half

Chopped fresh chives for garnish

Croutons for garnish (recipe follows)

In a large saucepan, melt butter over low heat. Add the parsnips, apples, and onion. Cover and cook until vegetables are tender, 7 to 10 minutes. Add the spices, garlic, salt, and pepper and cook for 2 minutes more, stirring constantly.

Add the stock or broth, cover, and simmer gently until the parsnips are tender, about 30 minutes.

Transfer to a blender or food processor in batches and process until smooth. If the mixture is too thick, dilute with additional stock or broth or water. Return to the same saucepan and whisk in the cream or half-and-half. Heat through over low heat. To serve, ladle soup into bowls and sprinkle with the chives and croutons.

Croutons

3 to 4 slices white bread
4 tablespoons butter

Makes 1 1/4 cups

Remove the crusts from the bread and cut into $1/2$-inch cubes. In a large skillet, melt the butter over medium heat. Add the bread cubes and sauté until golden brown. Drain on paper towels and season with salt and pepper to taste. For added crispness, place on a baking sheet and bake in a preheated 250°F oven for about 15 minutes.

Garlic Croutons: Add $1/2$ teaspoon minced fresh garlic to the butter and cook as above.

Celery and Apple Soup

Serves 10 as a first course

⇟⇟ The idea of combining vegetables with fruit harks back to the days when the Irish created meals out of necessity rather than creativity, a factor for which modern cooks can be grateful. Mayo-born Eliza Donohue serves this soup with brown bread at Beckett's Pub in the Boston suburb of Allston.

- 3 tablespoons unsalted butter
- 1 large onion, chopped
- 2 garlic cloves, minced
- 1 bunch celery, chopped
- 5 Granny Smith apples, peeled, cored, and sliced
- 6 cups homemade chicken stock or canned low-salt chicken broth
- Salt and freshly ground pepper to taste
- 1/2 cup light cream or half-and-half
- 3 tablespoons minced fresh parsley or 1 tablespoon dried

In a large saucepan, melt the butter over medium heat. Add the onions and garlic and cook until soft, 4 to 5 minutes. Add the celery and apples and cook for 5 minutes. Add the stock or broth and bring to a boil. Cover, reduce heat to a simmer, and cook, stirring occasionally, until the vegetables are tender, 25 to 30 minutes.

Transfer the solids to a blender or processor in batches and process until smooth. Return to the same saucepan and season with salt and pepper. Whisk in the cream or half-and-half. Heat through over low heat. To serve, ladle the soup into bowls and sprinkle with parsley.

The Ulster-American Connection

⇨⇦

Emigration was a way of life for Ulster people for more than three centuries, with the ports of Londonderry and Belfast the most popular embarkation points in the eighteenth century. The 250,000 Ulstermen who took a one-way passage in the eighteenth century were overwhelmingly Ulster Scots, descendants of the Presbyterians from Scotland who settled here in the seventeenth century at the behest of King James the First. In America they were known as the Scotch-Irish and were mostly Presbyterian. By the time of the Declaration of Independence, an estimated one sixth of the population of the thirteen colonies was Ulstermen.

The ancestral farmsteads and cottages of some of those Ulstermen who rose to positions of power in the New World have been preserved in various locations throughout Northern Ireland, most notably at the Ulster-American Folk Park at Camphill, Omagh, Country Tyrone. The Folk Park grew up around the cottage where Thomas Mellon, the Pennsylvania banker and millionaire, was born in 1813, and now contains log cabins, a replica of the Mellon's Pennsylvania farmstead, and other original rural Ulster buildings. The boyhood cottage of Archbishop John Hughes, the founder of Saint Patrick's Cathedral in New York, who was born a few miles away in 1797, was moved into the Folk Park and rebuilt stone by stone.

Also in County Tyrone, near Strabane, is the ancestral home of President Woodrow Wilson, whose great-grandfather, James, left for America in 1807, and the home of Gen. Ulysses S. Grant's maternal grandparents is located at Dergina, Ballygawley.

In Dreen, Cullybackey, County Antrim, you can visit the ancestral home of President Chester Alan Arthur, whose father left for America in 1815, and at Boneybefore, Carrickfergus, County Antrim, you can trace the background of Ulster-American emigration at the Andrew Jackson Centre, named for the American president whose parents emigrated in 1765.

Twelve men of Ulster descent made it to the White House, eleven as presidents (Chester A. Arthur, James Buchanan, Grover Cleveland, Ulysses S. Grant, Benjamin Harrison, Andrew Jackson, Andrew Johnson, William McKinley, James Polk, Theodore Roosevelt, Woodrow Wilson). The twelfth was Major General Robert Ross, who arrived in Washington, D.C., on August 14, 1814, fighting for the English. He burned the Capitol, then the White House, but not before he and his officers had consumed a hearty meal that had been intended as a victory dinner for President Madison.

The Ulster-American Folk Park is open daily from Easter to mid-September; Monday through Friday from mid-September to Easter.

Carrot Soup

Serves 6 as a first course, 4 as a main dish

〰〰 Finola and Denis Quinlan, chef-proprietors of the Courtyard (Schull, County Cork), a bakery/wine and cheese bar/pub, frequently use root vegetables in their soups. Carrots and a hint of cloves combine to create this deliciously sweet soup that's perfect as a first course, or to serve for lunch with a salad and brown soda bread (see pages 217, 220).

> 2 tablespoons olive oil
> 2 pounds carrots, peeled and sliced
> 1 large onion, chopped
> 6 garlic cloves, chopped
> 5 whole cloves
> 4 cups homemade chicken stock or canned low-salt chicken broth
> 1 tablespoon fresh lemon juice
> Pinch of sugar
> Salt and freshly ground pepper to taste
> 1/4 cup heavy (whipping) cream
> Minced fresh parsley or 6 whole sprigs for garnish

In a large saucepan, heat the oil over medium heat. Add the carrots, onion, garlic, and cloves, and cook until the onion is translucent, 5 to 8 minutes. Add 3 1/2 cups of the stock or broth, cover, and simmer, stirring occasionally, until the carrots are very soft, 25 to 30 minutes.

Remove the cloves from the stock or broth and discard. Transfer the mixture to a blender or food processor in batches and process until smooth. Return to the same saucepan and stir in the lemon juice and sugar. Heat through over medium heat. Season with salt and pepper and, if needed, thin with the remaining 1/2 cup stock or broth.

To serve, ladle the soup into bowls and drizzle the cream over. Sprinkle with minced parsley or place a sprig in the center of the cream.

Cream of Carrot and Parsnip Soup

**Serves 8 as a first course,
6 as a main dish**

⤳ At the Loaf & Ladle (483 East Broadway, South Boston, Massachusetts), Bernadette Healy, a Blackpool, County Cork, native, loves the spicy flavor of curry and uses it generously in what she describes as "one of my most popular soups." Healy opened her restaurant/coffee shop four years ago and her following increases daily.

12 tablespoons (1½ sticks) butter

4 carrots, peeled and diced

5 parsnips, peeled and diced

5 cups homemade chicken stock or canned low-salt chicken broth

2 cups all-purpose flour

2 teaspoons curry powder

½ cup orange juice

1 cup light cream or half-and-half

Freshly ground pepper to taste

Minced fresh parsley for garnish

In a large saucepan, melt the butter over medium heat. Add the carrots and parsnips and cook, stirring constantly, for 5 to 7 minutes. Add 1 cup of the stock or broth and continue to cook until the vegetables begin to soften and the liquid is reduced slightly, about 5 minutes.

In a bowl, combine the remaining stock or broth and flour and whisk until well blended. Add to the vegetables, reduce heat to low, and cook until the vegetables are tender, 10 to 12 minutes. Add the curry powder, orange juice, and cream or half-and-half and stir with a wooden spoon until the soup is hot, but not boiling. To serve, ladle the soup into bowls and sprinkle with pepper and parsley.

Cream of Cauliflower Soup

Serves 6 as a first course

The test kitchens of the National Dairy Council of Ireland are a great source of recipes that feature the country's world-class dairy products in combination with fresh produce, like this combination of hearty cauliflower, potatoes, and celery.

4 tablespoons butter

1 onion, chopped

2 boiling potatoes, peeled and cut into 1-inch pieces

1 head cauliflower, divided into florets

2 celery stalks, chopped

2 cups homemade chicken stock or canned low-salt chicken broth

2/3 cup light cream or half-and-half

Salt and freshly ground pepper to taste

Shredded Parmesan cheese for sprinkling

1/4 cup celery leaves for garnish

In a large saucepan, melt the butter over medium heat. Add the onion, potatoes, cauliflower, and celery and cook for 5 minutes. Stir in the stock or broth, bring to a boil, cover, and reduce heat. Simmer until the vegetables are tender, about 20 minutes.

Transfer the mixture to a blender or food processor in batches and process in until smooth. Return to the same saucepan and stir in cream. Heat through over medium heat. Season with salt and pepper.

To serve, ladle the soup into bowls and sprinkle with shredded cheese. Garnish with celery leaves.

Turnip and Brown Bread Soup

**Serves 8 as a first course,
6 as a main dish**

〰 Mulligan's of Mayfair (13–14 Cork Street) is one of London's best-known Irish restaurants, and this soup, a mélange of Irish favorites—turnips, carrots, and leeks—is one of its most popular dishes. The bread crumbs add sweetness and thicken the soup. Make this whenever you bake a loaf of brown soda bread, using part for the crumbs and the rest to serve with the soup. Since Irish brown bread is best used on the day it's baked, also keep this recipe in mind when you don't finish a loaf. Pop what's left into a freezer bag to make crumbs for this soup, or for a luscious brown bread ice cream (see page 218).

8 tablespoons (1 stick) plus 2 tablespoons butter

2 tablespoons olive oil

1 pound carrots, peeled and chopped

1 pound leeks (white and pale green parts only), washed and chopped

4 pounds turnips, peeled and cut into 2-inch pieces

Sprig of fresh thyme

6 cups homemade chicken stock or canned low-salt chicken broth

1 cup brown soda bread crumbs

Salt and freshly ground pepper to taste

2/3 cup light cream or half-and-half

2 tablespoons minced fresh parsley for garnish

In a large saucepan, melt the butter over medium heat. Add the olive oil, carrots, leeks, turnips, and thyme. Cover and cook, stirring frequently, until the vegetables begin to soften, 12 to 15 minutes. Add the stock or broth, cover, and simmer until vegetables are tender, about 1 hour.

Stir in the bread crumbs, cover, and simmer for 30 minutes. Remove from heat and let cool. Transfer to a blender or food processor in batches and process until smooth. Add the salt and pepper.   →

To serve, ladle the soup into bowls, swirl in the cream or half-and-half, and sprinkle with parsley. Serve with slices of toasted brown soda bread.

Onion and Murphy's Stout Soup

The French may have invented onion soup, but it took the Irish to give it a flavor of its own. At Langan's Bar and Restaurant in Manhattan, chef Gary Adler found that the addition of Murphy's Irish Stout gives the hearty soup a deep color and a malty flavor. Adler generally serves it with homemade garlic croutons and Blarney Irish cheese.

Serves 10 as a first course

2 tablespoons unsalted butter

3 large yellow onions, peeled and sliced

2 red onions, peeled and sliced

4 shallots, minced

2 garlic cloves, minced

2 bay leaves

1 teaspoon dried basil

1 teaspoon dried thyme

1 tablespoon firmly packed brown sugar

3 cups homemade beef stock or canned low-salt beef broth

1 cup Murphy's Stout or other Irish stout

Salt and freshly ground pepper to taste

Garlic Croutons, page 27

1 cup (4 ounces) shredded Swiss cheese, preferably Blarney Swiss (see Resources, page 277)

In a large saucepan, melt the butter over medium heat. Add the onions, shallots, garlic, and bay leaves and cook until the onions are translucent, 12 to 15 minutes. Add the basil, thyme, brown sugar, stock or broth, stout, salt, and pepper and bring to a boil. Cover, reduce heat to a simmer, and cook until the onions are tender, about 30 minutes. Add salt and pepper.

Preheat the broiler. Sprinkle 6 to 8 croutons into each of 10 ovenproof crocks, ladle the soup over, and sprinkle with cheese. Put the crocks on a small baking sheet or broiler pan and place under the broiler until the cheese melts and starts to brown, 1 to 2 minutes.

Part 2 From the Farm

There is an old saying in Ireland that you can

take the man away from the bog but you can't take

the bog away from the man. Most Irish men—and women—

have some connection with country life, and happy

memories of time spent on the farm.

MARY KINSELLA, *AN IRISH HOME COOKBOOK*

One of the ironies of early Irish immigration is that farming was just about the last form of employment that farmers sought in the New World. Because the land had been such a source of anguish, very few immigrants ventured far away from the port city they arrived in. Having had experience with only one crop, the potato, and knowing nothing of the farming methods here, the men took up picks and shovels and joined the American labor force. Many young Irish women found jobs as serving girls in the households of wealthy Bostonians, New Yorkers, and on Philadelphia's Main Line, working for low wages in exchange for room and board. Despite the cheerful attitude and loyalty of the young Irishwomen, however, their employers often complained that they were bad at cooking meat, since few of them had learned how in Ireland, being too poor to include meat in their diet.

Although the memories of the farm grew more and more distant for those who left it, they grow larger for us who seek to touch a part of our heritage. When I first visited Ireland in 1984, my grandmother's farm was my most important destination.

My family and I arrived on a particularly beautiful day in August and made our way east out of Killarney on the N72 and north up the narrow country lanes from the town of Rathmore to Bounard, a very small section of the town. Anyone who's gone in search of Irish roots knows it's not an easy task to locate what you think are genuine addresses, but up the road to Bounard we ventured, past the Meentogues School where my grandmother was recorded as pupil No. 366 on March 13, 1880, before stopping to ask directions to the farm.

"Would you know where the Sullivans live?" I asked an elderly man out for a stroll with his dog.

"Would that be O'Sullivan Mor, or O'Sullivan Beare?" the stranger answered, testing me on my knowledge of the two branches of the O'Sullivan clan of Munster.

"I only know their names are Kit and Mick," I told him, hoping that this wasn't exclusively Sullivan territory meaning I might be lost for days in the Kerry hills looking for my cousins.

"Ah, so you're looking for Kit and Mick, are you," he said with a knowing smile, and then the directions the Irish are so famous for giving began, with the hand and arm pointing this way and that, over the small bridge, up the hill, down the road, straight on, straight on, and there it is! The farm.

The Sullivan farm was only a few acres, with seven or eight milking cows, a few chickens, and the remains of the small cottage where my grandmother lived before leaving for America in 1898. When I pushed away the thickets that grew where windows had once been, I imagined the simple meals that must have been prepared and eaten there. A chicken on Sunday, perhaps; boiled bacon and cabbage another day; potatoes, oatmeal, eggs, and bread. Irish food.

Farmhouse cooking is easy to recapture: a few simple sauces, savory meat pies topped with shortcrust pastry, and hearty breakfasts with sausages, rashers, and puddings. Even Ireland's more progressive cooks are returning to rustic fare like black pudding, potted chicken, and coddle, with embellishments that bring ingredients from the Irish farm straight into the forefront of Irish cuisine. Those happy memories of country living are closer than you think.

Bacon and Cabbage

Serves 4 to 6

〰 Traditionally, the most important meat in Ireland is pork, which has been enjoyed there since medieval times. It was easy to keep a pig on the farm, and curing, or "salting," it was not only a good way to preserve the meat, but it also added a distinctive flavor. Only the leg of the pig is called ham; all other parts are known as bacon or pork, whether it's a thick slab, a loin, a joint, or "streaky rashers," which is what Americans think of as bacon. Boiled bacon and cabbage is probably the most popular of all traditional Irish dishes, and a parsley or mustard sauce is the usual accompaniment.

> 3 pounds boiling bacon (see Resources, page 277),
>   or smoked pork shoulder
> I head cabbage, cored and quartered
> 2 pounds boiling potatoes
> Whole-Grain Mustard Sauce or Parsley Sauce (recipes follow)

Put the bacon or smoked shoulder in a large pot of cold water. Bring the water to a boil, then cover and reduce heat to a simmer. Cook for 1½ hours (or 30 minutes per pound), skimming the water occasionally to remove foam.

About 30 minutes before bacon or smoked shoulder is cooked, add the cabbage. Cook until the cabbage is tender, but not soggy, about 20 minutes. Drain.

Meanwhile, in a large saucepan of boiling salted water, cook the potatoes in their jackets until tender, 12 to 15 minutes. Drain. Remove the bacon from the pot, reserving the boiling liquid for the sauce (see following recipes), and let it cool for 10 minutes. Transfer to a serving dish and surround with the cabbage and potatoes. Serve with whole-grain mustard sauce or parsley sauce.

Whole-Grain Mustard Sauce

Sauces are almost obligatory for boiled bacon, and two popular ones are a whole-grain mustard sauce, here made with one of the varieties of mustard produced by Lakeshore Foods (Nenagh, County Tipperary), or a classic parsley sauce, most delicious when made from the broth of the boiled bacon or smoked shoulder.

Makes about 2 cups

- **2 tablespoons butter**
- **1 onion, chopped**
- **1 garlic clove, crushed**
- **2 teaspoons whole-grain mustard, preferably Lakeshore brand (see Resources, page 277)**
- **2/3 cup dry white wine**
- **1 1/4 cups bacon or pork shoulder boiling liquid, homemade chicken stock, or canned low-salt chicken broth, plus more as needed**
- **1 1/4 cups light cream or half-and-half, plus more as needed**
- **Salt and freshly ground pepper to taste**

In a saucepan, melt the butter over medium heat. Add the onion and garlic and cook until soft, about 5 minutes. Stir in the mustard and wine and cook for 2 minutes. Add the boiling liquid or stock and cook to reduce by half. Add the cream and cook to reduce again by half. Add the salt and pepper and cook to a creamy consistency, about 5 minutes. Add more cream or boiling liquid, if needed, to make a smooth sauce. Serve warm.

Parsley Sauce

Makes about 1 1/2 cups

4 tablespoons unsalted butter

3 tablespoons all-purpose flour

1/4 cup bacon or pork shoulder boiling liquid, homemade chicken stock, or canned low-salt chicken broth

1 1/4 cups milk, heated

Salt and freshly ground pepper to taste

1/2 cup minced fresh parsley

In a saucepan, melt the butter over medium heat. Gradually stir in the flour with a wooden spoon and cook for 1 to 2 minutes. Add the boiling liquid or stock, then the milk. Bring to a boil and stir until slightly thickened. Add the salt, pepper, and parsley and cook, stirring constantly, until the sauce is smooth, 3 to 5 minutes. Serve warm.

Honey-Glazed Bacon
with Apple-Whiskey Sauce

Serves 4 to 6

⩞ A traditional meal of bacon and cabbage is considered delightful in Ireland, but a loin of bacon, boiled, then baked with honey and mustard and served with an apple–cream sauce, is an interesting variation. This is a great party dish because it can be prepared ahead of time and served cold with a warm sauce.

1 loin of bacon or smoked pork shoulder, about 3 pounds

2 celery stalks

1 carrot, peeled and chopped

1 to 2 bay leaves

1 teaspoon black peppercorns

1 tablespoon whole-grain mustard, preferably Irish
(see Resources, page 277)

1 tablespoon honey, preferably Irish
(see Resources, page 277)

Apple-Whiskey Sauce

1 tablespoon butter

3 apples, cored, peeled, and sliced

1/4 cup bacon or pork shoulder boiling liquid, homemade chicken stock, or canned low-salt chicken broth

2 tablespoons Irish whiskey

3 tablespoons light cream or half-and-half

1 tablespoon minced fresh tarragon

Salt and freshly ground black pepper to taste

In a large pot of cold water, combine the bacon or smoked shoulder, celery, carrot, bay leaves, and peppercorns. Bring to a boil, then cover and reduce heat to a simmer. Cook until fork tender, 60 to 75 minutes, skimming the water occasionally to remove foam.

Preheat the oven to 400°F. Transfer the bacon or shoulder to a roasting pan. Strain and reserve the boiling liquid. Cut off the rind and score the fat. Combine the mustard and honey in a small bowl and spread over the meat. Add 2/3 cup of the reserved broth to the roasting pan and bake for 20 minutes. Add more broth if necessary during cooking. Transfer to a serving plate.

To make the sauce: Melt the butter in a medium saucepan over medium heat. Add the apple slices and cook until golden, about 5 minutes. Add 1/2 cup of the reserved boiling liquid or stock, the whiskey, and cream, and boil, stirring constantly, until the sauce begins to thicken, 3 to 5 minutes. Add the tarragon and season with salt and pepper. To serve, slice the meat and serve with the sauce.

Pure Irish Honey

⥵

When Joe Gough's bee-keeping hobby grew to such an extent that he and his wife, Eilis, had more honey than they knew what to do with, they decided to turn hobby into enterprise and founded Mileeven, Ltd., a cottage-industry-of-sorts that now produces some of Ireland's best-known honey products. Located in the hills of south County Kilkenny overlooking the Comeragh Mountains and the Suir River Valley, Mileeven (from the Irish *mil aobhainn,* meaning "delicious or delightful honey") makes plain and creamed honey, honey flavored with Jameson Irish whiskey, honey flavored with Irish Mist liqueur, honey vinegar, nut and honey cakes, and their newest product, fresh fruit—blackberries, strawberries, and raspberries—preserved in honey, which is delicious blended with yogurt, on cereals, and spooned over vanilla ice cream or chocolate desserts. Long before modern jams and preserves came along, the fruits from the countryside were mixed with honey and served as "sweets," so it was inevitable that the newest honey product from Mileeven would be one that is almost as old as honey itself.

To find out where to buy Mileeven products in the United States, see Resources, page 277.

Glazed Bacon with Red Currant Sauce

Serves 4 to 6

≈≈ Another interesting glaze for loin of bacon or smoked pork shoulder is one made with red currant jelly and port wine. Once the meat is boiled, the preparation time is only 5 minutes. This, too, makes a great party meal, and leftovers are delicious served with salad and chutney.

- 1 loin of bacon or smoked shoulder, about 3 pounds
- 1 tablespoon mustard
- 1 tablespoon granulated brown sugar
- 2/3 cup reserved bacon or pork shoulder boiling liquid, homemade chicken stock, or canned low-salt chicken broth, plus more as needed

Red Currant Sauce

- 2/3 cup reserved bacon or pork shoulder boiling liquid, homemade chicken stock, or canned low-salt chicken broth
- 2 tablespoons red currant jelly
- 2 tablespoons port
- 2 tablespoons fresh red currants (optional)

Put the bacon or smoked shoulder in a large saucepan and cover with cold water. Bring to a boil, then cover and reduce heat to a simmer. Cook until fork tender, 60 to 75 minutes, skimming the water occasionally to remove the foam.

Preheat the oven to 400°F. Transfer the bacon or smoked shoulder to a roasting pan. Strain and reserve the boiling liquid. Cut off the rind and score the fat. Combine the mustard and brown sugar in a small bowl and spread over the meat. Add 2/3 cup of the boiling liquid or stock to the roasting pan and bake for 20 minutes. Add more liquid if necessary during cooking. Transfer the meat to a serving plate and keep warm.   →

To make the sauce: Pour the remaining 2/3 cup boiling liquid or stock into a small saucepan. Add the jelly, port, and red currants (if using), and cook over medium heat until thickened, 8 to 10 minutes.

To serve, slice the meat and pour the sauce over it.

Dublin Coddle

One of the oldest Irish recipes was traditionally served on Saturday night, when the man of the house might be a bit late arriving home from an afternoon at the pub. Regardless of what activities you might be indulging in, coddle, a hearty pork and potato casserole, is a good cold-weather meal, perfect for a crowd, and one that stands up well to reheating. Brown soda bread and a glass of stout or dry red wine are the recommended accompaniments.

Serves 6

I pound large pork sausages, preferably Irish bangers
(see Resources, page 277)

8 ounces slab bacon, preferably Irish (see Resources, page 277),
cut into 2-inch pieces

3 onions, sliced

1 1/2 pounds boiling potatoes, peeled and sliced

Freshly ground pepper to taste

1/4 cup minced fresh parsley

Preheat the oven to 350°F. Prick the sausages in several places with a fork. Put the sausages and bacon in a saucepan and add enough cold water to cover. Bring to a boil, then reduce heat and simmer until slightly tender, 10 to 15 minutes. Drain, reserving the liquid. Skim off the fat.

In a large Dutch oven, layer the sausages, bacon, onions, and potatoes, sprinkling each layer with pepper and parsley. Pour the reserved liquid over to just barely cover. Cover with a sheet of waxed paper, then the casserole lid, and bake until potatoes are tender, about 1 hour. Serve hot.

Beer-Braised Roast Pork

Serves 6   ⬦⬦   Another good Saturday night supper is one that combines two classic ingredients, pork and Guinness. The Guinness not only tenderizes the pork, but also creates a flavorful base for the gravy. Serve with potatoes in their jackets, applesauce, and Turnip and Potato Casserole (page 20).

I boneless pork loin roast, about 5 pounds
2 tablespoons vegetable oil
2 onions, sliced
Salt and freshly ground pepper to taste
1/4 cup minced fresh parsley
1 1/4 cups Guinness stout
2 tablespoons all-purpose flour

Wipe the meat with a damp cloth. In a heavy saucepan over medium heat, heat the oil. Add the meat and brown on all sides. Transfer to a Dutch oven or heavy casserole with a lid.

Add the onions to the pan and cook until soft, 3 to 5 minutes. Spoon the onions over the meat and sprinkle with salt, pepper, and parsley. Pour in the Guinness and bring to a boil. Reduce heat to low, cover, and cook until the roast is fork tender, 2 to 2 1/2 hours.

Transfer the meat to a platter. Add the flour to the pan juices and stir vigorously with a wooden spoon to remove any bits of meat. Cook until the juices have thickened, about 5 minutes.

Peppered Rack of Pork

Serves 6 to 8

⩘ On most farms, the best cuts of the pig were reserved for special occasions, and in my grandparents' time, those occasions were undoubtedly holidays like Christmas or Easter. Fortunately, we don't have to wait for such occasions to enjoy a succulent pork rib roast, known in Ireland as a rack of pork, here topped with a peppery coating spiked with orange zest and sweetened with honey combined with Irish Mist liqueur.

2 tablespoons peppercorns, coarsely crushed

2 garlic cloves, crushed

Grated zest and juice of 1 orange

2 teaspoons minced fresh thyme

1 tablespoon olive oil

1 pork rib roast, about 4 pounds

2 shallots, quartered

1/4 cup plus 1/3 cup water

2 tablespoons Mileeven's Irish Mist honey
(see Resources, page 277), or 1 tablespoon honey
mixed with 1 tablespoon Irish Mist liqueur

1 tablespoon butter

The day before cooking, mix the peppercorns, garlic, orange zest, thyme, and olive oil together in a small bowl. Press the mixture into the fat surface of the pork. Cover with plastic wrap and refrigerate overnight.

The next day, remove the pork from the refrigerator and let sit at room temperature for 2 hours.

Preheat the oven to 350°F. Transfer the pork to a roasting pan. In a small bowl, combine the orange juice, shallots, and the 1/4 cup water and pour over the meat. Cook until a meat thermometer inserted into the center registers 170°F, 1 1/2 to 2 hours, adding water during cooking, if necessary. If the topping browns too fast, cover the meat with aluminum foil, but remove it for the last 30 minutes. Pour on the Mileeven's honey or honey mixed with Irish Mist during the last 30 minutes.

Transfer the meat to a platter and let rest for at least 20 minutes. Return the pan to the stove over medium heat, bring the pan drippings to a boil, and stir vigorously with a wooden spoon to scrape up any browned bits of meat from the bottom of the pan. Add the 1/3 cup water and the butter to thicken the sauce. Slice the meat into 6 or 8 portions and serve with the sauce.

Spiced Pork Roast with Apple-Thyme Cream Sauce

〰 Award-winning Irish chef Gerry Galvin is a dedicated supporter of the use of the best local produce and suppliers in and around Moycullen, County Galway, where his Drimcong House is located. This autumn dish of a stuffed boneless pork loin, called a belly, or "lap," in Ireland, is spiced with a paste of apple chutney and Guinness-flavored mustard. Serve with mashed potatoes or Turnip and Potato Casserole (page 20) and a fresh green salad.

Serves 4

Stuffing

6 tablespoons butter

1 onion, chopped

3 garlic cloves, crushed

3 tablespoons minced fresh herbs (parsley, tarragon, thyme)

2 cups dried bread crumbs

1 egg, beaten

Salt and freshly ground pepper to taste

Apple Chutney Paste

2 tablespoons butter

2 tablespoons prepared apple chutney

1 tablespoon fresh lemon juice

2 garlic cloves, crushed

2 tablespoons Lakeshore Guinness-flavored mustard (see Resources, page 277) or 2 tablespoons whole-grain mustard mixed with 1 tablespoon Guinness stout

1 boneless pork loin, about 3 pounds

Apple-Thyme Cream Sauce

2 large Granny Smith apples, peeled, cored, and chopped

1 onion, chopped

2 garlic cloves, crushed

2 fresh thyme sprigs

2/3 cup dry white wine

2/3 cup homemade chicken stock or canned low-salt chicken broth

1¼ cups light cream or half-and-half

Fresh thyme sprigs for garnish

To make the stuffing: In a small saucepan, melt the butter over medium heat and cook the onion and garlic until soft, about 3 minutes. Stir in the herbs and bread crumbs and blend well. Remove from heat and let cool slightly. Stir in the egg, salt, and pepper.

To make the paste: In a small saucepan, melt the butter over medium heat. Remove from heat and add the remaining ingredients. Stir until smooth.

Preheat the oven to 300°F. Trim off any excess fat from the meat and prick the center section with a fork. Brush half the paste over one side of the pork. Spread the stuffing over the paste, then roll up the meat into a cylinder and tie it firmly with cotton string. In a large skillet over medium heat, heat the oil. Add the meat and brown quickly on all sides. Transfer to a rack in a roasting pan and cook, seam-side up, for 3 hours. Halfway through cooking, remove the meat and brush with the remaining paste. Turn it seam-side down and return it to oven to continue cooking.

To make the sauce: In a medium saucepan, combine all the sauce ingredients and bring to a boil. Reduce heat and simmer until the sauce begins to thicken, about 15 minutes. Discard the thyme. Transfer to a blender or food processor and process until smooth. Add additional stock or broth if necessary to adjust consistency.

To serve, slice the meat onto plates, surround with sauce, and garnish with thyme sprigs.

Bunratty Castle Pork Ribs
in Honey-Whiskey Sauce

⋙ You'll never be able to duplicate the entertainment from the Shannon Heritage castle feasts (at Bunratty, Knappogue, and Dunguaire), but you can recall your visit with these pork spareribs featured on the Bunratty menu.

**Serves 4 to 6
as a first course**

5 pounds pork spareribs

Honey-Whiskey Sauce

1 tablespoon vegetable oil

1 onion, peeled and sliced

1 garlic clove, minced

1/4 cup honey

1 cup Irish whiskey

1 teaspoon Worcestershire sauce

2 tablespoons tomato ketchup

Juice of 1 lemon

4 cups homemade chicken stock or canned low-salt chicken broth

1/2 cup demi-glace or concentrated chicken broth

Put the ribs in a large pot or Dutch oven and cover with cold water. Bring to a boil, then cover and reduce heat to simmer. Cook until fork tender, about 1 hour, skimming the water occasionally to remove the foam. Transfer to a large baking pan. Preheat oven to 350°F.

To make the sauce: In a medium saucepan over medium heat, heat the oil and cook the onion and garlic until soft, about 3 minutes. Stir in all the remaining ingredients except the demi-glace or concentrated chicken broth and bring to a boil. Cook until the sauce reduces by half, 10 to 15 minutes. Stir in the demi-glace. Pour half the sauce over the ribs and bake, turning once, until the ribs begin to brown, 30 to 40 minutes. Slice the meat into 4 or more ribs per person and serve with remaining sauce.

Black Pudding Roisín

Serves 4 as a first course

⇟⇟ Black and white puddings are among the more traditional by-products of a slaughtered pig (the blood is combined with oatmeal, other pork parts, and spices and stuffed into a sausage casing) and are an integral part of an Irish breakfast. Innovative chefs, however, are using black pudding more and more in luncheon and starter dishes, combining this distinctive sausage with everything from Cheddar cheese to garlic and chives. Chef Bill Dorton created this elegant dish for Dublin's Davenport Hotel dining room (Merrion Square) by combining black pudding with potatoes, cheese, and herbs. He tops it with a whiskey-mustard sauce and serves it on a bed of mixed greens. For fun, follow his method exactly as given.

2 large boiling potatoes, peeled

2 tablespoons vegetable oil

1 onion, chopped

1/2 garlic clove, crushed

1 teaspoon minced fresh parsley

1 fresh thyme sprig

8 ounces black pudding (see Resources, page 277), skinned and diced

1/2 cup (2 ounces) shredded Cheddar cheese, preferably Irish (see Resources, page 277)

Whiskey-Mustard Sauce

2 tablespoons butter

4 ounces slab bacon

3 green onions, green part only, chopped

2 teaspoons whole-grain mustard, preferably Irish (see Resources, page 277)

1 glass Irish whiskey

1 cup heavy (whipping) cream

→

4 tablespoons butter, melted

10 ounces mixed salad greens

Cook the whole potatoes in boiling salted water until almost tender, 15 to 17 minutes. Drain and let cool.

In a medium skillet over medium heat, heat the oil and sauté the onion and garlic until soft. Add the parsley and thyme. Slice the black pudding and, with your fingers, crumble it into the pan. With a wooden spoon, stir until pasty, about 5 minutes. Add the cheese and stir to blend, then remove from heat and let cool.

To make the sauce: In a medium skillet over medium heat, melt butter. Cut the bacon into small cubes and cook until crispy. Add the green onions, count to 10, then add the mustard. Take the whiskey, stand back, and tip a small amount (about 1/4 cup) into the pan. There will be a large flash. Drink the rest of the whiskey quickly to settle the nerves! Let cook until the flame subsides and the sauce starts to thicken. Add the cream and cook until the sauce is reduced, 3 to 5 minutes. Remove from heat.

Preheat the oven to 400°F. Grease a baking sheet. To assemble, slice the cooked potatoes 1/4 inch thick. Place four 3-inch-diameter pastry rings on the prepared pan. Starting with a potato slice, alternate layers of the black pudding mixture with potato slices, ending with the potato slice. (You should have about 4 layers in each ring.) Brush each potato slice with some melted butter. Bake until nicely browned, about 10 minutes. Run a spatula around the edges of the rings to loosen.

To serve, divide the salad greens onto 4 plates and place a black pudding ring on each. Pour sauce around the edges.

Black Pudding and Bacon Salad

Serves 4 as a first course

≈ A simpler way to use black pudding is in this salad with a warm bacon dressing, a recipe from the Irish Food Board (Bord Bia).

> 1 tablespoon olive oil
>
> 4 ounces bacon, preferably Irish (see Resources, page 277), finely chopped
>
> 8 to 12 slices black pudding (see Resources, page 277)
>
> 2 tablespoons balsamic vinegar or sherry vinegar
>
> Salt and freshly ground pepper to taste
>
> 10 ounces mâche or baby spinach leaves

In a large skillet over medium heat, heat the oil. Add the chopped bacon and cook until crisp, 4 to 5 minutes. With a slotted spoon, transfer the bacon to a plate. Return the pan to heat and cook the pudding slices on each side until crisp, about 10 minutes per side. Using a slotted spoon, remove the slices from the pan and keep warm.

Add the vinegar to juices in the pan and boil for 3 minutes, stirring constantly. Add the salt and pepper.

To serve, divide the greens onto 4 plates, add the pudding slices, and sprinkle with the bacon. Spoon some of the warm pan juices over the sausages. Serve immediately.

An Irish Farmhouse Breakfast

⋛⋚

Perhaps the word *farmhouse* is no longer completely accurate when describing an Irish breakfast, since cooks in every kitchen in Ireland, from castles in Clare to hotels in Dublin to bed and breakfasts throughout the country, pride themselves on what has become the benchmark of Irish hospitality. Once known as a "fry," the traditional Irish breakfast includes porridge, eggs, bangers, rashers, black and white pudding, potatoes, grilled mushrooms and tomatoes, and any number of homemade soda breads, both brown and white. Originally, this meal was intended to be hearty enough to sustain farmers through most of the workday, and the same intention holds true for visitors to Ireland today.

On my visits, I've always found that the best reason to get out of bed is to go to the dining room to see what specialty I might be able to indulge in before setting off to another location. Besides the traditional offerings, I've eaten kippers and scrambled eggs at Innishannon House in County Cork, smoked salmon and scrambled eggs at the Hibernian Hotel in Dublin, and a genuine Ulster fry at Beech Hill Country House in Derry. Other, more imaginative, variations on the traditional farmhouse breakfast have been devised by Irish-American chefs, which make wonderful additions to the breakfast table. To order real Irish ingredients, see Resources, page 277.

8 slices Irish bacon

4 bangers, or pork sausages

4 slices black pudding

4 slices white pudding

4 eggs

4 small tomatoes, halved

4 large white mushroom caps, halved

Freshly ground pepper to taste

In a large skillet over medium heat, cook the bacon, turning frequently, about 5 minutes per side. Using a slotted metal spatula, transfer the bacon to paper towels to drain. Place the bangers in the skillet and cook until browned on all sides, about 8 minutes. Add the tomatoes, mushrooms, and slices of pudding to the pan and cook until the pudding is browned on all sides. Transfer to warmed plates and keep hot. Fry the eggs. For an Ulster fry, serve with Joe Friel's Fadge, page 12. Serves 4.

Sunday Roast Chicken with Sage and Onion Dressing

Serves 4

Poultry has always been popular with the Irish, and even the poorest of Irish farmers kept a few hens and chickens around for the eggs and meat. Stewing or braising poultry was the most popular cooking method, since the birds selected for the pot were generally past their prime and needed a slow cooking method to tenderize them. Roasting was more often used for special occasions, like Sunday dinner. My mother prepared this dish using the black enamel roaster she inherited from her mother, along with her sage and onion dressing recipe.

Sage and Onion Dressing

3 small onions, chopped

I cup cubed day-old white bread or prepared stuffing mix

I teaspoon dried sage

1/2 teaspoon salt

2 tablespoons butter, melted

I roasting chicken, about 4 pounds

2 tablespoons butter at room temperature

Salt and freshly ground pepper to taste

To prepare the dressing: Cook the onions in boiling salted water until tender, about 15 minutes. Drain the onions, then transfer them to a large mixing bowl. Add the bread, sage, salt, and melted butter and stir to blend.

Preheat the oven to 350°F. Wash the chicken inside and out and pat dry with paper towels. Fill the cavity with the stuffing and secure with poultry skewers. Rub the chicken with the butter and sprinkle with salt and pepper. Roast, uncovered, until a meat thermometer inserted into the breast reaches 185°F, 60 to 75 minutes. Let chicken rest for 10 minutes before carving.

Roast Breast of Chicken with Cabbage and Bacon

Serves 4

⤲ Chicken boiled or braised with ham or bacon is another popular Irish dish. The flavors of poultry and pork combine exceptionally well and yield a delicious stock for soups and stews. As a tribute to tradition, many young chefs, like Warren Massey of Popjoy's (Terenure, County Dublin), rely on such classic combinations while experimenting with new ways to serve them. Massey says his aim is to serve "simple, elegant, and rustic dishes that let the produce speak for itself, are packed with flavor, and require very little processing." Here he teams up breast of chicken with the time-honored combination of bacon and cabbage in a modern dish that creates a flavorful sauce during the cooking.

6 slices bacon, cut into 1/4-inch strips

4 tablespoons cooking oil

4 boneless, skinless chicken breast halves

2 onions, sliced

2 garlic cloves, finely chopped

2 cups shredded Savoy cabbage

2/3 cup homemade chicken stock or canned low-salt chicken broth

2 tablespoons light cream or half-and-half

10 tablespoons (1 stick plus 2 tablespoons) butter

Salt and freshly ground pepper to taste

Preheat the oven to 375°F. In a medium skillet, cook the bacon over medium heat until crisp, 5 to 7 minutes. Drain on paper towels. Reserve.

In a large ovenproof skillet or flameproof casserole dish over medium-high heat, heat 2 tablespoons of the oil. Add the chicken, skin-side down, and brown lightly, 3 minutes per side. Transfer the pan to the oven and bake the chicken for 15 minutes.

Meanwhile, in a medium saucepan over medium-low heat, heat the remaining 2 tablespoons oil and sauté the onions and garlic until the onions are translucent, 3 to 5 minutes. Add the cabbage and mix well. Add the stock or broth, bring to a boil, and cook, stirring frequently, until the cabbage is tender, about 10 minutes. With a slotted spoon, transfer the cabbage to 4 heated plates. Boil the cooking liquid until reduced by half. Add the cream and cook to reduce by half again. Whisk in the butter. Strain the sauce and add the reserved strips of cooked bacon to the sauce.

Slice the chicken onto the cabbage and pour the sauce around it.

Chicken, Ham, and Leek Pie

~~ Plate pies, popular in Ireland and England, are traditional meat pies that originated in the fifteenth and sixteenth centuries when plates were still scarce and only the rich could afford knives and forks. With both a top and bottom crust, the pie was both plate and platter and could easily be eaten with or without utensils. Another feature of plate pies that cooks still find appealing is that almost any kind of leftover meat or vegetable can be combined for a filling. With the invention of cutlery, the bottom crust was often omitted, as in this recipe.

Serves 4

Pastry Dough

1/2 teaspoon salt

2 cups all-purpose flour

1 cup (2 sticks) cold unsalted butter

1/2 cup ice water

1 chicken, about 3 pounds

1 cup diced cooked ham

4 leeks (white and pale green parts only), washed and chopped

Pinch of ground nutmeg

Salt and freshly ground pepper to taste

3 tablespoons butter

1 onion, finely chopped

1/4 cup all-purpose flour

1 teaspoon Dijon mustard

1 1/2 cups homemade chicken stock or canned low-salt chicken broth

1/2 cup half-and-half

To make the dough: In a medium bowl, stir the salt and flour together. With a pastry cutter, 2 knives, or your fingers, cut or work the butter into the flour to the consistency of crumbs. Add the water slowly and stir into the flour mixture with a fork. Gather the dough and press it together until it forms a ball. Cover with plastic wrap and refrigerate for 20 to 30 minutes.

Meanwhile, put the chicken in a large pot with cold water to cover. Bring to a boil, reduce the heat to medium, cover, and simmer until tender, about 45 minutes. Drain and let cool to the touch. Cut the meat into thick slices or chunks. In a 6-cup deep-dish pie plate, alternate layers of chicken, ham, and leeks. Season the layers with nutmeg, salt, and pepper.

While the chicken is cooking, in a large saucepan melt the butter over medium heat. Add the onion and sauté until soft, about 3 minutes. Stir in the flour and mustard. Add the broth or stock and half-and-half slowly and, with a wooden spoon, stir until thickened. Pour the sauce over the meat and leeks.

Preheat the oven to 350°F. On a lightly floured board, roll the dough out 1 inch larger than the diameter of the pie dish you're using. Dampen the edges of the dish and place the pastry over the top. Press the edges of the pastry down well and crimp with a fork. Make cuts in the pastry to let the steam escape. Bake until lightly browned, 25 to 30 minutes. Cover the pastry with aluminum foil if the top browns too quickly.

Shepherd's Pie

Serves 4

≶ Most cooks today make shepherd's pie with ground beef, although the more traditional way is to use leftover cooked beef. Like plate pie, shepherd's pie can be made with either fresh, frozen, or leftover vegetables, but the special feature of shepherd's pie is, undoubtedly, its mashed-potato crust.

I cup diced raw or cooked carrots

I onion, sliced

1/2 cup fresh or partially frozen peas

3 cups diced cooked beef

Salt and freshly ground pepper to taste

I cup beef gravy

2 cups mashed potatoes at room temperature

I egg

2 tablespoons milk

If using raw carrots, cook them in boiling salted water until tender, 8 to 10 minutes. Drain and set aside. Meanwhile, cook the onions in boiling salted water until tender, about 5 minutes.

Preheat the oven to 350°F. In an 8-cup ovenproof casserole, combine the vegetables, beef, salt, and pepper. In a small saucepan, heat the gravy over low heat. Pour the gravy over the meat and vegetables. Bake, uncovered, for 20 minutes.

Pipe or spoon the mashed potatoes over the meat and vegetables. In a small bowl, beat the egg and milk together and brush over the potatoes. Return to the oven for 10 minutes, then place under the broiler to brown the potatoes for about 5 minutes.

Corned Beef and Cabbage

Serves 14 to 16

Corned beef and cabbage is, unquestionably, the quintessential Irish-American meal, even though I have it on good authority that it's eaten only in two counties in Ireland: Dublin and Cork. Chef Tom Ryan, of Boston's Durgin Park restaurant at Faneuil Hall, has been preparing the restaurant's famous corned beef and cabbage for thirty-five years, producing what you might say is definitely a beef of a different color. In "Yankee" or "Irish-style" corned beef, the brisket is cured with salt and brine and produces a gray corned beef, unlike the red sodium nitrite–cured corned beef you see vacuum wrapped in supermarket meat cases in other parts of the country.

According to Ryan, the secret to genuine "Irish-style" corned beef is all in the curing. "We corn it here in stainless steel barrels, and we just use kosher salt and water. To be sure you have enough salt in the brine, put a potato in the water. If it floats, you've got enough salt. If not, add more." The result is a mild, flavorful meat that is the centerpiece of this traditional boiled dinner. When Saint Patrick's Day falls on or near a weekend, Ryan says Durgin Park serves nearly one thousand pounds!

1 pound kosher salt

1 gallon water

1 fresh brisket of beef, about 7 to 8 pounds

6 whole bay leaves

8 to 10 black peppercorns

1 large head cabbage, cored and quartered

1 bunch carrots, peeled and thickly sliced

1 large turnip, cut into 2-inch cubes

8 large boiling potatoes, peeled and halved

→

In a large nonreactive pot, combine the salt and water. Add the brisket and let soak, covered, at room temperature, for a minimum of 48 hours. (The beef must be completely covered, so double the brine recipe if necessary.)

Lift the meat out of the pan with 2 large forks and pour out the brine. Add fresh water to the pan. Return the meat to the pan, add the bay leaves and peppercorns, and bring to a boil. Reduce heat to a simmer and cook, covered, until fork tender, 3 to 3 1/2 hours.

During the last 45 minutes of cooking, add the cabbage, carrots, turnip, and potatoes. (Alternatively, the carrots, turnip, and potatoes can be boiled separately.) Let the beef cool for about 15 to 20 minutes. To serve, carve the meat and place the potatoes, carrots, and turnip around it on a large platter. Serve the cabbage in a bowl.

Beef and Guinness Casserole

Serves 6

〰 Beef stew, with its combination of traditional ingredients—potatoes, carrots, beef, and stout—is a real Irish classic. As with all classics, there are as many variations as there are cooks, but this recipe from Frankie Sheedy, chef at his family's Spa View Hotel (Lisdoonvarna, County Clare) has always been my favorite. Serve this with boiled potatoes. It can be made a day ahead and reheated.

2 tablespoons vegetable oil

2 pounds round or rump beef, cubed

3 large onions, sliced

1/4 cup all-purpose flour

8 carrots, peeled and thickly sliced

1 bunch celery, thickly sliced

8 cups beef stock or canned low-salt beef broth

1 cup Guinness stout

1 teaspoon caraway seeds

1 tablespoon raisins

1 tablespoon tomato puree

Salt and freshly ground pepper to taste

2 tablespoons minced fresh parsley

In a large, heavy skillet over high heat, heat the oil. Add the meat and cook in batches, stirring constantly, until the meat is lightly browned on all sides, about 5 minutes per batch. Using a slotted spoon, transfer the meat to a large pot or Dutch oven.

In the same skillet, sauté the onions over medium heat until soft but not browned, about 5 minutes. Add the flour and stir to coat the onions. Transfer the onions to the pot or Dutch oven, then add all the remaining ingredients except the parsley. Cover and cook over low heat until the meat is tender, 2 to 2 1/2 hours. Taste and correct the seasoning and sprinkle with the parsley.

Gaelic Steak

⇕⇕ Beef is a lot more popular in Ireland today than it was in my grand-mother's time, when most farmers kept cows more for the milk than for meat, and Irish chefs never seem to tire of the versatility and adaptability of beef. One favorite is steak flamed with Irish whiskey, which has been fondly dubbed Gaelic steak. It's best to use a boneless cut like a fillet steak, but T-bones, sirloin steaks, or porterhouse steaks work just as well. Serve with buttered baby carrots, green beans, and boiled potatoes for a tri-colored garnish.

Serves 4

4 tablespoons butter

6 white mushrooms, sliced

1/2 cup diced onion

4 beef fillet steaks, about 4 ounces each

1/4 cup Irish whiskey

3/4 cup light cream or half-and-half

Salt and freshly ground pepper to taste

In a large skillet, melt 2 tablespoons of the butter over medium heat. Add the mushrooms and onions and sauté until soft but not browned, 3 to 5 minutes. With a slotted spoon, remove the vegetables and set aside.

Add the remaining 2 tablespoons butter to the skillet, add the steaks, and cook to desired doneness (5 minutes on each side for medium rare). Add the whiskey and let warm. Avert your face and light the whiskey with a long match. Swirl the steaks around in the pan until the flame subsides. Transfer the steaks to a warm plate. Add the cream or half-and-half, salt, and pepper and cook until the sauce reduces slightly. With a wooden spoon, stir the sauce to scrape up the browned bits from the bottom of the pan. Stir in the mushrooms and onions. Cook until the sauce is slightly thickened. Serve the steaks immediately with the sauce poured over the steaks.

Fillet of Baby Beef Stuffed with Spinach and Ham

Serves 4

≈ "What's freshest at the market" is what guides many Irish chefs to determine what they'll put on the menu on any given day, and if the ingredients are grown or raised organically, all the better. Sheila Sharpe cooks at Christy and Moira Tighe's Cromleach Lodge (Castlebaldwin, County Sligo) and relies on organically raised baby beef and smoked ham for this dish, which is served with an Irish whole-grain mustard sauce.

> 2 tablespoons butter
> 1/4 cup diced smoked ham
> 1 onion, finely chopped
> 1 carrot, peeled and finely diced
> 4 small white mushrooms, finely chopped
> 1 tablespoon light cream or half-and-half
> 1 garlic clove, crushed
> 1/4 cup cooked spinach, chopped
> Salt and freshly ground pepper to taste
> 4 beef fillet steaks, 4 ounces each
> Olive oil for brushing
> Whole-Grain Mustard Sauce (page 40)

In a medium skillet, melt the butter over medium heat. Add the ham, onion, carrot, and mushrooms and sauté until the vegetables are soft, 3 to 5 minutes. Add the cream or half-and-half, garlic, and spinach and stir to blend. Season with salt and pepper. Remove from heat and let cool.

Make a slit in the side of each steak to form a pouch. With a teaspoon, fill each pouch with 1/4 of the stuffing. Press to close, or secure with a toothpick. Brush both sides of the steaks with olive oil. In a large skillet over high heat, brown the meat, about 2 minutes per side. Reduce heat to medium and cook for 5 minutes per side for medium rare. Serve immediately on hot plates, with mustard sauce drizzled over the top.

Knaves of Beef Stuffed with Wild Mushrooms

⋙ Set in prime Irish beef country, Crookedwood House in Mullingar, County Westmeath, is home to the Kenny family, where you're likely to find chef Noel Kenny or his wife, Julie, out in the garden with their children when you arrive mid-afternoon. Kenny has an instinctive way of combining the wild foods around Crookedwood with the produce he grows in his large garden. Here he uses field mushrooms in the stuffing for his "knaves," or beef olives (a term the Irish use to describe stuffed beef roll-ups). Baked potatoes and Buttered Green Cabbage (page 22) are good accompaniments to this dish.

Serves 4

2 tablespoons butter

1 1/2 cups wild mushrooms, such as mixed cremini, portobellos, and shiitakes, chopped

1 teaspoon minced garlic

1 teaspoon minced fresh tarragon

1 cup dried bread crumbs

Salt and freshly ground pepper to taste

1 egg, beaten

8 slices beef round steak, 3 ounces each

2 tablespoons vegetable oil

2 cups homemade beef stock or canned low-salt beef broth

1 1/4 cups Guinness stout

Preheat the oven to 325°F. In a medium skillet, melt the butter over medium heat. Add the mushrooms and garlic and sauté until soft, about 3 minutes. Add the tarragon and bread crumbs and blend. Remove from heat, season with salt and pepper, and add the beaten egg. Mix well.

Lay out the slices of beef on waxed paper and season with salt and pepper to taste. Place $^1/4$ of the stuffing onto each piece, roll it up neatly, and secure with a toothpick.

In a large ovenproof skillet over medium-high heat, heat the oil and brown the meat on all sides. Add the stock or broth and Guinness and bake until the meat is tender, about 45 minutes, turning the meat once or twice during cooking.

To serve, place 2 pieces of rolled beef on each of 4 warmed plates and surround with some of the sauce.

Part 3 From the Dairy

Cheese making forms a central part
of any culture. You have only to look at the paintings of
the Renaissance, which always had a great big wheel of crumbling
cheese in among the figs and pomegranates, to know that
cheese is a staff of civilization as well as life.

HÉLÈNE WILLEMS, CHEESE MAKER, COOLEA, COUNTY CORK

Milk, cream, butter, and cheese. Fresh, natural, pure, and wholesome. Dairy products have always been important in the Irish diet, from the rich cream and butter added to flavor colcannon and champ, to the buttermilk that's mixed with soda as a leavening agent in soda bread. Irish people drink more milk than most other people in the world, and cream-laden desserts, from ice creams to puddings, are an integral part of many Irish meals. Cheese, however, was another story, and few recipes outside of a cheese-flavored white sauce, or rabbit—cheese melted with wine, ale, or milk—exist in Irish cookery books. Fortunately, all that has changed.

As the most natural way of preserving milk, cheese originated as an economical way of using up surplus milk. It was one of the earliest dairy products in Ireland, although the original variety was a soft-curd cheese made during summer and eaten immediately. For some reason, cheese production declined sometime during the late seventeenth century, and it wasn't until the 1930s that dairy cooperatives resumed the custom. In 1980, however, a new group of cheese makers began producing handmade cheese, and the "made in Ireland" stamp is now proudly affixed to more than thirty varieties.

From the tangy wave-blown pastures of West Cork to the mild meadows of the midlands and the east, Irish cheese makers are reviving the lost art of making cheese with character, flavor, and aroma that is as distinctive as the place it comes from. Using only the freshest, purest milk from small herds that graze on grass and herbs, these cheese makers allow intricate tastes and aromas to flower. From fluffy and creamy mild to long matured, hard, and rich, exciting varieties of Irish farmhouse cheese come from nearly every region of Ireland, and fortunately, a good number are also available in specialty foods shops in the United States and several can be ordered by mail.

While cheese purists might argue that the best way to enjoy a good Irish cheese is unadorned, with only a biscuit or, perhaps, a piece of fruit alongside to balance the flavor, more and more cooks are combining Irish cheeses with vegetables in tarts, flans, and soufflés; with fresh produce in salads and soups; and using them as stuffing or in sauces for meat and fish.

Other varieties of Irish cheese produced by dairy cooperatives like Kerrygold and Dairygold—Blarney, oak-smoked Blarney, vintage Cheddar, Irish Swiss, Skellig, and Tipperary Irish Cheddar—are also becoming perfect partners in an Irish kitchen and make great additions to a classic cheese board.

If the late Clifton Fadiman's suggestion that "cheese is milk's leap toward immortality" is true, then the Irish are headed in the right direction.

Classic Cheese Rabbit

Serves 4

≋ While this classic cheese dish certainly didn't originate in Ireland, it's one that people throughout the British Isles have eaten since earliest times and it still makes a quick and delicious sauce to serve over toast points, hard-boiled eggs, vegetables, ham, turkey, or potatoes. The secret to a good Welsh rabbit, as it's most familiarly known—yes, it's rabbit, not rarebit— has always been to use good quality Cheddar cheese, and to make a genuine Irish rabbit, use Bandon Vale, Ballycashel, or Blarney Vintage Cheddar, and Harp's Lager or Smithwick's Ale. You can drink what's left.

8 ounces Cheddar cheese, preferably Irish
   (see Resources, page 277)

1 tablespoon butter

1/4 teaspoon salt

1/2 teaspoon dry mustard

1 teaspoon paprika

1/2 cup ale, preferably Irish

1 egg, slightly beaten

1 teaspoon Worcestershire sauce

In a double boiler over simmering water, combine cheese, butter, salt, mustard, and paprika and cook, stirring occasionally, until the cheese melts. Add the ale, egg, and Worcestershire sauce and stir until thickened. Pour over toast points, or use as a sauce as suggested above.

Irish Fondue

⇝ Those old enough to remember when fondue was fashionable and everyone sat around the coffee table with forks in hand dipping bread cubes into a pot of bubbling cheese will also remember trying to cover the distance from the pot to your mouth without dripping cheese all over yourself. Leave it to the Irish to figure out a way to avoid all the mess by baking the cheese with the bread and serving it in finger-sized strips. It's a perfect Irish hors d'oeuvre.

Makes 36 pieces

8 tablespoons (1 stick) unsalted butter at room temperature

1/2 teaspoon dry mustard

1/2 teaspoon minced garlic

12 slices firm-textured white bread, crusts removed

2 cups (8 ounces) shredded Kerrygold Blarney or Swiss cheese (see Resources, page 277) or other Swiss cheese

3/4 teaspoon chopped fresh chives

1/2 teaspoon Worcestershire sauce

Salt and freshly ground pepper to taste

4 eggs

1 1/2 cups milk

2/3 cup dry white wine

2/3 cup heavy (whipping) cream

In a small bowl, blend the butter, mustard, and garlic together. Spread an equal portion on each slice of bread. Fit 6 slices, buttered-side down, into the bottom of a 9-by-13-inch glass baking dish.

In a small bowl, stir the cheese, chives, Worcestershire sauce, salt, and pepper together. Sprinkle over the bread. Place the remaining bread, buttered-side up, on top of the cheese.

In a medium bowl, whisk the eggs, milk, and wine together until well blended. Pour over the bread. Let sit for 30 minutes. Pour the cream over the top. Cover tightly with plastic wrap and refrigerate at least 12 hours or up to 24 hours.

Preheat the oven to 350°F. Bake, uncovered, until lightly browned and set, 60 to 70 minutes. Remove from oven and let rest for 15 minutes. Cut into finger-sized strips and serve hot.

Deep-Fried Irish Camembert

Makes 24 pieces

At Carrigbyrne Farmhouse (Adamstown, Enniscorthy, County Wexford), Patrick Berridge makes two soft French-style cheeses from whole cow's milk: St. Brendan's, a fresh-flavored Brie, and St. Killian, a creamy Camembert with mushroom scents. Berridge learned his cheese-making skills in a Camembert factory in Normandy, and now the Carrigbyrne cows provide milk for an Irish counterpart. Both of these creamy, mild-flavored cheeses can be eaten young and firm or ripe and soft, and have lately been turning up as delicious hors d'oeuvres, deep-fried in beer batter.

3/4 cup all-purpose flour

1/2 cup flat beer at room temperature

1/2 teaspoon salt

1 teaspoon vegetable oil

1 egg, separated

8 ounces Camembert cheese, preferably St. Killian (see Resources, page 277)

2 cups vegetable oil

In a medium bowl, whisk the flour, beer, salt, and oil together. There should be a few small lumps. Cover the bowl with plastic wrap and let sit in a warm place for about 3 hours.

→

Beat in the egg yolk. In a small bowl, beat the egg white until stiff, glossy peaks form. Fold into the beer batter.

Cut the cheese, rind and all, into about twenty-four 1-inch pieces. In a Dutch oven or deep fryer, heat the oil to 350°F. Dip the cheese pieces, one at a time, into the beer batter and drop, in batches, into the hot oil. Cook, turning as necessary with a wooden spoon, until golden brown. Remove each piece as soon as it is brown and drain on paper towels. Serve immediately.

Deep-Fried Knockalara Sheep Cheese

Knockalara is a fresh feta-style sheep cheese made by Wolfgang and Agnes Schliebitz on their farm in Knockalara (Cappoquin, County Waterford). Sheep cheese is a healthy alternative for those who suffer from allergies to cow's or goat's milk. Because its light tang marries beautifully with fruity olive oil, sheep cheese is ideal in salads, as in this recipe from the Schliebitzes. The cheese is served as a starter on toast rounds with cranberry conserve or mango chutney.

> 8 ounces Knockalara sheep cheese (see Resources, page 277) or feta cheese
>
> 1 egg, beaten
>
> 1½ teaspoons minced fresh thyme
>
> Salt and freshly ground pepper to taste
>
> 2 cups vegetable oil
>
> 1 cup dried bread crumbs
>
> Toast rounds for serving
>
> Cranberry conserve or mango chutney for serving

Serves 4 as a first course

Note:
Sean and Deirdre Fitzgerald also make a semi-hard variety of sheep cheese in Brickhill (Cratloe, County Clare). Their Cratloe Hills sheep cheese, made from the milk of their herd of pedigree Friesland ewes, is the first Irish sheep cheese made in the Republic. Like Knockalara, Cratloe Hills is also delicious in salads, especially with fresh fruit tossed with a light vinaigrette.

Cut cheese into 4 rounds or pieces. In a small bowl, whisk the egg, thyme, salt, and pepper together until well blended. In a Dutch oven or deep fryer, heat the oil to 350°F. Dip the cheese pieces into the bread crumbs and drop into the hot oil. Cook, turning as necessary with a slotted spoon or spatula, until golden brown. Transfer to paper towels to drain. Serve immediately on toast rounds, with cranberry conserve or mango chutney.

St. Tola Goat Cheese and Arugula Salad

Serves 4 ⋛⋚ Goat cheese is the choice of many Irish cooks, not only for the cheese board, but for use in hors d'oeuvres and first courses, especially salads. Derrick and Meg Gordon make their St. Tola soft goat cheese using milk from their organically fed goat herd at their farmhouse in Inagh (County Clare). Here, it's first marinated in olive oil and thyme, then baked and served with a tangy raspberry vinaigrette.

8 ounces St. Tola goat cheese (see Resources, page 277), or other fresh goat cheese

1/4 cup olive oil

Leaves from 3 fresh thyme sprigs

1 cup dried bread crumbs

Raspberry Vinaigrette

1/2 cup raspberry vinegar

2 teaspoons Dijon mustard

1/2 teaspoon salt

Freshly ground pepper to taste

1/4 cup walnut oil

1/4 cup olive oil

→

10 ounces arugula, stemmed, or 5 ounces arugula
and 5 ounces red-leaf lettuce

Salt and freshly ground pepper to taste

Garlic Croutons (page 27)

Cut the goat cheese into 4 rounds. Put the rounds in a shallow bowl and drizzle with the olive oil. Turn to coat both sides. Sprinkle with the thyme, cover with plastic wrap, and refrigerate for at least 12 hours or up to 24 hours.

Preheat the oven to 400°F. Lightly grease a baking sheet. Remove the cheese from the oil and dredge in the bread crumbs. Transfer to the prepared pan and bake until lightly browned, about 12 minutes. Do not turn.

To make the vinaigrette: In a small bowl, whisk vinegar, mustard, salt, pepper, and oils together until well blended.

To serve, divide the arugula or lettuce among 4 salad plates, top each with a warmed round of cheese, surround with croutons, and drizzle with vinaigrette.

Note:

Luc and Anne van Kampen also make Croghan, a semi-hard variety of goat cheese, at their farm in Ballyna-drishoge (Enniscorthy, County Wexford); Ina Koerner makes Ardsallagh, a semi-hard and full-fat creamy goat cheese at her farm in the Blackwater Valley (near Youghal, County Cork); and John and Anne Brodie make Boilie, tender, hand-rolled balls of soft goat cheese preserved in sunflower oil and flavored with herbs and garlic, at their Ryefield Farm (Virginia, County Cavan).

The Classic Cheese Board

⬦⬦

Crackers and cheese have always been the mainstay of the American cocktail hour. Europeans, on the other hand, usually serve fruit and cheese after dinner, either in place of or in addition to a sweet. Now the Irish favor it, too, especially since the Irish Farmhouse Cheesemakers Association was formed and top-notch European-style cheeses are being produced throughout the Emerald Isle. The cheese board, complete with fruit and biscuits, is now a fashionable ending to an Irish meal as well.

Choose at least one cheese from each of the major categories: a soft or semi-soft cheese like Adrahan, Dunbarra, Gubbeen, Durrus, Cooleeney, Lavistown, Milleens, St. Brendan, or St. Killian; a hard or semi-hard, waxed-rind variety like Baylough, Cahills, Carrigaline, Coolea, Kerry Farmhouse, Killorglin, Knockanore, Ring, or Round Tower; hard cheeses like Gabriel, Desmond, and Mizen; a semi-hard, Cheddar-style like Bandon Vale or Beal Lodge; a blue-veined cheese like Abbey blue Brie, Cashel or Chetwynd Blue, or Blue Rathgore; and a goat or sheep cheese like Ardsallagh, Boilie, Cratloe Hills, Croghan, Knockalara, Orla, Shamrock Rathgore, or St. Tola.

Several cheese makers also make smoked and herb-flavored varieties, which you might like to add to a cheese board. They include Abbey smoked Brie; Baylough oak-smoked, or flavored with garlic and herbs, or with fresh garlic; Cahills herb blend; Coolea, flavored with herbs, nettles, and garlic; Killorglin, flavored with garlic, cumin, and cloves; Kerry farmhouse, flavored with garlic, chives, nettle, and hazelnut; Knockanore oak-smoked, or flavored with garlic and herbs; and Round Tower with herbs. For an extraordinary treat, add one of the adventurous hard cheeses produced by Cahills that are marbled with red wine, whiskey, or stout!

The flavor and character of most cheeses come through best when served at room temperature. Remove slicing cheese, goat cheese, and blue cheese from the refrigerator at least 30 minutes before serving. Remove soft cheeses like Camembert from the refrigerator at least 2 hours before using.

To find out where to buy farmhouse cheese in the United States, see Resources, page 277.

Irish Farmhouse Cheese Parcels with Root Vegetable Salad

Serves 2

〰〰 Terry McCoy, chef-proprietor of the Red Bank Restaurant (Skerries, County Dublin), one of the great characters of contemporary Irish cuisine, is an enthusiast of local produce and an innovator in ways to prepare it. When he was a contender in the 1996 Guinness Chef of the Year Competition, he turned to his colleagues in the dairy industry for inspiration. In this recipe, McCoy pays tribute to some of the industry's "first ever" products, including Veronica and Norman Steele's Milleens, a soft, washed-rind cheese that set the standard for farmhouse cheese production; Louis and Jane Grubb's Cashel Blue, the first Irish farm blue cheese; and Jeffa Gill's rind-washed, semi-soft Durrus. His suggestion for serving it on a root vegetable salad is yet another indication of the happy marriage of all kinds of Irish produce.

1 parsnip, peeled and cut into julienne

1 carrot, peeled and cut into julienne

1 zucchini, peeled and cut into julienne

Herb Dressing

1/2 teaspoon salt

1/2 teaspoon freshly ground pepper

2 teaspoons sugar

1/4 cup minced fresh herbs such as parsley, tarragon, thyme

2 tablespoons white wine vinegar

1/2 cup olive oil

1 egg yolk

2 sheets filo dough, thawed

6 ounces Durrus cheese (see Resources, page 277)
   or other semi-soft cow's cheese such as Munster

6 ounces Cashel blue cheese (see Resources, page 277)
   or other firm blue cheese

6 ounces Milleens cheese (see Resources, page 277)
   or other Camembert-style cheese

1 egg yolk beaten with 1 tablespoon water

2 tablespoons vegetable oil

2 tablespoons sherry vinegar

In a small bowl, combine the parsnip, carrot, and zucchini.

To make the dressing: In a blender or food processor, combine the salt, pepper, sugar, herbs, vinegar, olive oil, and egg yolk, and process until smooth. Mix about half of the dressing with the vegetables and reserve the rest.

Preheat the oven to 400°F. Stack the filo dough on a pastry board and cut into two 6-by-6-inch pieces. Cut each cheese into 2 rectangular slices and stack the cheeses in the center of each rectangle of filo with the blue cheese in the middle. Wrap up in the dough like an envelope to create a "parcel" and brush all over with the egg yolk mixture.

In a large skillet over medium heat, heat the oil. Cook the parcels on all sides until the dough begins to brown lightly, 3 to 5 minutes per side. Transfer to an ovenproof casserole dish and bake until the cheese melts and the pastry puffs up and turns golden brown, about 5 minutes.

To serve, arrange the salad like a haystack on 2 serving plates. Put a cheese parcel on top of each and spoon some of the dressing over the top. Drizzle a few drops of sherry vinegar around the edge of the plates.

Irish Whole-Grain Mustard

⇟⇟

U ntil Hillary Henry came along, the Irish were poor mustard eaters, except for the occasional dab of Colman's English mustard on a ham sandwich. Henry's grandfather is reputed to have taken mustard sandwiches along when hunting, which may explain the interest in mustard that led her to establish Lakeshore Foods in 1986. Located in the picturesque Tipperary village of Ballinderry, near Lough Derg, the largest lake on the River Shannon, Lakeshore Foods produces a range of fine-quality whole-grain mustards made in the traditional French manner. The all-natural mustards include traditional, horseradish, and honey-flavored, as well as three flavored with Irish spirits: Guinness stout, Irish whiskey, and Bunratty Meade. All the varieties are versatile and appear frequently in contemporary Irish cooking.

To find out where to where to buy Lakeshore products in the United States, see Resources, page 277.

Boilie Salad with Crabmeat and Salmon

Serves 4

〰 Boilie is the trade name of John and Anne Brodie's tender hand-rolled balls of soft cow or goat cheese, which are preserved in sunflower oil and delicately flavored with herbs and garlic. Mark Phelan, chef at Dunraven Arms Hotel in Adare, one of County Limerick's most charming hotels, combines what he calls "little pearls of Boilie" with fresh crabmeat, slivers of barbecued salmon, and a whole-grain mustard dressing.

Whole-Grain Mustard Dressing

1 tablespoon walnut oil

1/3 cup olive oil

1/2 teaspoon whole-grain mustard, preferably Irish (see Resources, page 277)

1/4 teaspoon mustard seeds

1/4 teaspoon pink peppercorns

1/2 teaspoon chopped fresh chives

10 ounces mixed salad greens and endive

1 avocado, peeled, pitted, and sliced lengthwise

8 slices barbecued or smoked salmon

12 rounds Boilie goat cheese (see Resources, page 277) or 8 ounces other oil-cured goat cheese

8 crab claws, shelled, or 8 ounces fresh crabmeat

To make the dressing: In a small bowl or screw-top jar, combine all the ingredients and whisk or shake until well blended. Refrigerate for 15 to 30 minutes.

Divide the greens and endive among 4 plates. Arrange slices of avocado, salmon, cheese rounds, and crabmeat on the greens and spoon the dressing over.

Coleslaw with Blue Brie Dressing

Serves 8 as a first course

A slice of Brie with a biscuit and an apple is a delicious way to serve the creamy soft-ripened cheese named, according to legend, for the place where the Emperor Charlemagne first tasted it, the priory of Reuil-en-Brie in France. A relatively new variation on classic Brie is blue Brie, a delightful blend of the texture of Brie with the flavor of blue. While there are several producers of blue Brie in France, only Pat and Joan Hyland make Irish blue Brie from pasteurized full cream milk and specialized cultures. Named for the ancient Aghaboe Abbey close to their farm in Ballacolla (County Laois), the Hylands refer to their unique cheese as "a high-quality fashion piece, one that can be eaten casually or dressed up to add an elegant touch to any meal." This old-fashioned coleslaw with a dressing of blue Brie and cream is a perfect example.

I Granny Smith apple, cored and peeled

I tablespoon fresh lemon juice

I small head green cabbage, quartered and cored

I small head red cabbage, quartered and cored

I carrot, peeled

I red bell pepper, seeded, deribbed, and diced

1/2 cup green onions, thinly sliced

Salt and freshly ground pepper to taste

I tablespoon caraway seeds

Blue Brie Dressing

4 ounces Abbey blue Brie cheese (see Resources, page 277)
   or other creamy blue cheese, cut into cubes

I cup heavy (whipping) cream

1/2 teaspoon sugar

2 tablespoons cider vinegar

Salt and freshly ground pepper to taste

2 tablespoons olive oil

Using the large holes of a box grater, shred the apple into a large bowl and toss with the lemon juice to prevent discoloring. Shred the green cabbage, red cabbage, and carrot into the bowl. Add the bell pepper, onions, salt, pepper, and caraway seeds and toss.

To make the dressing: In a blender or food processor, process the cheese and cream until smooth. Add the wine vinegar, salt, and pepper and blend again for 30 seconds. With the machine running, gradually add the oil and blend until the sauce thickens, about 15 seconds. Pour over the salad and toss until thoroughly coated. Refrigerate for at least 1 hour or for up to 12 hours.

Two Dairy Dressings

For a taste from the dairy in simple salad terms, these two traditional dressings—one with buttermilk, the other with blue cheese—can be used on mixed lettuces, in cabbage salads like coleslaw, or in fruit salads.

Buttermilk Dressing

Makes 1 1/2 cups

3/4 cup buttermilk
3/4 cup mayonnaise
1 shallot, minced
1 garlic clove, minced
Salt and freshly ground pepper to taste
1/8 teaspoon curry powder
1 tablespoon minced fresh basil
1 tablespoon minced fresh parsley
1 teaspoon minced fresh thyme

In a medium bowl, whisk the buttermilk, mayonnaise, shallot, and garlic together until smooth. Add all the remaining ingredients and whisk again. Refrigerate for at least 1 hour or up to 12 hours.

Blue Cheese Dressing

1 cup mayonnaise

1/2 cup plain low-fat yogurt or sour cream

2 teaspoons white wine vinegar

Freshly ground pepper to taste

8 ounces Cashel blue cheese (see Resources, page 277)
  or other firm blue cheese

1 tablespoon minced fresh chives

Makes 2 cups

In a medium bowl, whisk the mayonnaise and yogurt together until smooth. Add the vinegar and pepper and whisk again. Fold in the cheese and chives. Season with more pepper, if desired. Refrigerate for at least 1 hour or up to 24 hours.

Mushrooms Stuffed with Cashel Blue

Cashel blue, the first Irish farmhouse blue cheese, is made from the milk of the Friesian herd of Louis and Jane Grubb at Beechmount, Fethard, County Tipperary. In this savory first course, it is stuffed into mushroom caps, which are then fried to a golden brown.

Serves 2 as a first course

6 large white mushrooms, stemmed

4 ounces Cashel blue cheese (see Resources, page 277)
  or other firm blue cheese

Flour for dredging

1 egg, beaten with 2 tablespoons water

1 1/2 cups dried bread crumbs

2 cups vegetable oil

5 ounces salad greens

Vinaigrette

1 tablespoon balsamic vinegar

4 tablespoons extra-virgin olive oil

1 tablespoon minced garlic

1 teaspoon Dijon mustard

Salt and freshly ground pepper to taste

Mustard-Meade Dip

1/2 cup mayonnaise

1/4 cup Lakeshore whole-grain mustard with Bunratty Meade
(see Resources, page 277) or 1/4 cup whole-grain mustard mixed
with 1 tablespoon mead

1 teaspoon minced fresh dill

Wash the mushrooms and dry with paper towels. (Reserve the stems for soups or omelettes.) With a small spoon, stuff the mushroom caps with the cheese. Dredge in flour. Dip mushrooms in the egg mixture, then in the bread crumbs.

To make the vinaigrette: In a small bowl, combine all the ingredients. Whisk to blend and set aside.

To make the dip: In a small bowl, whisk the mayonnaise, mustard, and dill together until smooth. Set aside.

In a Dutch oven or deep fryer, heat the oil to 350°F. Drop the mushrooms, in batches, into the hot oil. Cook, turning as necessary with a wooden spoon, until golden brown, 3 to 5 minutes. Using a slotted spoon, transfer to paper towels to drain.

To serve, divide the greens between 2 plates. Place 3 hot mushrooms on top of each, drizzle with vinaigrette, and pass the mustard-meade dip.

Abbey Blue Brie Omelette

≋ Irish cheese makers have adapted many traditional cheese-making skills from their French counterparts, so it's only logical that recipes for tarts, flans, omelettes, and soufflés would follow. Most of the egg and cheese dishes in this book are substantial enough for a luncheon or light supper when served with a fresh salad and a loaf of bread, and the combinations are quite unusual.

2 cups packed fresh spinach leaves

2 tablespoons water

8 eggs

Salt and freshly ground pepper to taste

2 large tomatoes, peeled, seeded, and chopped (see Note)

1 tablespoon olive oil

Pinch of nutmeg

6 ounces Abbey blue Brie cheese (see Resources, page 277)
   or other soft blue cheese

1/2 cup light cream or half-and-half

Minced fresh parsley for garnish

Preheat the broiler. In a saucepan over medium heat, cook the spinach in the water until wilted, about 2 minutes. Drain and chop. Pat dry.

In a large bowl, beat the eggs, salt, and pepper together and stir in the tomatoes.

In a nonstick 10- or 12-inch ovenproof skillet over medium heat, heat the olive oil. Pour in the egg mixture. Stir in the spinach and sprinkle with nutmeg. Slice the cheese on top, pour the cream or half-and-half over, and cook, without stirring, until the eggs begin to firm around the edges. Place under the broiler until the mixture firms and the top browns lightly, about 5 minutes. With a rubber spatula, gently loosen the sides of the omelette. Cut into wedges and serve immediately, sprinkled with parsley.

Serves 8 as a first course, 4 as a main dish

Note:
To peel and seed tomatoes, put them in a pot with 2 quarts of boiling water for about 30 seconds. Remove, cool under running water, and peel. The skins will slip off easily. To seed the peeled tomatoes, cut them in half across their equator (consider the cored stem end as the North Pole). Hold each half over a bowl, cut side down, and lightly squeeze to remove the seeds, using the tip of your paring knife if needed.

It All Began with Brisket

⪤

Milleens, an original Irish farmhouse cheese, is produced in Eyeries (in County Cork) by Veronica and Norman Steele, the founders of Cáis, the Irish Farmhouse Cheesemakers Association. It was first made in 1978 as a practical way to use up the excess milk produced by their one-horned cow named Brisket. Here's Veronica's version of how it all began:

"…and then one day we bought a farm and a cow. Her name was Brisket, and she only had one horn. She lost the other one gadding down a hill, tail waving, full of the joys of spring. Her brakes must have failed. We had to put Stockholm tar on the hole right through the hot summer. And all the milk she had, three gallons a day! Wonder of wonders, and what to do with it all…

"So for two years I made Cheddars. They were never as good as the ones in Castletownbere had been, but they were better than the sweaty vac-packed bits. Very little control at first, but each failed batch spurred me on to achieve control. I was hooked. Once I had four little truckles [little rounds of cheese] on a sunny windowsill outside, airing themselves, and Prince (our dog) stole them and buried them in the garden. They were nasty and sour and over-salted anyway. Those were the days.

"So one day Norman said, 'Why don't you try making a soft cheese for a change.' So I did. It was a quare hawk [eccentric, odd] all right, wild, weird, wonderful. Never to be repeated. You can never step twice into the same stream….

"So there was this soft cheese beginning to run. We wrapped up the last of it and away it went with the vegetables and pies to Sneem and the Blue Bull restaurant where it made its debut. Not just any old debut, mind you. As luck would have it, Declan Ryan, of Arbutus Lodge Hotel in Cork, was having dinner there that very night. Attracted no doubt by Annie Goulding's growing reputation, Declan had ventured forth to sample the delights of Sneem, and the greatest delight of them all was our humble cheese. An original Irish farmhouse cheese! At last, the real thing, after so long. Rumour has it that there was a full eclipse of the sun and many earth tremors when the first Milleens was presented on an Irish cheese board."

Chetwynd Blue and Cauliflower Flan

Serves 8 as a first course, 4 as a main dish

≋ Chetwynd blue is a semisoft mild blue cheese made by Jerry Beechinor at Castlewhite Farmhouse (Waterfall, County Cork). Its blue veins develop during three weeks of maturing, but the cheese may ripen for up to four months to a pronounced flavor and a distinctive pink skin. Its piquant flavor pairs well with other distinctive tastes like cauliflower and Cheddar cheese, as in this recipe from the National Dairy Council. Woodford Dairy in Belfast, Northern Ireland, also makes blue Rathgore, an off-white cheese made from local goat's milk, which has a creamy, buttery flavor ideal for cheese boards, cooking, dips, dressings, and sauces.

Pastry Shell

Pinch of salt

1/2 cup all-purpose flour

6 tablespoons (3/4 stick) cold butter

1/4 to 1/2 cup cold water

1 cauliflower, cut into florets

2 tablespoons butter

1 onion, chopped

2 tablespoons all-purpose flour

1 cup milk

Salt and freshly ground pepper to taste

4 ounces Chetwynd blue cheese (see Resources, page 277) or other soft blue cheese, crumbled

1/4 cup (1 ounce) shredded Kerrygold Irish Cheddar cheese (see Resources, page 277) or other Cheddar cheese

Preheat the oven to 425°F.

To make the pastry shell: In a small bowl combine the salt and flour. Using a pastry blender, 2 knives, or your fingers, cut or work the butter into the flour to the consistency of fine crumbs. Stir in the water with a fork until all the flour is moistened. Form into a ball with your hands. On a lightly floured board, roll the pastry out to a thickness of 1/4 inch. Fit the pastry into a 9-inch pastry ring or springform pan. Prick the bottom of the pastry. Line the pastry with aluminum foil or waxed paper and fill with pie weights or dried beans to weigh down the crust. Bake for 10 minutes. Remove from the oven and remove the foil and weights or beans. Let cool on wire rack. Reduce the oven temperature to 375°F.

Cook the cauliflower in boiling salted water until tender, 10 to 12 minutes. Meanwhile, in a small skillet, melt the butter over medium heat and cook the onions until soft, 3 to 5 minutes. Stir in the flour and cook for 1 minute. Gradually add the milk and cook, stirring frequently, until the sauce begins to thicken. Add the salt and pepper.

Sprinkle the blue cheese over the pastry crust. Pour the cauliflower mixture over and sprinkle with the Cheddar cheese. Bake until the top begins to brown, about 30 minutes. Let cool for 5 minutes. To serve, cut into wedges.

Cheddar, Bacon, and Oatmeal Soufflé

〰️ When the Irish Food Board invites chefs to create dishes for a special meal, most rise to the occasion effortlessly, as evidenced by this breakfast soufflé by fourth-generation Irish-American Michael Foley, chef/proprietor of Printer's Row Restaurant in Chicago. Foley, a member of Euro-Toques, the prestigious European chef's organization, is a lot like his Irish counterparts in the group, who continually seek out the best in local and regional fare. This soufflé includes three very Irish ingredients: traditional bacon, oatmeal, and Cheddar cheese, and although it was intended for an Irish breakfast, it's elegant enough for a luncheon or light supper.

**Serves 4 to 6
as a main dish**

2 tablespoons unsalted butter

1/2 cup chopped bacon, preferably Irish (see Resources, page 277)

1 cup milk

3/4 cup quick-cooking oatmeal, preferably McCann's brand
(see Resources, page 277)

1/2 cup (2 ounces) shredded Cheddar cheese, preferably Irish
(see Resources, page 277)

1/3 cup low-fat cream cheese

4 eggs, separated

1 tablespoon minced fresh parsley

1 teaspoon Dijon mustard

1/4 teaspoon salt

1/2 teaspoon cayenne pepper

Freshly ground pepper to taste

Generously butter an 8-inch soufflé dish. Dust with flour and set aside.

In a small skillet, cook the bacon over medium-high heat until slightly crisp. Transfer to paper towels to drain.

In a medium saucepan, melt the remaining butter over medium heat, add the milk, and heat until almost boiling. Slowly stir in the oatmeal. Cook, stirring constantly, until thick, about 4 minutes. Remove from heat and whisk in the Cheddar and cream cheeses until blended. Stir in the bacon, egg yolks, parsley, mustard, salt, cayenne, and pepper.

In a large bowl, beat the egg whites until soft peaks form. Gently fold the beaten whites into the oatmeal mixture in thirds until blended. Spoon into the prepared dish and place in a cold oven. Turn heat to 350°F and bake, undisturbed, until the center is still slightly soft but the soufflé has risen and set, about 40 minutes. Serve immediately.

Cheddar Colcannon Torte

≈ Michelin chefs Paul and Jeanne Rankin of Roscoff, their Belfast restaurant (Shaftesbury Square), like to experiment with traditional ingredients to produce sophisticated dishes. This torte is a beautiful blend of tradition and invention.

Serves 8

1/2 head Savoy cabbage, cored and shredded

3 tablespoons butter

6 slices bacon, diced

4 baking potatoes, peeled and cut into 1/4-inch slices

Salt and freshly ground pepper to taste

2 cups (8 ounces) shredded Cheddar cheese, preferably Kerrygold (see Resources, page 277)

Preheat the oven to 400°F. Grease a 9-inch pie plate or tart pan.

In a medium saucepan, blanch the cabbage in boiling salted water for 2 minutes. Drain and plunge into cold water. Drain again and transfer to paper towels to dry.

In a medium skillet, melt the butter over medium heat. Add the bacon and cook until browned. With a slotted spoon, transfer the bacon to a bowl and reserve the bacon drippings in the pan. Add the cabbage to the bacon and toss gently. Sprinkle the potatoes with salt and pepper, and toss in the bacon drippings.

Layer 1/3 of the potatoes in the prepared pan. Sprinkle with 1/3 of the cheese, top with half the cabbage mixture, and sprinkle with another 1/3 of the cheese. Add another 1/3 of the potatoes, the remaining cheese, then the remaining cabbage mixture. Top with remaining potatoes. Cover with a sheet of parchment paper or aluminum foil and bake for 45 minutes. Remove from the oven and let cool for 30 minutes or to room temperature. To serve, cut into wedges and serve with a fresh green salad.

Pasta Baked with Cheese and Stout

**Serves 8 as a first course,
4 as a main dish**

⇘⇙ Irish pasta? Why not? While it doesn't ooze tradition, it's just about as creamy and delicious as old-fashioned macaroni and cheese can get. When chef Robert Mignola of Manhattan's Post House created this dish for an Irish Food Board luncheon, he not only used clover-shaped pasta and three varieties of Irish cheese, he flavored the sauce with Guinness stout for a most unusual flavor.

8 ounces clover- or pinwheel-shaped pasta

3 teaspoons butter

2 teaspoons minced shallots

3/4 cup Guinness stout

2 cups heavy (whipping) cream

1/2 cup (2 ounces) shredded Kerrygold Blarney cheese (see Resources, page 277) or other semi-soft cheese like Gouda

1/2 cup (2 ounces) shredded Swiss cheese, preferably Kerrygold (see Resources, page 277)

1/2 cup (2 ounces) Cheddar cheese, preferably Kerrygold vintage Cheddar (see Resources, page 277)

3/4 cup dried bread crumbs

In a large pot of boiling salted water, cook pasta until al dente, about 10 minutes. Drain and set aside. →

In a medium saucepan, melt 1 teaspoon of the butter over medium heat. Add the shallots and cook until soft, about 3 minutes. Add the Guinness and cook until reduced by half, about 5 minutes. Add the cream and cook until reduced by half, about 5 minutes longer. Remove from heat and let cool to room temperature.

In a large bowl, combine the cooked pasta, cheeses, and Guinness mixture and stir to blend. Preheat the oven to 350°F. Grease a 9-by-13-inch baking dish or 6 ramekins and pour the pasta mixture into the prepared dish(es).

In a small saucepan, melt the remaining 2 teaspoons butter. Combine with the bread crumbs and spoon over the top of the pasta. Bake until the cheese begins to bubble and the top browns lightly, about 20 minutes for individual ramekins and 30 minutes for the baking dish.

Chicken Cashel Blue with Gaelic Sauce

Serves 4

≋≋ The French master chef Escoffier lists in his *Guide Culinaire* more than forty recipes for chicken breast, by far the most versatile and popular meat the world over. It's easily adaptable to any national cuisine, and it works well with Irish dairy products, like this easy-to-prepare dish from Bailey's of Cashel, a charming restaurant situated in the shadows of the ancient Rock of Cashel (County Tipperary).

4 boneless, skinless chicken breast halves

4 ounces Cashel blue cheese (see Resources, page 277)
  or other firm blue cheese

Flour for dredging

1 teaspoon garlic salt

1 egg beaten with 1 tablespoon milk

1 cup dried bread crumbs

2 cups vegetable oil

Watercress sprigs for garnish

Gaelic Sauce

2 tablespoons olive oil

1 onion, chopped

8 fresh white mushrooms, chopped

2 tablespoons Irish whiskey

1/4 cup heavy (whipping) cream

Preheat the oven to 350°F. Cut a small pocket into the side of each chicken breast. Roll the cheese into 4 equal cylinder shapes and stuff 1 into the pocket of each chicken breast. Dredge the chicken in flour, dip in the egg mixture, and coat with the bread crumbs.   →

In a large skillet over medium heat, heat the oil. Add the chicken and cook on both sides until lightly browned, 5 to 7 minutes. Transfer to a baking sheet and bake for 10 minutes.

To make the sauce: In a small skillet over medium heat, heat the oil and sauté the onion and mushrooms until soft, 3 to 5 minutes. Add the whiskey and cook until slightly reduced. Add the cream and cook until slightly thickened.

To serve, place a few spoonfuls of sauce on each of 4 serving plates, top with a chicken breast and garnish with the watercress.

Chicken with Cooleeney Sauce

Serves 4

Cooleeney is a rich Camembert cheese hand made by Jim and Breda Maher using milk from their Fresian herd in Moynes (Thurles, County Tipperary). Their cheese, made from raw milk and ripened in special maturing rooms for two weeks, is hand turned daily to produce the characteristic mold that develops on traditional Camembert. Maturing time for Cooleeney is anywhere from six to twelve weeks, depending on the size of the cheese, but connoisseurs might wish to ripen the cheese further until it becomes runny and full-flavored. They might further argue that it's somewhat sinful to use it in a cream sauce, but the Mahers believe it should be eaten according to taste, as in this unusual chicken dish that's flavored with vermouth and garnished with walnuts. Serve this with brown rice and a green vegetable.

4 boneless, skinless chicken breast halves

Freshly ground pepper to taste

1/3 cup homemade chicken stock or canned low-salt chicken broth

1 leek, white part only, washed and sliced

1/2 cup heavy cream

4 ounces Cooleeney Camembert cheese (see Resources, page 277) or other Camembert, chopped

1/3 cup sour cream

1/3 cup dry vermouth

1/3 cup walnut pieces

Preheat the oven to 400°F. Place the chicken breast halves in a baking pan, sprinkle with pepper, and bake for 25 minutes, turning once. Add the stock or broth and cook for 10 minutes. Remove from the oven and drain the cooking liquid into a medium saucepan. Set the chicken aside and keep warm.

Add the leek to the saucepan with the cooking liquid and cook until slightly softened, about 3 minutes. Add the cream and cheese and cook, stirring constantly, until the cheese melts. Reduce heat and simmer until the sauce begins to thicken, 3 to 4 minutes. Stir in the sour cream and vermouth and cook until smooth and hot.

To serve, place 1 chicken breast on each of 4 plates, pour some sauce over, and sprinkle with some of the walnuts.

Cashel Blue and Celery Soup

≋ The chef at Kilcoran Lodge Hotel, a former hunting lodge in Cahir, County Tipperary, relies on local produce and cheese, especially Cashel blue, a tasty addition to this creamy soup.

Serves 8 as a first course, 6 as a main dish

8 tablespoons (1 stick) butter

1 bunch celery, trimmed and finely chopped

2 tablespoons all-purpose flour

8 cups homemade chicken stock or canned low-salt chicken broth

2/3 cup heavy (whipping) cream

2 ounces Cashel blue cheese (see Resources, page 277)
 or other firm blue cheese, crumbled

Salt and freshly ground pepper to taste

Minced fresh parsley for garnish

Croutons (page 27)

In a large saucepan, melt the butter over medium heat. Add the celery and cook, stirring frequently, until soft, about 10 minutes. Add the flour, stock or broth, and cream and boil until slightly thickened, about 10 minutes. Add the cheese, salt, and pepper and cook until the cheese melts and is well blended, about 5 minutes.

To serve, ladle the soup into bowls, sprinkle with parsley, and top with croutons.

Baked Cheddar and Scallion Soup

≋ This homespun version of the classic French onion soup is another innovation of the talented husband-and-wife team of Paul and Jeanne Rankin, proprietors of Roscoff (Belfast, County Antrim), authors of *Gourmet Ireland,* and stars of the PBS show of the same name.

Serves 4 to 6 as a first course

4 tablespoons unsalted butter

1 1/2 pounds onions, sliced

1 1/2 cups dry white wine

3 tablespoons all-purpose flour

9 cups homemade chicken stock or canned low-salt chicken broth

Bouquet garni: 2 fresh parsley sprigs, 1 thyme sprig, 1 bay leaf, and 1 chervil sprig, tied together in a cheesecloth bag

Salt and freshly ground pepper to taste

1 egg yolk

7 tablespoons light cream or half-and-half

2 3/4 cups (11 ounces) Blarney Irish Cheddar cheese (see Resources, page 277) or other Cheddar cheese

2 cups green onions, green parts only, thinly sliced

8 to 12 slices day-old baguette, toasted

In a large saucepan, melt 2 tablespoons of the butter over medium heat and sauté the onions until soft, 3 to 5 minutes. Add the wine and cook until the wine has almost evaporated, 8 to 10 minutes.

Meanwhile, in another large saucepan over low heat, melt the remaining 2 tablespoons of the butter. Add the flour and cook, stirring constantly, for 2 minutes. Let cool slightly, then whisk in the stock or broth and cook until slightly thickened. Add this mixture to the onions along with the bouquet garni. Simmer gently for about 30 minutes. Season with salt and pepper. (At this point, the soup may be pureed in a blender or food processor to make a smooth and thick soup, or leave the onion slices whole.)

To serve, preheat the oven to 400°F. Place 4 to 6 individual ovenproof bowls on a baking sheet. In a small bowl, whisk the egg yolk and cream or half-and-half together. Add 2 tablespoons of this to each bowl. Divide half the cheese and half the green onions among the bowls. Ladle in the hot soup and float 2 slices of toasted baguette on each serving. Top with the remaining green onions and cheese. Bake for about 5 minutes, or until bubbling and crusty brown. Serve at once.

Part 4 From the Hillside

The more carrots you chop, the more
turnips you slit, the more murphies you peel, the
more onions you cry over, the more bullbeef you butch,
the more mutton you crackerhack, the more potherbs you pound,
the fiercer the fire and the longer your spoon and the harder
you gruel with more grease to your elbow, the
merrier fumes your new Irish stew.

JAMES JOYCE, *FINNEGANS WAKE*

⌄⌃

Whether in memories or photographs, the visual images of rural Ireland are warm and beckoning. From the forty shades of green that color the land to the tiny specks of white sheep that graze on mile-high mountains, the Irish countryside continues to evoke a nostalgia for the way things used to be. A thatched-roof cottage sits remotely at the base of a hill, a thin pencil of smoke swirling from its chimney. You wonder what's cooking in the cast-iron pot hanging over the fire.

For centuries, the principal cooking utensils in Irish country cottages were the iron pot and black iron skillet, both of which have been used in various forms since the time of the Celts. The pot was filled with water, and whatever meat, grain, or vegetable was available was added for day-long cooking. Usually the meat was kid or mutton, but bacon was often added for additional flavor. Today, lamb is the meat of choice in Ireland's national dish, Irish stew, although the debate continues about whether to add carrots and turnips for color and flavor.

Myrtle Allen, hostess at Ballymaloe House (Shanagarry, County Cork), author, and an internationally recognized chef who established her reputation by reviving traditional Irish dishes, says the common practice is to include carrots south but not north of Tipperary.

In *Myrtle Allen's Cooking at Ballymaloe House,* Allen writes, "I spent one period of my life going around asking everyone I met, 'Do you put carrots in your Irish stew?' The answer was invariably, 'yes.' My mother always put carrots in her stew; everyone in Shanagarry did, too. I found carrots going into Irish stew as far north as Tipperary [even though] the classic version has no carrots."

Carrots or not, as with a number of old-world recipes, there are as many variations as there are cooks, so add what suits you.

Beyond the homey stew, other lamb dishes, whether a roast, a rack, or a chop, turn up virtually everywhere, and everyone has a local favorite—Wicklow, Kerry, Connemara, Mount Errigal, or lamb from the Mountains of Mourne—which they claim is best in the land. But short of being there in person to decide for ourselves, local lamb can be just as rewarding when it's dressed up to look Irish.

Irish Stew

⇔⇔ The original one-pot meal, Irish stew is great pub grub and a whole-some cold-weather meal. The combination of lamb, onions, potatoes, and stock is so popular, in fact, that it's spawned interesting variations that use lamb shanks instead of lamb cubes, turnips instead of carrots, and stout instead of stock. Most agree, however, that this recipe is a classic version.

2 tablespoons vegetable oil

2 pounds boneless stewing lamb, cut into chunks and trimmed

2 to 3 onions, sliced

2 carrots, peeled and sliced (optional)

I small turnip, peeled and sliced (optional)

2 to 3 large baking potatoes, thickly sliced

Salt and freshly ground pepper to taste

I tablespoon minced fresh thyme or I teaspoon dried

2 tablespoons minced fresh parsley, plus I tablespoon for garnish

1¹/₂ cups water, homemade lamb stock, or canned low-salt beef broth

In a large Dutch oven or flameproof casserole over medium heat, heat the oil. Cook the lamb in batches on all sides until all the meat is browned. In the same pan, alternate layers of meat, onions, and potatoes, ending with potatoes. (If using carrots and turnip, add them with the onions.) Sprinkle each layer with salt, pepper, thyme, and some of the parsley. Add the water, stock, or broth and cover tightly with a lid. Cook until the meat is tender, 2 to 2¹/₂ hours. (Alternatively, bake the stew in a preheated 300°F oven for the same amount of time.)

Check the pan occasionally and add more water or stock, if necessary, to make sure you have a thick gravy. Before serving, brown the pota-toes under the broiler for a few minutes and sprinkle with the remaining parsley.

Lamb and Vegetable Soup

〰〰 A lighter version of Irish stew, this soup raises no arguments about whether or not to add carrots; in fact, they are required, along with turnip, cabbage, and leeks. This soup is even better made a day in advance and reheated.

Serves 6

1¹/₂ pounds shoulder lamb chops, trimmed of excess fat

1 large onion, chopped

2 bay leaves

5 cups water

2 to 3 carrots, peeled and sliced

¹/₂ turnip, peeled and diced

¹/₄ head white cabbage, cored and shredded

2 to 3 leeks, white part only, washed and thinly sliced

1 tablespoon tomato puree

2 tablespoons minced fresh parsley

Salt and freshly ground pepper to taste

In a large saucepan, combine the lamb, onion, and bay leaves. Add the water and bring to a boil over medium heat. Skim the residue from the soup, then reduce heat and simmer, covered, for 1 to 1¹/₂ hours. Skim again, if needed.

With a slotted spoon, transfer the lamb to a cutting board. Trim off all meat, cut it into small pieces, and discard the bones. Return the meat to the broth. Add all the remaining ingredients and simmer for 30 minutes more. Serve with whole-wheat bread and a green salad.

Dingle Pie

⇧⇩ I first traveled to Ireland in 1984, arriving, coincidentally, on the first day of one of Ireland's oldest events, the Puck Fair, held annually in Killorglin, County Kerry. From as early as 1613, when a local landowner received a royal patent "to hold a fair in Killorglin on Lammas Day (August 1) and the day after," the fair has been held to trade livestock and to celebrate the first day of the harvest. Changes in the Gregorian calendar altered the dates slightly, so the event now runs August 10 to 12. The "king" of the fair is a large male goat, King Puck, who is installed on a lofty platform over the market square, where he reigns supreme for three days nibbling on cabbage. The townspeople celebrate with Guinness and Dingle pies, which are traditional Kerry mutton pies made with a rich crust originally flavored with mutton drippings and served with a mutton broth. The pies can also be made with lamb, as in this recipe from Máire De Barra, a public house at the Pierhead in Dingle, County Kerry, and have been celebrated in song by Paul Creightin, a Dubliner now living on the peninsula.

They look so neat,
They're packed with meat,
They surely are the best.
They'd warm the cockles
of your heart,
And put hair upon your chest.
The poor ole vegetarians,
They can't believe their eyes,
At the crowds outside
De Barra's
Waiting for her mutton pies.

Shortcrust Dough

1 teaspoon salt

2 cups all-purpose flour

1 cup (2 sticks) cold butter, cut into small pieces

1/2 cup ice water

1 pound stewing lamb, finely chopped

Salt and freshly ground pepper to taste

1 onion, finely diced

2 carrots, diced

3 teaspoons minced fresh thyme or 1 teaspoon dried

1 egg, beaten with 1 tablespoon milk

Lamb Broth for reheating (recipe follows) (optional)

→

To make the dough: In a medium bowl, combine the salt and flour. With a pastry cutter, 2 knives, or your fingers, cut or work the butter into the flour to the consistency of coarse crumbs. Gradually stir in the water with a fork until all the flour mixture is moistened. Knead the dough with your hands until you can form a ball. Divide the dough in half and form each into a flattened disk. Cover each disk with plastic wrap and refrigerate for 20 to 30 minutes.

Season the lamb with salt and pepper. In a bowl, mix the chopped lamb, onion, carrots, and thyme together.

Preheat the oven to 350°F. Grease a baking sheet. On a floured board, roll out 1 dough disk and, using a small plate or bowl as a measure, cut into 6 rounds about 4 inches in diameter. Spoon 1 to 2 tablespoons of the meat mixture and vegetables into the center of 3 rounds. Dampen the edges with a little milk or water. Cover each round with another dough disk and, with a fork, crimp the edges all around. Dampen the edges again with a little milk or water. Brush some of the egg mixture over the pies, and cut a slit into the lid of each pie to let the steam escape. Repeat with the remaining dough and filling. Place the pies on the prepared pan. Bake until browned, about 1 hour. Serve hot, at room temperature, or reheated in lamb or mutton broth.

Lamb Broth

> **1 pound lamb bones**
> **Salt and pepper to taste**

Put lamb bones in a large saucepan with water to cover. Season with salt and pepper and bring to a boil. Reduce heat to a simmer and cook, covered, for 1 hour. Place the Dingle pies in the broth for 10 minutes to heat.

Makes 2 cups

Jack Barry's Lamb Kidneys

Serves 4 as a first course

〰〰 My grandfather James Barry was a Cork native, possibly from Butte-vant where the Barry name is among the most common. The noble family of Barry was most probably of Norman origin, and the first Barrys reportedly came to Ireland near the end of the eleventh century. Jack Barry, the proprietor of Barry's Butcher Shop in Kinsale, County Cork, may be a distant relative, but Brian Cronin, proprietor of Kinsale's award-winning Blue Haven Hotel, says with absolute certainty that Barry "supplies the best of Irish beef and lamb." As a tribute, Cronin has named one of his popular dishes after the well-known butcher.

1 teaspoon vegetable oil

8 lamb kidneys, halved

2 shallots, finely diced

2 tablespoons brandy

1 cup homemade beef stock or canned low-salt beef broth

2 teaspoons whole-grain mustard, preferably Lakeshore brand (see Resources, page 277)

Salt and freshly ground pepper to taste

1 tablespoon cold butter

10 ounces mixed salad greens

In a large skillet over medium heat, heat the oil. Add the kidneys and cook until lightly browned, about 5 minutes. Add the shallots and cook until soft, about 3 minutes. Add the brandy, let warm, avert your face, and light with a long-handled match. Shake the pan until the flames subside. Pour in the stock or broth and boil rapidly until reduced and syrupy, 3 to 5 minutes. Reduce heat, add the mustard, salt and pepper, and whisk in the butter to thicken. (Do not allow to boil.) Remove from heat.

Divide the salad greens among 4 plates. Arrange the kidneys on top and pour the sauce over. Sprinkle with freshly ground pepper to taste.

Lamb Shanks Braised in Stout

Serves 6

〰〰 When the Fitzpatrick Manhattan Hotel (687 Lexington Avenue) holds its annual Irish cooking contest to find "the best recipe on this side of the Atlantic," the entries are usually top-notch adaptations of meals served "across the pond." Most come with stories of who first prepared it, or of cousins who make it whenever "Yanks" come to call. Long Islander Larry Ryan was the 1997 winner with this version of a classic French peasant dish. He told the judges, "I decided if the French can slow-cook lamb shanks in Cabernet Sauvignon or Burgundy, then the Irish can surely turn to Guinness to flavor the broth." I think you'll agree with his decision.

6 lamb shanks

Flour for dredging

Salt and freshly ground pepper to taste

1/3 cup olive oil

12 small white onions, peeled

3 large carrots, peeled and sliced

3 celery stalks, sliced

1 garlic clove, minced

Pinch of dried rosemary

Pinch of dried thyme

1 cup Guinness stout

3/4 cup homemade beef stock or canned low-salt beef broth

12 small red potatoes

Lightly moisten the lamb shanks with water. In a large bowl or plastic bag, combine the flour, salt, and pepper and dredge the meat in the mixture. In a large skillet over medium heat, heat the olive oil. Add the lamb shanks and cook on all sides until browned, about 10 minutes. Transfer to a Dutch oven or flameproof casserole.

Add the onions, carrots, celery, garlic, rosemary, and thyme to the skillet and cook over medium heat for 5 minutes, stirring to scrape up the browned bits from the bottom of the pan. Pour the vegetables and pan juices onto the lamb. Add the Guinness and stock or broth, cover, and simmer for 45 minutes. Add the potatoes, re-cover, and cook until meat is fork tender, 1½ to 1¾ hours.

To serve, place 1 lamb shank in the center of each of 6 shallow soup bowls and spoon some vegetables and broth around.

It Takes a Village to Prepare a Meal

⬧⬦⬧

Amateur Chef Larry Ryan's narrative of the origins of his recipe for lamb shanks braised in Guinness is worth repeating:

"One of the things my wife, Patty, and I enjoy about our summers on the Loop Head in County Clare is watching the gathering and the preparing of our evening meal. Pat Gavin and Danielle Dequin, our hosts for the lion's share of our evening meals, are the owners of the Long Dock, a two-hundred-year-old pub on West Street, in the village of Carrigaholt, which translates from the Irish as the 'rock of the fleet.' The village lies on a small bay in the Shannon estuary on Ireland's west coast.

"Many mornings find us sipping coffee on one of the tables on the sidewalk in front of the Dock. The sun chases the chill from the breeze that stirs up from the Shannon as we peruse that day's edition of the *Independent,* or the latest copy of the *Clare Champion.* Small, colorful delivery vans continuously stop and replenish the inventories of the two shops and the six pubs, while an occasional tractor speeds to the next hayfield to be mowed….

"Course by course, entree by entree is delivered throughout the day, usually by a local supplier. A farmer comes by with a supply of freshly harvested produce: potatoes, carrots, onions, cabbage, parsley. Michael O'Connell chugs up from the pier in the fish co-op forklift with a load of salmon right off one of the boats that call Carrigaholt home….

"In the afternoon, the aroma of brown bread baking at the Dock mingles with the scents of sea air and burning turf. As I sit having a slow Guinness at an available outside table, Patty returns from the butcher in Kilrush with, among other victuals, choice lamb shanks. My inspiration! In a minute, I'm off for the vegetables, a bit more Guinness, and the makings of our evening meal!"

Chops in Locke's

Serves 6

〰〰 Lamb chops are perfect for marinating, especially less-expensive chops like shoulder (round bone or blade), and for grilling. This marinade calls for Locke's Irish whiskey, a new addition to the Irish whiskey market, and plenty of thyme, "that chef of seasoners," so-called by James Joyce, who likened history to an Irish stew, influenced by thyme!

Marinade

I cup Irish whiskey, preferably Locke's brand
(see Resources, page 277)

1 1/2 cups olive oil

2 garlic cloves, minced

2 shallots, minced

3 sprigs fresh thyme or I teaspoon dried

1/2 teaspoon dried rosemary

1/2 teaspoon cayenne pepper

1/2-inch piece fresh ginger, grated

Salt and freshly ground pepper to taste

6 shoulder lamb chops

To make the marinade: Combine all the ingredients in a small bowl or screw-top jar and whisk or shake well to blend. Reserve half of the marinade for basting. Place the lamb chops in a shallow dish, pour the remaining marinade over, cover, and refrigerate for at least 8 hours or up to 12 hours.

Remove the chops from the marinade. Let sit at room temperature for 1 hour. Light a fire in a charcoal grill, or preheat a gas grill or broiler. Grill or broil the chops for 5 minutes on each side for medium rare, and brush with the reserved marinade once or twice.

"Grilled" Lamb Chops and Tomatoes with a Garlic Crust

Serves 2

≈≈ When the Irish say "pop something under the grill," they generally mean to cook it under the broiler. While the meat is cooking, boil a few new potatoes.

2 loin lamb chops (see Note)

Salt and freshly ground pepper to taste

3 tablespoons olive oil, plus more for sprinkling

2 slices brown soda bread, store-bought or homemade (see page 217)

1 1/2 teaspoons fresh minced parsley

3/4 teaspoon fresh chopped chives

1/8 teaspoon dried thyme

1 garlic clove, minced

Grated zest and juice of half an orange

2 large tomatoes, halved crosswise

Preheat the broiler, placing the rack 4 to 5 inches from the heat source. Spray a small baking sheet with olive oil cooking spray.

Using 1 tablespoon of the olive oil, brush both sides of each chop with oil and season with salt and pepper. Place the chops on the prepared pan and broil on one side for 5 minutes.

Meanwhile, in a blender or food processor, process the brown bread, herbs, garlic, orange zest, and salt and pepper to the consistency of fine bread crumbs. Transfer to a small bowl, add the orange juice and remaining 2 tablespoons olive oil, and blend thoroughly.

Turn the chops over and spread 1 tablespoon of the crumb topping over each. Place the tomatoes on the baking sheet with the lamb chops and

Note:

If you wish to serve 2 chops per person, double the ingredients for the topping.

spoon the remaining topping over the tomato halves. Sprinkle a few drops of olive oil over the topping. Set rack at the position farthest from the heat, and broil the chops and tomatoes until the crust is crisp, 7 to 8 minutes. Serve "straightaway," with new potatoes.

Honey-Mustard Lamb Chops

Serves 4   ⟩⟩ The combination of honey and mustard turns up in everything nowadays, from salad dressing to pretzels. Both flavors are especially good with lamb, as this simple recipe proves.

> 8 loin lamb chops, trimmed of excess fat
>
> I garlic clove, halved
>
> I tablespoon minced fresh rosemary
>
> Freshly ground pepper to taste
>
> 1/4 cup honey, preferably Mileeven brand (see Resources, page 277)
>
> 2 tablespoons whole-grain mustard, preferably Lakeshore brand (see Resources, page 277)
>
> Fresh rosemary sprigs for garnish
>
> Lemon slices for garnish

Preheat the broiler, placing the rack 3 to 4 inches from the heat source. Rub the chops on both sides with the cut side of the garlic. Press the rosemary and pepper into both sides of the chops.

In a small bowl, blend the honey and mustard together. Spread half of the honey-mustard mixture on top of each chop and broil the chops for 4 minutes. Turn the chops, spread with the remaining honey-mustard mixture, and cook for 2 minutes on the second side for medium rare. Serve immediately, garnished with the rosemary sprigs and lemon slices.

Mount Errigal Lamb
Wrapped in Buttermilk Bread

Serves 4

⩔⩔ For the more ambitious cook, this succulent lamb dish—made with what the chef calls Ireland's finest, Mount Errigal spring lamb from John Duffy of Raphoe, County Donegal—is a variation of a classic but with a distinctly Irish twist. Created by chef Neil McFadden of the Old Dublin Restaurant (Francis Street, Dublin), the lamb is braised in stock with a good dash of spirits, wrapped in bacon slices, then encased in a buttermilk dough. Prepare this dish for an impressive special-occasion Irish meal. Serve it with broccoli or Brussels sprouts, and thick-sliced carrots.

- 2 tablespoons vegetable oil
- 1 boneless shoulder of lamb, rolled and tied (see Resources, page 277)
- 1 carrot, peeled and sliced
- 1 onion, sliced
- 1 celery stalk, sliced
- 1 1/4 to 1 1/2 cups lamb stock, Lamb Broth (page 108), or canned low-salt chicken broth
- 2 tablespoons Bunratty poitín (see Resources, page 277) or Irish whiskey
- 10 slices bacon, preferably Irish (see Resources, page 277)

Buttermilk Dough

- 2 cups sifted all-purpose flour
- 1/2 teaspoon salt
- 1/2 package (1 teaspoon) active dried yeast
- 1 tablespoon vegetable oil
- 1/4 cup boiling water
- 1/2 cup buttermilk

1 egg mixed with 1¹/₂ tablespoons water

2 tablespoons sesame seeds

Salt and freshly ground pepper to taste

In a Dutch oven or flameproof casserole over medium heat, heat the oil. Add the lamb and brown quickly on all sides, about 10 minutes. Transfer to a plate. Add the carrot, onion, and celery to the pan to make a bed for the lamb. Return the meat to the casserole and add enough stock or broth to come about 2/3 of the way up the meat. Add the poitín or whiskey. Reduce heat to simmer, cover, and cook until the meat is tender, about 2 hours. Transfer the lamb to a plate and let cool. Set aside. Let the cooking liquid stand for 10 minutes, then skim off the fat. Strain and set aside. When the lamb has cooled, remove the string and wrap the meat in the bacon. Set aside.

To make the dough: Preheat the oven to 400°F. In a large bowl, combine the flour, salt, and yeast. Mix the oil, water, and buttermilk together, add to the dry ingredients, and mix well. On a lightly floured surface, knead until a smooth, elastic dough is formed, about 5 minutes. (A little extra flour or liquid can be added, if necessary.) Roll the dough out to make a piece big enough to wrap around the meat. Lay the meat in the center and roll the dough around it.

Lightly oil a baking sheet large enough to hold the meat and place the meat in center. Let it rest until the dough has puffed up to twice its size, 10 to 15 minutes. Mix the egg and water together to make a wash. Brush the egg mixture over the dough and sprinkle with the sesame seeds. Bake for 15 minutes, then reduce heat to 325°F and bake until the dough is golden brown, about 30 minutes. Remove from the oven.

Boil the cooking liquid over medium-high heat until reduced by half. Season with salt and pepper.

To serve, cut 1 thick slice per serving and spoon 1 tablespoon of the reduced cooking liquid over the top. Pass the rest in a serving dish.

Loin of Lamb Wrapped in Puff Pastry

Serves 4

〰 A simpler version of what could be called lamb "Wellington" uses frozen puff pastry and the tender loin portion of lamb, which you should have your butcher cut for you. American chef Robert Mignola of Manhattan's Post House Restaurant also combines lamb and bacon, and serves three slices of lamb per person, arranged in the shape of a shamrock with a watercress stem. A whiskey-mustard sauce is spooned around the lamb.

- 1 tablespoon vegetable oil
- 2 boneless loins of lamb, about 12 ounces each (see Resources, page 277)
- 6 slices bacon, preferably Irish (see Resources, page 277)
- 1 box frozen puff pastry, thawed
- 1 egg mixed with 1 tablespoon water
- 1 bunch watercress for garnish

Whiskey-Mustard Sauce

- 1 teaspoon butter
- 1 shallot, diced
- 1/4 cup Irish whiskey
- 3/4 cup homemade chicken stock or canned low-salt chicken broth
- 2 tablespoons whole-grain mustard, preferably Lakeshore brand (see Resources, page 277)

Preheat the oven to 400°F. Line a baking sheet with parchment paper.

In a heavy pot large enough to hold both loins, heat the oil over medium heat. Add the lamb and brown it quickly on all sides, about 10 minutes. Transfer to a plate to cool. Reserve the pan for the sauce.

Note:

This recipe is pictured on the front cover.

Wrap each loin in 3 slices of bacon. Divide the puff pastry in half and carefully roll out each half to a piece about 1/4 inch thick and large enough to wrap 1 loin. Lay a loin in the center of each pastry and roll up the pastry over the meat. Pinch the edges. Brush the egg mixture over the pastry.

Place the loins on the prepared pan and bake until pastry is golden brown, about 30 minutes for medium rare. Remove from the oven and let the meat rest for 10 minutes.

Meanwhile, make the sauce: In the reserved pan, melt the butter over medium heat and sauté the shallots until soft, 2 to 3 minutes. Add the whiskey and stir to scrape up the browned bits from the bottom of the pan. Cook until the whiskey is reduced by half, about 2 minutes. Add the stock or broth and cook to reduce by half again, about 5 minutes. Stir in the mustard.

To serve, cut each loin into 6 slices. Arrange 3 slices on each plate in the shape of a shamrock and garnish with a watercress sprig as the stem. Spoon the warm sauce around the lamb.

Marinated Loin of Kerry Lamb
with Herbed Potato Galettes

✒✒ Michael and Geraldine Rosney, proprietors of Killeen House (Aghadoe, Killarney), feature Kerry lamb on their menu. Their chef, Paul O'Gorman, often marinates a loin of lamb first, then roasts it quickly. He serves it with herbed potato cakes he calls *galettes*.

Serves 8

2 cups dry red wine

3 garlic cloves, minced

2 fresh thyme sprigs

I shallot, minced

I bay leaf

I loin of lamb, about 4 pounds (see Resources, page 277)

1¹/₂ pounds boiling potatoes, peeled and cut into 2-inch pieces

10 tablespoons (I stick plus 2 tablespoons) butter

2 tablespoons minced fresh chives

2 tablespoons minced fresh parsley

I tablespoon minced fresh tarragon

Salt and freshly ground pepper to taste

2 tablespoons vegetable oil

2 cups lamb stock, Lamb Broth (page 108)
   or canned low-salt chicken broth

I tablespoon honey

The day before cooking, combine the wine, 2 cloves garlic, 1 thyme sprig, the shallots, and bay leaf in a large bowl. Add the lamb, cover, and refrigerate overnight.

The next day, remove the lamb from the refrigerator and let sit at room temperature for 1 hour. Meanwhile, cook the potatoes in boiling salted water until tender, 12 to 15 minutes. Drain and mash. Add 8 tablespoons butter, the remaining garlic clove, the chives, parsley, tarragon, salt, and pepper and, with a wooden spoon, mix well. Let cool, then shape into cakes about 1½ inches in diameter. Set aside.

Preheat the oven to 375°F. Remove the lamb from the marinade and pat dry. In a large skillet over medium heat, heat the oil and brown the lamb quickly on all sides, about 10 minutes. Transfer to a baking pan and bake for 20 minutes (for medium rare).

Meanwhile, in a large skillet, melt the 2 tablespoons butter over medium heat and cook the potato cakes for 3 to 4 minutes on each side, or until golden brown. Transfer to a baking sheet and keep warm in the oven.

In a saucepan, cook the lamb stock or broth over medium heat until reduced by half, 5 to 8 minutes. Add the remaining thyme sprig and the honey and cook until thickened, about 5 minutes.

To serve, carve the lamb into medallions. Place a potato galette in the center of each plate, surround with lamb slices, and spoon some of the sauce around the edge.

Legs of Lamb, Irish Style

〰 Lamb always lends itself well to special occasions, and a leg of lamb is one of the easiest meats to cook. Coating a leg with herbs or garlic and serving it with a sauce to complement its distinctive flavor makes a perfect Irish Sunday dinner. Here are three different ways to give a leg of lamb a definite Irish touch: Centurion Lamb combines the classic mint jelly sauce with Irish Mist liqueur; Lakeshore Lamb blends whole-grain Irish mustard with soy sauce and ginger; and Lamb Folláin is marinated in a tasty combination of orange-whiskey marmalade and orange juice. All start with a five- to seven-pound leg of lamb, but most of the sauces and marinade recipes are enough to coat a larger leg if necessary.

Centurion Lamb

1 leg of lamb, 5 to 7 pounds

2 garlic cloves, slivered

Salt and freshly ground pepper to taste

1 lemon, sliced thin

1 cup mint jelly

3/4 cup Irish Mist liqueur

Serves 6 to 8

Preheat the oven to 325°F. Make slits in the meat and insert the garlic. Sprinkle the meat all over with salt and pepper, place in a shallow baking pan, and arrange the lemon slices all over the surface of the lamb. Roast for 1 hour and 15 minutes.

Meanwhile, in a small saucepan, blend the mint jelly and 1/2 cup of the Irish Mist over medium heat. Cook to a sauce consistency, about 10 minutes. Remove from heat.

Remove the lamb from the oven, discard the lemon slices, and brush with the sauce. Roast again, basting every 15 minutes until a meat thermometer inserted into the thickest part of the lamb registers 170°F (medium rare), 175°F (medium), or 180°F (well done), 1 1/4 to 1 1/2 hours. Remove from the oven and keep warm.

In a small saucepan, heat the remaining 1/4 cup Irish Mist over low heat. Pour over the roast, avert your face, and light the pan drippings with a long-handled match. When the flame subsides, transfer the lamb to a serving platter and allow to rest for 15 minutes before carving. Return the pan drippings to a small saucepan over medium heat, stir thoroughly, and heat until warm. Serve as a sauce for the meat.

Lakeshore Lamb

Serves 6 to 8

This mustard-coated leg of lamb is delicious served hot with traditional accompaniments like potatoes and vegetables, but it's also great cold for a picnic or luncheon, sliced thin and served in pita pockets with chutney or with chopped lettuce, cucumber, and tomato dressed in vinaigrette.

1 leg of lamb, 5 to 7 pounds

2 garlic cloves, slivered

Salt and freshly ground pepper to taste

1/2 cup whole-grain mustard, preferably Lakeshore whole-grain mustard with Bunratty Meade (see Resources, page 277)

2 tablespoons mead, preferably Bunratty Meade (see Resources, page 277)

3 tablespoons soy sauce

1 teaspoon dried rosemary

1/4 teaspoon ground ginger

1/4 cup olive oil

Preheat the oven to 325°F. Make slits in the meat and insert the garlic slivers. Sprinkle the meat all over with salt and pepper. In a blender or food processor, process the mustard, mead, soy sauce, rosemary, ginger, and olive oil until smooth. Coat the lamb with the mixture and let sit at room temperature for 1 to 2 hours.

Place the lamb in a shallow baking pan and roast until a meat thermometer inserted into the thickest part of the lamb registers 170°F (medium rare), 175°F (medium), or 180°F (well done), 2 1/2 to 3 hours. Transfer the lamb to a serving platter and let rest for 15 minutes before carving.

Lamb Folláin

Folláin Irish whiskey marmalade is one of the few Irish marmalades that are made in small batches from the finest natural ingredients—Seville and sweet oranges, lemons, and sugar—and is fortified with one of the finest local ingredients, Jameson Irish whiskey. Delicious on toast, biscuits, and scones and wonderful in combination with other ingredients in marinades and sauces, it's particularly tasty as a coating for leg of lamb. Folláin (from the Irish word meaning "wholesomeness") preserves, marmalades, jams, and chutneys are made by Peadar and Maureen Ó Lionáid in Cúil Aodha (Coolea), in the Gaeltacht (Irish-speaking area) of County Cork. Their products contain no artificial preservatives or colorings.

Serves 6 to 8

3 tablespoons Folláin orange-whiskey marmalade (see Resources, page 277) or orange marmalade mixed with 1 teaspoon Irish whiskey

2 tablespoons grated orange zest

2 tablespoons minced garlic

3 tablespoons olive oil

1/2 cup orange juice

3 tablespoons minced fresh chives

Salt and freshly ground pepper to taste

1 leg of lamb, 5 to 7 pounds

In a saucepan, combine the marmalade, orange zest, garlic, olive oil, orange juice, chives, salt, and pepper and cook over low heat until the marmalade melts and the sauce is smooth, 5 to 8 minutes.

Place the lamb in a shallow dish and pour the marinade over, reserving 1/4 cup for basting. Turn to coat, cover, and refrigerate for at least 12 hours or up to 24 hours. Turn the lamb 2 to 3 times during marinating to coat evenly.

Remove the lamb from the refrigerator and let sit at room temperature for 1 hour. Preheat the oven to 325°F.

Remove the lamb from the marinade and pat dry. Place the lamb in a shallow baking pan and roast until a thermometer inserted into the thickest part of the lamb registers 170°F (medium rare), 175°F (medium), or 180°F (well done), 2 1/2 to 3 hours, basting 2 or 3 times with the reserved marinade. Transfer the lamb to a serving platter and let rest for 15 minutes before carving.

Butterflied Leg of Lamb

Serves 6 to 8

≈≈ Butterflied leg of lamb (ask your butcher to bone and flatten the leg), is perfect for both broiling or grilling. You'll love this recipe from County Mayo, by way of Sharon Mullaney of Spring Lake Heights, New Jersey. For her entry into the Fitzpatrick Manhattan Hotel's annual cooking contest, Mullvaney submitted this luscious lamb recipe from her cousin Sheila of Swinford, her father's hometown.

Mullaney says, "Sheila broils it in the oven, but I find that it's even more delicious when cooked over a charcoal grill."

1/2 cup olive oil

1/3 cup Irish whiskey

1/4 cup fresh lemon juice

I small onion, finely chopped

I garlic clove, minced

I teaspoon salt

I teaspoon sugar

I teaspoon paprika

I teaspoon dried rosemary

I teaspoon dried oregano

1/2 teaspoon freshly ground pepper

I butterflied leg of lamb, 6 to 7 pounds (see Resources, page 277)

→

In a small bowl, combine all the ingredients except the lamb and mix well. Place the lamb in a shallow dish and pour the marinade over, reserving 1/4 cup for basting. Turn to coat, cover, and refrigerate for at least 12 hours or up to 24 hours. Turn the lamb 2 to 3 times during marinating to coat evenly.

Remove the lamb from the refrigerator and let sit at room temperature for 1 hour. Light a fire in a charcoal grill or preheat a gas grill. Transfer the lamb to the cooking rack over a hot fire and grill for about 1 hour for medium rare, turning every 15 minutes and basting with the reserved marinade.

Rack of Lamb

⇕⇕ For an elegant meal, a rack of lamb can't be beat. It's not difficult to manage, even for a dinner party, when it can be cooked earlier in the day and finished in the oven for 20 minutes during the first course. This Irish classic needs little adornment, although the Irish Food Board (Bord Bia) suggests a lightly flavored breadcrumb topping. Serve with Potato Soufflé (see page 13), fresh green beans, or baby carrots.

Serves 8

2 racks of lamb, about 2 pounds each (see Resources, page 277)
Salt and freshly ground pepper to taste
Pinch of cayenne pepper
1 cup (2 sticks) butter at room temperature
1 tablespoon dry mustard
3 cups dried bread crumbs
3 garlic cloves, minced
1/4 cup minced fresh parsley
2 teaspoons minced fresh rosemary

Preheat the oven to 400°F. Remove the fat and meat from the tips of the bones and scrape the bones clean (or ask your butcher to "French" the racks). Wrap aluminum foil around the tips of the bones to prevent them from burning. Remove all but a very thin layer of fat from the lamb.

Score the remaining fat to make a lattice pattern, which will help hold the coating during the final roasting. Season the lamb with salt, pepper, and cayenne. Place the racks in a roasting pan and bake for 20 minutes. Remove from the oven and let cool to room temperature.

Meanwhile, in a small bowl, mix 3/4 cup of the butter and mustard together to make a smooth paste. Spread it over the fatty side of the lamb. In a small bowl, combine the bread crumbs, garlic, parsley, and rosemary. Melt the remaining butter and add it to the bread-crumb mixture. Mix well. With your fingers, press the bread crumb mixture into the mustard paste. Keep the racks at room temperature until ready for the final roasting.

Reheat the oven to 400°F. About 20 minutes before serving time, return the meat to the oven and roast for 20 minutes. To serve, remove the foil from the tips of the bones and garnish with paper frills, if desired. Carve the meat into cutlets, allowing 2 to 3 per person.

Part 5 From the Waters

Sláinte an bradáin chugat. (May you be as healthy as the salmon.)

OLD IRISH SAYING

⇘⇙

My knowledge of Irish is very poor, so when a Dublin friend toasted me with *"Sláinte an bradáin chugat,"* I had to be told that it was a wish for me to enjoy the same strength, agility, and long life as the salmon, the noblest of Irish fish.

Folklorists have absolutely no doubt of the salmon's superiority, for they tell the tale of the ancient Irish hero Finn MacCool, who reportedly gained the gift of knowledge simply from cooking and tasting a salmon!

The association of salmon with Irish heroes is not confined to legend alone, and at feasts of Gaelic chieftains, salmon, roasted on a spit over an open fire and basted with wine, honey, and herbs, was often the centerpiece of the meal. Served with a glass of mead, it was truly a meal fit for a king.

Salmon is not the only fish with national identity in a country with hundreds of miles of coastline, thousands of miles of sparkling rivers, and acres of pristine loughs. In the Republic, Dublin prawns, Galway oysters, Bantry mussels, and Kenmare scallops are world famous, and in Ulster, their counterparts hail from places like Portavogie, Carling-ford, Ardglass, and Murlough Bay. Herrings from Sligo and brown trout from Lough Corrib are near legendary, and Lough Neagh eels were rated "the fairest and the fattest" by Archbishop Laud in the seventeenth century.

For those of us who live away from Ireland's shores yet yearn for a taste from its waters, the closest catch—whether it's mussels from Maine, oysters from Chesapeake Bay, or salmon from the Pacific Northwest—can be turned into an Irish meal. In this chapter you'll find traditional recipes for native Irish fish that can be adapted for what's freshest in the local market. Try one, bake up a loaf of brown soda bread, and enjoy a glass of mead or a pint of Guinness. You'll be pleasantly surprised to discover that you don't have to travel all the way to Ireland or wait until Saint Patrick's Day to enjoy a delightful Irish seafood meal.

Poached Salmon

If the salmon is the noblest Irish fish, when it's poached whole and served with one of the following colorful and flavorful sauces, it's also the most impressive. A fish poacher is ideal for this recipe, but a deep roasting pan will also work.

Serves 8 as a main dish, 12 as a first course

2 tablespoons minced fresh dill

1/2 cup dry white wine

1/2 cup fish stock or clam broth

1 small carrot, peeled and sliced

1 celery stalk with leaves, cut into 4 pieces

1 small onion, sliced

1 salmon, 5 to 8 pounds, cleaned, gutted, and scaled

Lemon slices, fresh dill, and fresh parsley for garnish

Choice of sauces (recipes follow)

In a small saucepan, combine the dill, wine, stock or broth, carrot, celery, and onion. Bring to a boil, then reduce heat and simmer, uncovered, for 20 minutes.

If using a poacher, add the poaching liquid to it. Place the salmon on a double thickness of cheesecloth, twist the ends to form handles, and place the fish in the hot liquid. Cover the poacher and simmer (do not boil) about 10 minutes for each inch of the thickness of the fish (25 to 30 minutes for a 5-pound fish).

Without a poacher, preheat the oven to 300°F. Place the salmon on a double thickness of buttered aluminum foil large enough to make a packet to enclose the fish. Pour the poaching liquid over the salmon and fold up the sides of the foil to make a container. Pull up the lengthwise sides and crimp the edges together all around. Bake for 25 to 30 minutes for a 5-pound fish. Remove from the oven and let the salmon sit in its foil packet for about 20 minutes.

Using 2 metal spatulas, remove the fish from the poacher or from the aluminum foil packet to a serving plate and discard the poaching liquid. Carefully remove the skin from both sides. Cut the fish along the backbone. Garnish with lemon slices and herb sprigs. Serve at room temperature with one or more of the sauces. When the top side is eaten, turn the fish over to serve the remaining half.

Sauces for Salmon

〰〰 From a casual picnic to a formal dinner, poached salmon pairs well with a sauce of sorrel, a tangy vegetable frequently mentioned in Irish literature; a leek butter sauce spiked with tarragon; a spinach-flavored green mayonnaise; watercress sauce; or a simple mix of mayonnaise and Dijon mustard accented with fresh dill.

Sorrel Sauce

2 shallots, minced

2 tablespoons dry white vermouth

1/4 cup dry white wine

1/4 cup water

3 egg yolks

1 cup (2 sticks) butter

1 to 2 cups sorrel leaves, cut into thin strips

Salt and freshly ground pepper to taste

Makes about 2 cups

In a small saucepan, combine the shallots, vermouth, wine, and water and boil until almost all the liquid has evaporated and the shallots are soft, about 10 minutes. Strain, reserving both the shallots and the liquid. Transfer the shallots to a blender or food processor, add the egg yolks, and process on high for 30 seconds. Return to the saucepan.

In a medium saucepan, melt the butter over medium heat and stir in half the sorrel leaves. When the butter is almost boiling, whisk the mixture in a very thin stream into the egg yolk mixture. As the sauce begins to thicken, whisk in the salt and pepper and the remaining sorrel. Keep warm in a double boiler over hot water, or reheat over gentle heat.

Leek-Tarragon Butter

Makes about 1¹/2 cups

1 shallot, minced

1 leek, white part only, sliced

3 tablespoons white wine vinegar

3 tablespoons dry white wine

12 tablespoons (1¹/2 sticks) butter, cut into tablespoon-sized pieces

1¹/2 teaspoons minced fresh tarragon or ¹/2 teaspoon dried

Salt and freshly ground pepper to taste

In a small saucepan, combine the shallots and leeks with the vinegar and wine and boil over medium heat until the liquid is reduced to 2 tablespoons, about 10 minutes. Reduce heat and whisk in the butter, 1 tablespoon at a time. Add the tarragon, salt, and pepper. Keep warm in a double boiler over hot water, or reheat over gentle heat.

Green Mayonnaise

Makes 2¹/2 cups

2 packed cups fresh spinach leaves, cooked, drained, and finely chopped

1 teaspoon Dijon mustard

1 teaspoon fresh lemon juice

1 tablespoon minced fresh parsley

1 teaspoon minced fresh chives

1¹/2 teaspoons minced fresh tarragon or ¹/2 teaspoon dried

1¹/2 teaspoons minced fresh basil or ¹/2 teaspoon dried

2 cups reduced-fat mayonnaise

In a blender, combine all the ingredients except the mayonnaise and process until smooth. Stir into the mayonnaise and whisk until smooth.

Watercress Sauce

4 tablespoons butter

1/2 cup minced shallots

2 large bunches watercress, washed and stemmed

1 1/2 cups heavy (whipping) cream

Salt and freshly ground pepper to taste

Makes about 2 cups

In a large skillet, melt the butter over medium-low heat. Add the shallots and sauté until soft, about 3 minutes. Add the watercress and stir until wilted, 3 to 5 minutes. Add the cream, salt, and pepper, and bring to boil. Remove from heat, cool slightly, transfer to a blender or food processor, and process until smooth. Keep warm in a double boiler over hot water, or reheat over gentle heat.

Dill-Mustard Sauce

1 cup reduced-fat mayonnaise

2 tablespoons Dijon mustard

3 tablespoons minced fresh dill

Makes 1 1/4 cups

In a blender, combine all the ingredients and process until smooth.

Salmon Cakes

Serves 4 to 5 as a main dish, 8 to10 as a first course

〜〜 I'd like to be able to reflect on the luscious salmon meals from my Irish-American childhood, but I'm afraid my memories are of my mother's creamed salmon and peas, which she served on saltine crackers or toast points, and her salmon cakes, both made with canned salmon rather than fresh. Replacing canned with fresh salmon in the recipes makes a world of difference, however, and these salmon cakes are particularly good when served with one of the sauces suggested for the poached salmon.

1/2 cup dry white wine

1/2 cup fish stock or clam broth

1/2 cup water

2 shallots, minced

2 to 3 celery leaves

1 fresh parsley sprig

1 pound salmon fillet, boned

1 pound boiling potatoes, peeled and cut into 2-inch pieces

1/4 cup milk

3 teaspoons minced fresh tarragon or 1 teaspoon dried

3 tablespoons minced fresh parsley, plus sprigs for garnish

1 teaspoon lemon pepper

1/4 teaspoon salt

1 egg beaten with 1 tablespoon water

Flour for dredging

1 cup dried bread crumbs

1/2 cup vegetable oil

Lemon slices for garnish   →

In a large nonreactive skillet, combine the wine, stock or broth, water, shallots, celery leaves, and parsley. Bring to a boil over medium heat and add the salmon, skin-side down. Cover, reduce heat, and simmer until the fish flakes when tested with a fork, about 10 minutes. Remove from heat and let the fish cool in the poaching liquid for 15 minutes. With 2 slotted spoons or spatulas, gently lift the salmon from the liquid to a plate. Remove the skin and flake the fish.

Meanwhile, cook the potatoes in boiling salted water until tender, 12 to 15 minutes. Drain and mash.

In a medium bowl, combine the flaked salmon and mashed potatoes. Add the milk, tarragon, parsley, lemon pepper, and salt and mix well. Add the egg and mix again. Refrigerate for 10 minutes.

Shape the mixture into 8 to 10 evenly sized cakes. Lightly dredge in flour, pass through the egg mixture, then coat with the bread crumbs. In a large skillet over medium heat, heat the oil and cook the cakes in batches until browned, 3 to 5 minutes per side. Serve immediately, garnished with parsley sprigs and lemon slices, or transfer to a baking sheet and keep warm in a preheated 200°F oven until ready to serve. Serve a sauce alongside.

Finn McCool and the Salmon of Knowledge

Dubliner Stephen Houlihan, of Finn McCool/Sea Love Seafoods Company, tells this story of how the legendary Irish warrior gained his magical powers:

"Finn McCool, or Fionn mac Cumhaill, has been a celebrated hero in Irish literature for over one thousand years. He's always portrayed as a great warrior and seer, but is best known for his gift of wisdom, which he acquired from a salmon.

"As a seven-year-old boy, Finn met a seer called Finneigeas on the banks of the Boyne River. Finneigeas had dedicated the past seven years of his life to trying to catch the Salmon of Knowledge, which reportedly swam in the river. Legend had it that the first person to taste it would be blessed with all the knowledge in the world.

"And so it was that while Finn was there, Finneigeas caught the salmon, and with much joy he immediately put it on the spit, entrusting Finn to cook it, but warning him not to taste it. Like any watchful cook, after a time Finn went to test for doneness, using his thumb. Naturally, he burned himself, and to ease the pain he stuck his blistered thumb into his mouth, and thus became the first person to taste the salmon. When Finneigeas looked at the boy's face, he saw the wisdom shining in it and knew that the salmon was no longer any good to him. Ever after that, if Finn needed to know something, he put his thumb into his mouth and the knowledge came to him. Lucky guy!"

Salmon and Spinach Terrine

One of the nicest ways to begin a meal is with a chilled terrine of fish. This salmon-cod combination, flavored and colored with fresh spinach leaves, is a favorite at Eniscree Lodge, a charming country retreat perched on a County Wicklow hillside in Eniskerry. Served with brown soda bread, the terrine is perfect for a luncheon dish or as a first course for dinner.

Serves 8 as a first course or a luncheon dish

4 cups packed fresh spinach leaves

I pound cod, skinned and boned

I cup dried bread crumbs

3 eggs

1 1/4 cups light cream or half-and-half

One 12-ounce fresh salmon fillet, boned and skinned

1/2 teaspoon ground nutmeg

Salt and freshly ground pepper to taste

Mixed salad greens for serving

Cherry tomatoes for garnish

Preheat the oven to 350°F. Blanch the spinach in boiling salted water until the leaves are limp, 1 to 2 minutes. Drain and plunge into cold water. Drain again and squeeze spinach dry. Transfer the spinach to a blender or food processor. Add the cod, bread crumbs, eggs, and cream or half-and-half and process until smooth.

Line an 8-by-3¾-by-2½-inch glass loaf pan with aluminum foil and brush lightly with cooking oil. Spoon half the spinach mixture into the pan. Cut the salmon into ½-inch-thick crosswise slices. Lay the slices of salmon on top of the spinach mixture and sprinkle with nutmeg, salt, and pepper. Spoon the remaining spinach mixture over the top. Cover with another piece of greased foil, place the loaf pan in a baking dish, and add hot water to come two thirds up the sides of the loaf pan. Bake for 1¼ hours. Remove both pans from the oven and let the terrine cool in the water bath for 2 to 3 hours. Remove from the water bath and refrigerate for at least 12 hours or up to 24 hours.

To serve, loosen the sides of the terrine with a warm knife and unmold onto a serving plate. Cut into 8 slices and serve over a bed of mixed greens garnished with cherry tomatoes.

Roasted Salmon Wrapped in Bacon

Serves 4

〜〜 Irish chefs have found countless ways to use salmon, in elaborate creations like napoleons, as well as in simple dishes that incorporate other classic Irish ingredients like bacon and cabbage. Chef Jonathan Parker of the Manhattan Ocean Club livened up salmon fillets for a recent Irish Food Board luncheon by wrapping them in bacon and topping them with a colorful sauce. Serve this dish with boxty, champ, or colcannon.

4 salmon fillets, about ¹/2 pound each

4 slices bacon, preferably Irish (see Resources, page 277)

Salt and ground white pepper to taste

4 tablespoons canola oil

4 tablespoons unsalted butter at room temperature

1 cup fish stock or clam broth

2 teaspoons minced fresh chives

2 teaspoons minced fresh parsley

Juice of ¹/2 lemon

Fresh chervil sprigs for garnish

Preheat the oven to 425°F. Wrap each salmon fillet with 1 slice of bacon and secure with toothpicks. Season with salt and pepper.

In an ovenproof skillet large enough to hold all 4 fillets, heat 2 tablespoons of the oil over medium-high heat. Place the salmon fillets in the skillet, skin-side down, and bake until opaque on the outside but translucent in the center, about 10 minutes. Transfer to a serving plate and lightly cover with aluminum foil to keep warm.

Meanwhile, in a small saucepan, bring the stock or broth to a simmer. Discard any cooking liquid from the skillet. In the same skillet, melt the remaining 2 tablespoons canola oil with the 4 tablespoons butter over medium heat. Add the stock or broth, chives, parsley, lemon juice and stir up to remove any browned bits from the bottom of the skillet. Cook until slightly thickened.

To serve, transfer the salmon to 4 warmed plates, spoon some of the sauce over to the top, and garnish with fresh chervil.

Roasted Salmon with Leeks

Serves 4

≋ Leeks, a popular member of the onion family, are one of the oldest Irish vegetables and combine well with everything from potatoes to fish. Here they're used as a bed for salmon steaks.

> 3 large leeks, white part only, cut into 1/4-inch-thick slices
> 2 tablespoons water
> 1 tablespoon olive oil
> 1 teaspoon finely shredded lemon zest
> 2 teaspoons minced fresh dill, plus dill sprigs for garnish
> 4 salmon steaks, about 8 ounces each
> 1/4 teaspoon ground pepper
> 2 tablespoons fresh lemon juice
> Lemon wedges for garnish

Preheat the oven to 425°F. In an ovenproof casserole large enough to hold all 4 steaks, combine the leeks, water, olive oil, lemon zest, and dill. Cover with a lid or aluminum foil and bake for 20 minutes, stirring once halfway through. Remove from the oven, push the leeks aside, and add the salmon steaks to the dish.

→

Spoon the leeks evenly over the fish and season with salt, pepper, and lemon juice. Bake, uncovered, until the salmon is opaque on the outside but translucent in the center, 10 to 12 minutes. To serve, divide the leeks among 4 plates and top with a salmon steak. Garnish with dill sprigs and lemon wedges.

Salmon with Bacon and Cabbage

≋ Once a homespun, old-fashioned meal, bacon and cabbage is now paired with other meats (see Roast Breast of Chicken with Cabbage and Bacon, page 58) or fish, for a striking combination of flavors. Young chefs James and Margaret Nicholas, who share cooking duties at Beech Hill Country House (County Londonderry), like bacon and cabbage with salmon, to which they add a peppercorn sauce.

Serves 4

2 cups cored and shredded Savoy cabbage

2 tablespoons dry red wine

1 teaspoon green peppercorns

1 cup homemade chicken stock or canned low-salt chicken broth

4 tablespoons unsalted butter, plus 2 tablespoons (optional)

4 salmon fillets, boned

8 slices bacon, preferably Irish (see Resources, page 277), chopped

Blanch the cabbage in boiling salted water for 2 minutes. Drain and plunge into cold water. Drain again and transfer to a plate.

In a small saucepan, combine the wine and peppercorns and cook over medium heat until the wine is reduced to 1 tablespoon, 5 to 8 minutes. Add the stock or broth and cook to reduce to about 3/4 cup. Remove from heat and keep warm.

Preheat the oven to 350°F. In a large skillet, heat 2 tablespoons of the butter over medium heat and cook the salmon, skin-side down, for 3 minutes. Transfer to a baking sheet and bake, skin-side up, until opaque on the outside but translucent in the center, 8 to 10 minutes. Set aside and keep warm.

In another large skillet over medium heat, cook the bacon until browned, 5 minutes. With a slotted spoon, transfer the bacon to paper towels to drain. In the same skillet, melt the remaining 2 tablespoons butter over medium heat, add the cabbage, and cook until heated through. Add the 2 tablespoons butter to the sauce to thicken it, if you like.

To serve, place a bed of cabbage on each plate. Place a salmon fillet on top, spoon some sauce over, and garnish with some bacon bits.

Smoked Salmon on Oatmeal Pancakes with Cucumber-Dill Sauce

Serves 4 as a first course or a luncheon dish

For centuries, salmon has been smoked in Ireland using time-honored techniques that capture and enhance the flavor and texture of this legendary fish. Irish smoked salmon, which acquires its inimitable dark orange color and subtle flavor from the traditional oak-smoking method, seems to suit every occasion, from an informal brunch to a sumptuous banquet, and while its price is usually "quite dear," as the Irish say, a little goes a long way toward creating an elegant and impressive dish. As an appetizer, salmon purists prefer to eat it with only a squeeze of lemon and a slice of brown soda bread. Here, it tops oatmeal pancakes for a first course or luncheon dish.

1/2 cup all-purpose flour

1 tablespoon steel-cut oats, preferably McCann's brand (see Resources, page 277), toasted (see page 229)

Pinch of salt

1 teaspoon active dry yeast

1/4 cup warm (105° to 115°F) water

Cucumber-Dill Sauce

1 cucumber, peeled, seeded, and sliced

Salt for sprinkling

1/4 cup sour cream

1 tablespoon minced fresh dill

1/2 teaspoon honey

Juice of 1/2 lime, plus lime slices for garnish

Freshly ground pepper to taste

2 tablespoons vegetable oil

8 slices smoked salmon, preferably Irish (see Resources, page 277)

In a small bowl, combine the flour, oats, salt, and yeast. Stir in the warm water and mix to blend. Cover with plastic wrap or a damp towel and set aside in a warm spot for 1 hour.

To make the sauce: Put the cucumber in a colander over a bowl, sprinkle with salt, and let drain for 15 to 20 minutes. In a small bowl, blend the sour cream, dill, honey, lime juice, and pepper together. Set aside.

In a large skillet or griddle over medium heat, heat the oil. Drop the pancake batter, 1 tablespoonful at a time, onto the pan or griddle and cook until browned, 2 to 3 minutes per side.

To serve, stir the cucumber into the sour cream mixture. Place 2 pancakes on each plate, top with 2 slices of smoked salmon, and drizzle some cucumber-dill sauce over the top. Garnish with lime slices.

Lemon Sole and Lobster Terrine

Serves 8 as a first course or a luncheon dish

〰〰 At Springfort Hall, a classic eighteenth-century Georgian country house in Mallow, County Cork, chef Ita Smith uses smoked salmon to wrap a luscious mixture of lemon sole and lobster and serves slices of the terrine with a sauce of yogurt and fresh herbs. Brown soda bread is a good accompaniment.

8 ounces cooked lobster meat

2 eggs

3 egg whites

3 cups heavy (whipping) cream

1 teaspoon salt

1 pound lemon sole fillets

1 pound smoked salmon, preferably Irish
   (see Resources, page 277), sliced

Garden Herb-Yogurt Sauce

1/4 teaspoon minced fresh chives

1/4 teaspoon minced fresh dill

1/4 teaspoon minced fresh chervil

1/4 teaspoon fennel seeds

1 cup plain yogurt

Lettuce, tomato slices, and cucumber slices for garnish

In a blender or food processor, process the lobster meat, 1 egg, and 1 egg white until smooth. Transfer to a small bowl and, with a wooden spoon, blend in 1 cup of the cream and 1/2 teaspoon of the salt. Cover and refrigerate. Repeat the process with the lemon sole and remaining egg, egg whites, 2 cups cream and 1/2 teaspoon salt.

Preheat the oven to 300°F. Line the bottom and sides of an 8-by-3³/4-by-2¹/2-inch glass loaf pan with half the salmon slices. Spoon in half the sole mixture and smooth with a spatula. Cover with the lobster mixture and smooth, then add the remaining sole mixture and smooth. Cover top with remaining smoked salmon. Cover the terrine with greased waxed paper, then aluminum foil. Place in a baking pan. Add hot water to the baking pan to come two thirds up the sides of the terrine. Place in the oven and bake until the terrine is firm, 1 hour and 15 minutes.

Remove both pans from the oven and let the terrine cool in the water bath for 2 to 3 hours. Remove from the water bath and refrigerate for at least 12 hours or up to 24 hours.

To make the yogurt sauce: In a small bowl, stir all the ingredients together until blended. Cover and refrigerate until ready to use.

To serve, loosen the sides of the terrine with a warm knife and unmold onto a serving plate. Cut into 8 slices. Garnish with lettuce, tomato, and cucumber and serve with the yogurt sauce.

Smoked Mackerel Bake

Serves 4 as a first course or a luncheon or light supper dish

In addition to salmon, many other varieties of smoked fish are popular in Ireland, including cod, eel, haddock, and trout. Simple, delicious, and ready in under 20 minutes, this smoked mackerel dish, a recipe from An Bord Iascaigh Mhara (The Irish Sea Fisheries Board), is perfect as a first course or as a quick supper with a tossed green salad and white or brown soda bread.

2 smoked mackerel fillets, boned, skinned, and flaked

2 to 3 tomatoes, peeled, seeded, and diced (see page 88)

2/3 cup heavy (whipping) cream

Freshly ground pepper to taste

1/4 cup shredded Cheddar or Swiss cheese, preferably Irish (see Resources, page 277)

Fresh parsley sprigs for garnish

Preheat the oven to 400°F. Lightly oil 4 ramekins. Divide the mackerel evenly among the prepared ramekins. Add the diced tomatoes and spoon some of the cream into each dish. Sprinkle with the black pepper and shredded cheese. Place the ramekins on a baking sheet and bake until lightly browned, about 10 minutes. With a spatula, unmold each serving and turn onto a serving plate. Garnish with parsley sprigs.

Warm Trout Smokies with Lemon Sauce

Serves 8 as a first course

Connemara (County Galway) has hundreds of lakes, streams, and bays that provide for the choice seafood served at Cashel House Hotel, situated at the head of Cashel Bay. Hoteliers Dermot and Kay McEvilly pride themselves on the seafood selection available in the dining room of their mid-nineteenth-century country house, like this creamy combination of smoked trout and cheese enlivened with a creamy lemon sauce.

1 1/2 pounds smoked trout, boned, skinned and flaked

1 cup heavy (whipping) cream

2 tablespoons shredded Cheddar cheese, preferably Irish
   (see Resources, page 277)

Lemon Sauce

1 cup heavy (whipping) cream

1 cup fish stock or clam broth

1/2 cup dry white wine

Zest of 1/2 lemon, finely chopped

Salt and freshly ground pepper to taste

Lemon slices for garnish

Preheat the oven to 350°F. Lightly oil 8 ramekins.

In a medium saucepan, combine the trout and cream and cook, stirring frequently, over medium heat, until the cream thickens, 5 to 7 minutes. (Do not allow to boil.) Divide the creamed trout evenly among the prepared ramekins and sprinkle with the cheese. Place the ramekins in a baking pan and add hot water to come halfway up the sides of the ramekins. Bake until the mixture is set, about 30 minutes.

To make the lemon sauce: In a small saucepan, combine the cream, stock or broth, and wine. Cook over medium heat until reduced by half. Add the lemon zest and pepper. Stir thoroughly.

To serve, spoon the warm sauce onto 8 plates. With a knife, loosen the smokies and place 1 in the center of each plate. Garnish with lemon slices.

Smoked Haddock with a Cheese Crust

Serves 6 as a first course or a luncheon dish

Bushmill's Inn, a hotel/restaurant in the County Antrim town of the same name, is part of a coaching inn that dates back to 1608 when the famous Old Bushmills Distillery was granted the world's first license to distill whiskey. Chef Patricia Wilson likes to rely on local ingredients in her cooking, and suggests local smoked haddock, Cheddar cheese from nearby Coleraine, and Caffrey's ale in this smoked haddock dish with a cheese crust. Innkeepers Roy Bolton and Richard Wilson serve this for lunch with boiled new potatoes, or as a first course on lettuce leaves with tomatoes.

3 cups (12 ounces) shredded Cheddar cheese, preferably Irish
(see Resources, page 277)

1/3 cup light ale

1 tablespoon all-purpose flour

1 teaspoon dry mustard

2 tablespoons dried bread crumbs

Salt and freshly ground pepper to taste

1 egg

1 egg yolk

6 pieces smoked haddock, about 6 ounces each

Fresh parsley sprigs

In a double boiler over barely simmering water, combine the cheese and ale and cook until the cheese melts, 5 to 7 minutes. (Do not boil.) Stir in the flour, mustard, and bread crumbs and cook until the mixture comes away from the sides of the pan, about 5 minutes. Season with salt and pepper and let cool. Transfer to a blender or food processor and process until smooth. With the machine running, add the egg, then the egg yolk. Transfer to a small bowl, cover, and refrigerate for 30 minutes.

Preheat the oven to 350°F. Butter an ovenproof casserole dish large enough to hold the haddock pieces in one layer.

On a pastry board, roll the cheese mixture out to a smooth thickness of about 1/4 inch. Place the haddock into the prepared dish and cut pieces of the cheese pastry to fit on top of the haddock pieces (trim the edges). Bake, uncovered, until the haddock is heated through, about 10 minutes. Place under the broiler to brown the crust. To serve, lift the haddock pieces out of the dish with a spatula and garnish with fresh parsley sprigs.

Old-fashioned Fish Bake

Serves 4

⩔ Aside from geography and legend, another important historical influence on fish in the Irish diet was the Catholic Church. By the Middle Ages, there were at least 150 "fish days" on the calendar, designed in part for the purpose of religious fasting. It's no surprise, then, that eating fish on Fridays was a tradition that most Irish-American Catholics grew up with as well (until July 2, 1970, when the requirement was lifted), and clever cooks had enough variations for accessible fish like flounder, cod, haddock, and sole to keep their families happy week after week. Along with traditional fish and chips, a fish "bake" has also been a long-standing Irish recipe and one with many variations. Serve it with boiled potatoes and a green vegetable or salad.

2 tablespoons butter

1 to 1 1/2 pounds haddock, boned and cut into 2-inch chunks

2 leeks, white and pale green parts only, washed and sliced

2 tablespoons all-purpose flour

1 1/4 cups milk

2 tablespoons heavy (whipping) cream

Salt and freshly ground pepper to taste

1 bay leaf

1 tablespoon minced fresh parsley, plus fresh parsley sprigs for garnish

2 tablespoons shredded Cheddar cheese

→

Preheat the oven to 350°F. Use 1 tablespoon of the butter to grease an ovenproof casserole large enough to hold the fish in one layer. Place the fish in the prepared pan, skin-side down.

In a medium saucepan, melt the remaining 1 tablespoon butter over medium heat and cook the leeks until they soften, 3 to 5 minutes. Stir in the flour and cook until smooth, 1 to 2 minutes. Whisk in the milk and cream, salt and pepper to taste, add the bay leaf and parsley, and bring to a boil, stirring constantly, until the sauce is smooth. Spoon the sauce over the fish. Cover with a lid or aluminum foil and bake for 25 minutes.

Remove from the oven, uncover, sprinkle the cheese over the fish, and place under the broiler until browned, 3 to 5 minutes. Garnish with parsley sprigs.

Fish Bake with Spinach: Stem 10 ounces of fresh spinach and cook it, covered, in 2 tablespoons of boiling water until wilted, about 2 minutes. Drain and pat dry. Layer the spinach over the haddock and proceed as above.

Fish Bake with Potato Crust: Prepare the fish and bake as in the main recipe for 15 minutes. Omit the shredded cheese and add a layer of warmed mashed potatoes. Bake for 10 minutes, then place under the broiler until browned, 3 to 5 minutes.

Seafood Festivals

A seafood festival is a great excuse for a party, and in Ireland, where they pay great homage to shellfish, there's genuine revelry to be had at any of these: the Bantry Mussel Fair, Bantry, County Cork, in May; the Clarenbridge Oyster Festival, Clarenbridge, County Galway, the first weekend in September; and the Galway International Oyster Festival, Galway City, the third weekend in September.

Stuffed Paupiettes of Sole with Chive Sauce

Serves 4

⋛⋚ A combination of crabmeat and smoked salmon makes an elegant stuffing for fish served at Christy and Moira Tighe's Cromleach Lodge Country House Hotel (Castlebaldwin, County Sligo). Moira, the chef, says she aims for "the look of nouvelle, the quality of haute, and the portions of Irish generosity," a goal that this dish attains.

I tablespoon butter

I ounce fresh crabmeat

Pinch of grated fresh ginger

1½ tablespoons fresh lemon juice

6 ounces smoked salmon, preferably Irish (see Resources, page 277)

Pinch of cayenne pepper

¼ cup heavy (whipping) cream

Salt and freshly ground pepper to taste

12 fillets of sole

½ cup water

½ cup dry white wine

Chive Sauce

¼ cup dry white wine

I teaspoon white wine vinegar

¼ cup fish stock or clam broth

2 tablespoons unsalted butter, diced

¼ cup minced fresh chives

Fresh chervil sprigs for garnish

Preheat the oven to 350°F. In a small skillet, melt the butter over medium heat. Gently stir in the crabmeat and ginger and cook for about 3 minutes. Stir in half the lemon juice and set aside to let cool. →

In a blender or food processor, process the smoked salmon, remaining lemon juice, cayenne, and cream until smooth.

Season the sole with salt and pepper. Spread each fillet with 1 tablespoon of the salmon mixture and top with a spoonful of the crabmeat mixture. Carefully roll the fillets into cylinders and brush with a little lemon juice. Place the fillets in a shallow ovenproof dish with the water and wine, cover with aluminum foil, and bake until the sole is firm, 8 to 10 minutes.

To make the sauce: In a small saucepan, cook the wine, vinegar, and stock or broth over medium-high heat until reduced by half. Add the cream and cook to reduce further, 3 to 5 minutes. Whisk in the butter until it melts completely. Stir in the chives. Keep warm over a bowl of hot water.

To serve, spoon the warm chive sauce onto 4 plates and arrange 3 paupiettes on each. Garnish with a sprig of fresh chervil.

Fillets of Sole Bonne Femme

Serves 4

〰〰 At Fitzpatrick's Castle Hotel in Killiney, County Dublin, head chef Sean Dempsey's eclectic cooking sets the standard for the restaurants in the other branches of the Fitzpatrick family's hotel empire—in Ireland, at Bunratty and Cork—and in Manhattan, where chef Willon Gibbs maintains Dempsey's signature dish, a delicate sole with a rich velouté sauce and border of piped Duchess potatoes, on his daily luncheon. The term "bonne femme" refers to a home-style dish, cooked simply and accompanied by several vegetables or a thick sauce.

2 tablespoons butter

4 white mushrooms, sliced

I tablespoon minced shallots

3 pounds Dover sole

Salt and freshly ground pepper to taste

3/4 cup dry white wine

I cup fish stock or clam broth

Cream Sauce

4 tablespoons butter

3 tablespoons all-purpose flour

1/4 teaspoon salt

1/4 teaspoon ground pepper

I cup reduced poaching liquid (above)

1/3 cup heavy (whipping) cream

3 egg yolks

Duchess Potatoes (page 14) at room temperature   →

In a small skillet, melt the butter over medium heat and sauté the mushrooms and shallots until soft, 3 to 5 minutes. Set aside.

In a buttered ovenproof casserole dish large enough to hold all the fish in one layer, fold or roll the fillets and cover them with the mushroom mixture. Combine the wine and stock or broth and pour over the fish. Cover with a piece of greased aluminum foil and poach over medium heat for 10 minutes. Transfer the fillets to a serving dish and keep warm.

Strain the poaching liquid into a small saucepan, reserving the vegetables. Cook the poaching liquid over medium heat until reduced to 1 cup. Spoon the reserved vegetables over the fish.

To make the sauce: In a small saucepan over medium heat, melt 2 tablespoons of the butter. Stir in the flour, salt, and pepper and blend well. Cook 2 to 3 minutes. Add the reduced poaching liquid and bring to a boil. Cook, stirring constantly, until the sauce begins to thicken, about 2 minutes. Remove from heat and stir in the cream.

Melt the remaining 2 tablespoons butter. In a double boiler over barely simmering water, whisk the egg yolks. Gradually whisk in the melted butter. Cook, stirring constantly, for 2 to 3 minutes. Stir the egg mixture into the sauce.

To serve, preheat the broiler. Using a pastry bag with a 1-inch opening, pipe the potatoes around the edge of 4 plates, place the sole fillets in the center, and cover with the cream sauce. Place the plates under the broiler until the potatoes and sauce are lightly browned, 1 to 2 minutes.

Fish and Chips

≈≈ What better way to recapture an Irish moment than with a traditional fish "fry," pub grub at its finest! It's a meal that made places like Leo Burdock's in Dublin famous and one that can easily be duplicated at home. An electric deep fryer or skillet is perfect for this, since the oil temperature can be controlled to keep the outside from burning before the inside is thoroughly cooked. The correct temperature also prevents too much oil absorption, since the food seals almost instantly.

1 egg yolk

1/4 cup beer

1/4 cup water

1/2 teaspoon salt, plus salt to taste

3/4 cup all-purpose flour

4 large baking potatoes, peeled

Canola oil for frying

1 egg white

1 pound haddock, boned, skinned, and cut into 2-inch chunks

Freshly ground pepper to taste

Malt vinegar for serving

Lemon wedges for garnish

In a small bowl, whisk together the egg yolk, beer, water, and 1/2 teaspoon salt. Whisk in the flour until smooth. Set aside for 30 minutes.

Cut the potatoes into 1/2-inch-thick strips or slices and place in a bowl of cold water to prevent discoloring. →

Fill an electric skillet, deep fryer, or Dutch oven 2/3 full with oil and heat it to 375°F. While the oil is heating, beat the egg white until soft peaks form, then fold it into the batter to lighten it. Dip the fish in the batter and fry, in batches, until golden brown, 4 to 5 minutes. Using a slotted spatula, transfer the fish to paper towels to drain. Place the fillets on a baking sheet and transfer to a 200°F oven to keep warm.

Drain the potatoes and pat dry with paper towels. Strain the oil used to fry the fish. In the same pan used to fry the fish, reheat the oil to 375°F. Fry the potatoes, in batches, until brown, 3 to 5 minutes. Serve immediately with the fish, with malt vinegar and lemon wedges alongside.

Oven-Fried Fish and Chips: Dip the fish fillets in 1/2 cup milk or 2 tablespoons plain yogurt and dredge in quick-cooking oatmeal, preferably McCann's brand (see Resources, page 277). Bake in a preheated 500°F oven until the fish is golden brown, 8 to 10 minutes.

Stuffed Fillets of Plaice

Serves 4

≈ Plaice is a flat white fish similar to flounder. It poaches well in wine or stock, and although most often served fried, like my first Irish meal in Galway, it's also delicious when lightly stuffed with bread crumbs or, as here, with vegetables.

2 tablespoons butter

1 small onion, chopped

6 ounces white mushrooms, chopped

2 plum tomatoes, seeded and chopped

1½ pounds fillets of plaice or flounder

2 tablespoons dried bread crumbs

2 tablespoons shredded cheese

Preheat the oven to 375°F. Lightly oil an ovenproof casserole large enough to hold the fillets in one layer.

In a large skillet, melt the butter over medium heat. Stir in the onion, mushrooms, and tomatoes and sauté until the onion is translucent, 3 to 5 minutes. Add the fish to the prepared casserole and divide the vegetables onto half of each fillet. Fold over or gently roll up. Sprinkle with the bread crumbs and shredded cheese. Bake until fish is firm and the bread crumbs are lightly browned, about 25 minutes.

Oysters In and Out of Season

⋙⋘

Given the cost of a dozen oysters today, it's hard to believe the prized mollusk was once considered "famine food" and associated with poverty and hard times. Carried in panniers by donkeys along dirt-track roads, the seaweed-wrapped shellfish were sold not by the dozen, but by the barrelful, and were often given away free by Dublin publicans and innkeepers. Native wild oysters are still synonymous with Galway Bay, where they fatten in its clear and clean waters. Today they're enjoyed everywhere throughout the year, even in months with no "r" in them (as the rule for eating oysters used to forbid), since more and more oysters are being farm-raised in Ireland and elsewhere. Water temperatures can be controlled through aquaculture to prevent spawning, a condition that leads to "mushy" oysters.

The question of how to eat oysters, however, remains controversial, with purists insisting that the only way to indulge is uncooked and straight from the shell with a squeeze of lemon and a pint of Guinness. Others prefer them grilled, in stews, or in creamy sauces.

Gratin of Oysters on Creamed Leeks with Guinness Hollandaise

Serves 6 as a first course

Chef Brian Loughlin and his wife, Anne, operate Le Chateaubrianne in Bundoran, County Donegal, a popular seaside resort set on a ragged crescent inlet of Donegal Bay. Local ingredients predominate, and as one Irish food guide reports, "they're cooked with a nicely judged balance of simplicity and imagination." This delectable oyster dish is just one example of chef Loughlin's style, and easy enough to duplicate even without benefit of the view of Donegal Bay.

24 large oysters in the shell

2 tablespoons butter

2 tablespoons water

2 leeks, white and pale green parts only, washed and sliced

2/3 cup heavy (whipping) cream

Salt and freshly ground pepper to taste

Guinness Hollandaise

12 tablespoons (1 1/2 sticks) butter

Reserved oyster liquid

1/2 cup Guinness stout

3 egg yolks

Juice of 1/2 lemon

Shuck the oysters over a small bowl. Strain and reserve the liquid and the deeper half of each shell.

In a medium saucepan, combine the butter and water and cook over medium heat until the butter has melted. Add the leeks and cook until slightly tender, 3 to 5 minutes. Add the cream and cook, stirring constantly, to reduce until slightly thickened, 3 to 5 minutes. Season with the salt and pepper and keep warm in a bowl over hot water. →

To make the hollandaise: In a small saucepan, melt the butter over low heat. In another small saucepan, combine the reserved oyster liquor and Guinness and bring to a boil over medium heat. Cook until reduced to about 2 tablespoons. Transfer the mixture to a blender or food processor. With the machine running, add the egg yolks and lemon juice, then slowly drizzle in the melted butter and process until thickened.

Preheat the broiler. Place the reserved oyster shells on a bed of coarse salt on a baking sheet. Divide the creamed leeks evenly among the shells and top each with an oyster. Spoon some of the hollandaise sauce over each. Heat under the broiler until the sauce is browned and bubbling, about 3 minutes. Serve 4 oysters per person.

Scallop Pie with Potato Crust

〰〰 This Irish version of coquilles St. Jacques is as tasty as the original, but the potato crust gives it a wholesome touch. It's nice served as a main-dish casserole or in individual baking shells as a first course.

Serves 8 as a first course, 4 as a main dish

> **3 boiling potatoes, peeled and cut into 1-inch pieces**
> **1 pound bay scallops**
> **1¼ cups milk**
> **2 tablespoons butter**
> **1 tablespoon all-purpose flour**
> **Salt and freshly ground pepper to taste**
> **8 ounces white mushrooms, sliced**
> **¼ cup dry sherry**

Preheat the oven to 350°F. Cook the potatoes in boiling salted water until tender, 12 to 15 minutes. Drain and mash. Set aside.

Rinse the scallops and pat dry with paper towels. In a small skillet, bring the milk to a simmer over medium heat, add the scallops, and cook until opaque, 12 to 15 minutes. Strain and reserve the scallops and liquid.

In a small saucepan, melt 1 tablespoon of the butter over medium heat. Stir in the flour, then gradually whisk in the reserved liquid. Cook 2 to 3 minutes. Season with salt and pepper. Reduce heat to a simmer, add the mushrooms, and cook until the sauce thickens, about 10 minutes. Stir in the sherry and scallops.

Pour the mixture into an ovenproof casserole dish or spoon into 8 oven-proof scallop shells and cover with the mashed potatoes, making sure they cover the mixture right to the edges. Dot with the remaining 1 table-spoon butter. Bake until the top begins to brown, 15 to 20 minutes.

Grilled Scallops with Chanterelles and Brown Butter Vinaigrette

Serves 4 as a first course

⋛⋚ The bounty of fish and shellfish from the waters surrounding North-ern Ireland's Ards Peninsula is enormous. From the deep waters of Strang-ford Lough, divers handpick big, beautiful scallops that the local people call clams. Within hours of the catch, chef Donal Keane has them on the table at the Portaferry Hotel (Portaferry, County Down), combining them with chanterelles that he handpicks from the forests surrounding the nearby Mount Stewart Estate, a fascinating eighteenth-century house and garden on the east shore of Strangford Lough near Greyabbey (County Down). For this recipe, choose scallops that are $2^{1}/_{2}$ to $3^{1}/_{2}$ ounces each, if possible. →

Note:

This recipe is pictured on the back cover.

8 tablespoons (1 stick) plus 1 tablespoon butter

8 ounces chanterelles or other wild mushrooms, halved (see
  Resources, page 277)

1 tomato, peeled, seeded, and chopped (see page 88)

2 tablespoons balsamic vinegar

12 sea scallops

Champ (page 8)

Light a fire in a charcoal grill, or preheat a gas grill or a broiler. In a medium skillet, heat 2 tablespoons of the butter over medium heat. Add the chanterelles and cook quickly until lightly colored, 2 minutes. With a slotted spoon, transfer the chanterelles to a plate.

In a small saucepan, melt the remaining butter over medium heat and cook until it turns nutty brown, 5 minutes. Add the tomato and vinegar and stir to blend.

Place the scallops in a grilling basket and cook over a hot fire until opaque, about 2 minutes on each side. Or cook under the broiler, turning once.

To serve, place a large spoonful of Champ on each plate, top with 3 scallops, and spoon some sauce over. Scatter some of the chanterelles or mushrooms over the sauce.

Monkfish on a Causeway
of Leeks with Mussel Sauce

Serves 4

This dish is named for a Northern Ireland phenomenon, the Giant's Causeway, forty thousand basalt columns rising out of the sea, which some believe was clearly a giant's work. The story goes that the ancient Ulster warrior Finn McCool fell in love with a lady giant who lived on Staffa, an island in the Hebrides, and he put the stones there at the top of County Antrim as a highway to bring her across to his native land! Legend aside, Paul McKnight, head chef at the sumptuous Culloden Hotel (Holywood, County Down), creates his own "causeway" of leeks, which he uses as a platform for monkfish medallions and a creamy mussel sauce. For added local color, McKnight suggests deep-fried dulse (edible seaweed) as a garnish. If it's available in your region, give it a try.

12 large mussels, scrubbed and debearded

2/3 cup dry white wine

1 garlic clove, minced

2 tablespoons minced fresh parsley

8 tablespoons (1 stick) plus 2 tablespoons butter

1 1/4 cups heavy (whipping) cream

1 leek (white and pale green parts only), washed
 and sliced in a variety of widths

4 monkfish fillets, about 6 ounces each

Fried dulse or fresh parsley sprigs for garnish   →

In a medium saucepan, combine the mussels, wine, garlic, parsley, and the 2 tablespoons of the butter. Cover and cook over medium heat until the mussels open, 5 to 8 minutes. Remove the pan from the heat. With a slotted spoon, transfer the mussels to a plate, remove the mussels from the shells, and discard the shells. Discard any mussels that do not open. Return the saucepan to medium heat with its cooking liquid, stir in the cream, and cook until the liquid is reduced by half, 5 to 8 minutes. Stir in 2 tablespoons of the butter and cook until the sauce thickens, about 5 minutes. Add the reserved mussels and remove from heat.

In a medium skillet, heat the remaining 6 tablespoons butter. Add the leeks and sauté until tender but not separated, 5 minutes. With a slotted spoon, transfer the leeks to a plate.

Slice each monkfish fillet into 4 medallions. Return the same skillet to medium heat and cook the medallions until opaque, 5 to 7 minutes.

To serve, preheat the broiler. Place 4 monkfish slices on a bed of leeks and spoon some mussel sauce over. Place the plates under the broiler until the sauce browns lightly and bubbles, about 3 minutes. Garnish with the dulse or parsley.

Mussels in Murphy's

Serves 6 as a first course, 4 as a main dish

〰〰 Mussels are, of course, the main attraction at the annual Mussel Fair in Bantry, County Cork. Many of the pubs use longtime fair organizer Eileen O'Shea's recipe which calls for steaming the mussels in Murphy's Irish stout, the local brew from Lady's Well Brewery, Cork City, and the fair's sponsor. The suggested accompaniment is . . . you guessed it, a pint of Murphy's stout.

> 4 tablespoons butter
>
> 2 large onions, chopped
>
> 1 12-ounce bottle stout, preferably Murphy's brand
>
> 2 tablespoons minced fresh parsley
>
> Salt and freshly ground pepper to taste
>
> 6 pounds mussels, scrubbed and debearded

In a large pot, melt the butter over medium heat. Add the onions and cook until soft, 2 to 3 minutes. Add the stout and bring to a boil. Add 1 tablespoon of the parsley, salt, pepper, and mussels. Cover and cook until the mussels open, 8 to 10 minutes, stirring once or twice. Discard any that don't open. Ladle the mussels into large bowls and sprinkle with the remaining parsley.

Cockles and Mussels Alive, Alive-O

Since shellfish is extremely perishable and couldn't be transported any great distance, the practice of gathering it and eating or cooking it almost immediately was a necessity in Ireland before the days of refrigeration. From this came the tradition of selling cooked shellfish, like the cockles and mussels Molly Malone sang about as she walked the streets of Dublin selling them from her barrow. Such cooked shellfish were a favorite food in pubs and taverns, most often washed down with a pint of ale or stout. The tradition remains very much alive today.

Maggie's Cockles and Mussels

≈ Mark Whelan, chef-proprietor of the Whelan family restaurant in Manhattan, loves this recipe for cockles (tiny round clams) and mussels, because it reminds him of the days when he used to pick them up on the beach in Donegal as a kid. At Maggie's Place (21 East 47th Street), which his Dublin-born parents, Teddy and Maggie, opened in 1974, Whelan likes to initiate innovative new menus while maintaining traditional Irish fare. Serve this with crusty bread to sop up the broth.

Serves 4 as a first course, 2 as a main dish

1 tablespoon olive oil

2 garlic cloves, minced

2 pounds mussels, scrubbed and debearded

1 pound cockles or littleneck or Manila clams

Juice of $1/2$ lemon

$1/4$ cup dry white wine

4 tablespoons unsalted butter

$1/2$ tablespoon minced fresh parsley

$1/2$ tablespoon minced fresh thyme

Freshly ground pepper to taste

1 tomato, seeded and diced

In a large saucepan over medium heat, heat the olive oil. Add the garlic and sauté until soft but not browned, 2 to 3 minutes. Add the mussels, cockles or clams, lemon juice, and wine. Cover and steam until the shells open, 8 to 10 minutes, stirring once or twice. Discard any shellfish that do not open. Add the butter and let it melt on top.

To serve, ladle the cockles and mussels into serving bowls and sprinkle with the parsley, thyme, pepper, and diced tomato.

Fish Soup

Serves 4 as a first course

〰〰 Like the farmhouse soups made of ingredients from the land, traditional Irish fish soups and stews rely on what's "on hand." The following soup is a basic recipe that can be varied depending on available fish, including clams, mussels, scallops, or cod, or smoked fish like salmon or haddock.

2 tablespoons diced salt pork

I onion, diced

1½ teaspoons butter

I teaspoon minced fresh thyme

2 tablespoons all-purpose flour

2 large boiling potatoes, peeled and diced

2 cups fish stock or clam broth

2 bay leaves

1½ pounds cod or haddock fillets, skinned
   and cut into chunks

1½ cups half-and-half

Salt and freshly ground pepper to taste

¼ cup minced fresh parsley

In a soup pot, cook the salt pork over low heat until it begins to brown, 3 to 5 minutes, stirring frequently. Add the onion, butter, and thyme and sauté until the onion is soft but not browned, about 3 minutes. Stir in the flour. Add the potatoes, stock or broth, and bay leaves. Simmer, covered, until the potatoes are fork tender, about 20 minutes. With a slotted spoon or spatula, remove the bay leaves and salt pork. Add the fish and half-and-half. Simmer, uncovered, for about 10 minutes. Season with the salt and pepper and sprinkle with the parsley.

Smoked Haddock and Potato Soup

⇔⇔ When the Irish Food Board invited Manhattan chefs to create some new recipes for them, the results were spectacular. This traditional fish chowder recipe, from chef David Amorelli of Cité (120 West 51st Street), is enhanced with smoked haddock and Irish bacon.

Serves 8 as a first course, 4 as a main dish

3 slices bacon, preferably Irish (see Resources, page 277), diced

1/2 cup diced shallots

3 garlic cloves, minced

4 cups fish stock or clam broth

2 to 3 boiling potatoes, peeled and quartered

1 bay leaf

3/4 teaspoon minced fresh thyme or 1/4 teaspoon dried

Salt and freshly ground pepper to taste

8 ounces smoked haddock, cut into chunks

2 cups heavy (whipping) cream

1/4 cup minced fresh parsley

In a soup pot, sauté the bacon over medium heat until lightly browned, 3 to 5 minutes. Add the shallots and garlic and sauté until translucent, about 3 minutes. Stir in the stock or broth, potatoes, bay leaf, thyme, salt, and pepper and cook, covered, until the potatoes are tender, about 20 minutes. Add the smoked haddock, cover, remove from heat, and let sit for 5 minutes.

Transfer the soup to a blender or food processor in batches and process until smooth. Return to the same soup pot over low heat, add the cream, and gently heat through. To serve, ladle the soup into bowls and sprinkle with the parsley.

Mussel Soup with Oatmeal-Herb Crust

**Serves 6 as a first course,
4 as a main dish**

Chef James Bowe, of Dublin's famous Catering College on Cathal Brugha Street, sprinkles a crunchy oatmeal topping over his traditional mussel soup.

1/2 cup water

1/4 cup dry white wine

1 pound mussels, scrubbed and debearded

2 tablespoons vegetable oil

6 slices bacon, preferably Irish (see Resources, page 277), diced

3 leeks, white and pale green parts only, washed and sliced

2 onions, finely chopped

2 to 3 boiling potatoes, peeled and diced

4 cups homemade chicken stock or canned low-salt chicken broth

1 1/2 teaspoons minced fresh thyme or 1/2 teaspoon dried

2 tablespoons butter

1/2 teaspoon minced fresh chives,

1/2 teaspoon minced fresh parsley

1/2 teaspoon minced fresh dill

1/4 cup steel-cut oats, preferably McCann's brand (see Resources, page 277)

Salt and freshly ground pepper to taste

In a large saucepan, combine the water and wine and bring to a boil. Add the mussels, cover, and steam until the mussels open, about 5 minutes. Discard any mussels that don't open. With a slotted spoon, transfer the mussels to a small bowl. Remove the mussels from the shells. Discard the shells and reserve the mussels and their cooking liquid.

→

In a soup pot, over medium heat, heat the oil and sauté the bacon, leeks, and onions until the onions are translucent, 3 to 5 minutes. Add the potatoes and cook for 2 minutes. Stir in the stock or broth and thyme and bring to a boil. Reduce heat and simmer for 15 minutes. Stir in the mussels and reserved cooking liquid and cook for 4 to 5 minutes.

Meanwhile, in a small skillet, melt the butter over medium heat. Add the oatmeal and herbs and stir until oatmeal is toasted to a golden brown.

To serve, ladle the soup into bowls and sprinkle the toasted oatmeal over the top.

Caragh Crab and Tomato Soup

At Caragh Lodge, a peaceful country house overlooking Caragh Lake in County Kerry, chef-proprietor Mary Gaunt provides fishing boats, ghillies (fishing guides), and permits for fishing guests, and is more than willing to cook the day's catch for them. Otherwise, guests can enjoy any number of dishes made with local fish, like this delightful crab and tomato soup, lightly flavored with a hint of sherry.

Serves 6 as a first course

12 large tomatoes

1 onion, chopped

2 shallots, minced

1/2 cup water

1 teaspoon curry powder

1 1/4 cups homemade chicken stock or canned
    low-salt chicken broth

2/3 cup tomato sauce

1 tablespoon dry sherry

Tabasco sauce to taste

4 ounces fresh lump crabmeat

1¹/4 cups light cream or half-and-half

Salt and freshly ground pepper to taste

Minced fresh parsley for garnish

In a soup pot, combine the tomatoes, onion, shallots, and enough water to cover the bottom of the pot so that the tomatoes won't brown. Bring to a boil, then reduce heat and simmer until the vegetables are soft but the tomato skins are still intact. Transfer to a blender or food processor, in batches if necessary and process until nearly smooth. Strain through a sieve and press the solids through with the back of a large spoon.

Return to the soup pot and add the curry powder, stock or broth, tomato sauce, sherry, Tabasco, and crabmeat. Bring to a boil over medium heat. Remove from heat, stir in 1 cup of the cream or half-and-half, and season with salt and pepper. Reheat gently, but do not boil.

To serve, ladle the soup into bowls and swirl in the remaining cream. Sprinkle with parsley.

Sing a song of sixpence, a pocket full of rye,

Four-and-twenty blackbirds, baked in a pie.

OLD NURSERY RHYME

⟡

Frankly, my mother never baked a blackbird pie, never made a rabbit stew, and never roasted a venison. Her only foray into the world of game cooking was when she took what she thought to be a considerable culinary risk and roasted Cornish game hens once for Sunday dinner. We thought she was trying to skimp on the grocery bill by serving us miniature chickens until she explained that she had read in the "Confidential Chat" section of the *Boston Globe* that Cornish game hens were the "new" thing to serve.

Although the hens were about the "wildest" meal my mother ever made, Irish country people have long relied on wild game for seasonal food. Because so many parts of Ireland were wild and uncultivated, hunting—rabbit, pigeon, quail, pheasant—was both a sport and a way to add variety to the diet. The most prized game meat, venison, however, was reserved for the gentry, as the hunting rights were granted only to landowners.

One of the delights of game cooking, whether the meat is roasted or cut up for stew or pie, is the sauce or stuffing that accompanies it. The strong flavors of venison call for the sweetness of red currant jelly or the richness of Cumberland sauce made with oranges, lemons, and port. Game birds seem to require cranberry-based sauces, fruit chutneys, savory stuffings, and game chips (homemade potato chips). The first goose of the season was traditionally eaten on Michaelmas Day, September 29, when the birds are still young and tender, and again on Christmas, when they've grown to about twelve pounds. Stuffed with potatoes and accompanied with homemade applesauce, a roasted goose makes for a spectacular meal, as does turkey, now as popular for Christmas in Ireland as it is here.

Due to the seasonal nature of game and the modern propensity for supermarket shopping, the idea of a wild Irish meal might seem as remote as Ireland itself. Not so. Cornish hen, duck, and turkey are, of course, readily available in markets either fresh or frozen, and now game like quail, pheasant, squab, goose, and wild duck, as well as rabbit, brown hare, and red and roe venison is being farm-raised and can be ordered by mail from specialty-meat purveyors for a taste of Ireland "from the wild."

Roast Turkey with Sage, Onion, and Celery Stuffing and Bread Sauce

Serves 12

≈≈ In much the same way that Christmas cake, with its covering of marzipan and royal icing, is nearly obligatory for the holiday in Ireland, a roasted turkey with a savory stuffing and bread sauce is, likewise, *the* Christmas dinner. Although some households still prefer goose and ham, since the turn of the century turkey has taken over as the centerpiece of the holiday meal. Bread sauce, though not Irish in origin (it was first recorded in Scotland in the eighteenth century) is often served with game birds and poultry and is an interesting alternative to gravy.

10 to 12 cups bread cubes

1 turkey, 12 to 14 pounds

1 cup (2 sticks) butter

2 onions, chopped

4 celery stalks, chopped

1/2 cup minced fresh parsley

1 teaspoon salt

2 tablespoons ground pepper

2 tablespoons dried sage

2 tablespoons dried thyme

1 1/2 cups homemade chicken stock or canned low-salt chicken broth

Bread Sauce

2 cups milk

1/3 cup fine dried bread crumbs

1 onion, stuck with 6 to 8 cloves

1 teaspoon salt

Pinch of cayenne pepper

3 tablespoons unsalted butter

1/2 cup coarse dried bread crumbs

→

The day before cooking, put the bread cubes in a large bowl and leave uncovered overnight to dry out.

The next day, wash the bird inside and out and pat dry with paper towels. In a large skillet, melt the butter over medium heat and sauté the onions and celery until the onions are translucent, 7 to 8 minutes. Add the parsley, salt, pepper, sage, thyme, and half the bread cubes. Cook until the cubes begin to brown lightly, 5 minutes. Transfer the mixture to the bowl with the remaining bread cubes and mix well. Stir in the stock or broth.

Preheat the oven to 325°F. Pack the stuffing loosely into the bird's neck and body cavities. Truss the bird with cotton string, place in a rack in a roasting pan, and roast for 3½ to 4½ hours. Test for doneness by moving the drumstick gently. When the bird is done, the joint will move easily. Remove from the oven and let sit for 20 minutes.

Meanwhile, make the bread sauce: In a double boiler over warm water, heat the milk. Stir in the fine bread crumbs and the onion. Cook for 30 minutes. Remove the onion. Stir in the salt, cayenne pepper, and 2 tablespoons of the butter. In a small skillet, melt the remaining 1 tablespoon butter. Add the coarse bread crumbs and cook until lightly browned. Transfer the sauce to a serving bowl and sprinkle with the crumbs.

Remove and discard the trussing string from the turkey. Remove the stuffing and transfer it to a serving bowl. Carve the turkey and serve it with the stuffing and bread sauce.

Christmas Goose with
Chestnut Stuffing and Port Sauce

Serves 6 to 8

Before the introduction of the turkey to Europe and Ireland in the eighteenth century, a plump goose was the bird of choice for festive occasions like Christmas. Because goose is so fatty, a tart or dry stuffing, such as chestnut or potato, is usually recommended.

1 goose, 10 to 12 pounds

1 lemon, halved

1/2 teaspoon salt

1/2 teaspoon ground pepper

1 large onion, sliced

1 carrot, peeled and sliced

1 celery stalk, sliced

Chestnut Stuffing

4 pounds chestnuts

4 teaspoons vegetable oil

6 cups chicken stock or canned low-salt chicken broth

3 tablespoons butter at room temperature

1 onion, chopped

3/4 cup dried bread crumbs

1 tablespoon minced fresh parsley

3 teaspoons minced fresh thyme or 1 teaspoon dried

1 tablespoon minced fresh chives

1 1/2 teaspoons minced fresh sage or 1/2 teaspoon dried sage or poultry seasoning

Salt and freshly ground pepper to taste

1/2 cup water

1 cup port

→

Port Sauce

Reserved goose pan juices
¹/₂ cup port
I cup homemade chicken stock or canned low-salt chicken broth
3 tablespoons all-purpose flour

Remove all visible fat from the body cavity of the goose. Wash the goose inside and out and pat dry with paper towels. Rub inside and out with the cut sides of the lemon and season with salt and pepper. Prick the skin all over with a fork. Spread the onion, carrot, and celery in the bottom of a roasting pan. Set the goose aside while preparing the stuffing.

To make the stuffing: Cut a slit into the flat side of each chestnut. In a saucepan over medium heat, heat the oil, add the chestnuts, and cook, stirring constantly, to heat the chestnuts and loosen the skin from the shells, 3 to 5 minutes. Drain and let cool just to the touch. Remove and discard the shells and inner skins.

Using the same pan, combine the stock or broth and the chestnuts. Cook over medium heat until the chestnuts are tender, 20 minutes. Drain, reserving the liquid. Chop half the chestnuts and mash the rest.

In a small skillet, melt 2 tablespoons of the butter over medium heat. Add the onion and sauté until translucent, about 7 minutes. Add the onion mixture to the chestnuts along with the bread crumbs, parsley, thyme, chives, sage, salt and pepper. Stir in enough reserved liquid to moisten the crumbs. Let cool.

Preheat the oven to 425°F. Stuff the goose loosely with the chestnut stuffing. Truss with cotton string and rub all over with the remaining tablespoon of softened butter. Place the goose on a rack over the vegetables. Bake for 25 minutes, spooning off the excess fat 2 or 3 times during cooking. Reduce heat to 350°F and add 1/2 cup of the reserved liquid and the water to the roasting pan. Cover with aluminum foil and bake for 1 hour. Remove the foil, add the port to the pan juices, and bake, basting with the pan juices, until the skin is crisp and a thermometer inserted into the thickest part of the breast registers 170°F (a total of about 3 hours). Transfer the goose to a serving platter, reserving the pan juices, and let rest for 20 minutes. Remove and discard the trussing string. Remove the stuffing and transfer the stuffing to a serving dish.

To make the port sauce: Skim the fat from the reserved pan juices. Place the roasting pan over medium heat, add the port, and stir to scrape up the browned bits from the bottom of the pan. In a small bowl, whisk the stock or broth into the flour, then stir into the pan. Reduce heat and cook until the sauce thickens, 5 minutes. Strain and serve with the goose.

Michaelmas Goose with Potato Stuffing

Serves 6

⇟⇞ The Irish tradition of eating the first goose of the season on September 29, Michaelmas Day, may have died out slightly, but the recipe for young goose with potato stuffing is one that can be used whenever the mood strikes. The potato stuffing is a traditional one that can also be used for duck.

> 1 goose, 8 to 9 pounds
> Salt to taste
> 1 pound baking potatoes, peeled and cut into 1-inch pieces
> 4 tablespoons butter
> 2 onions, chopped
> 1/2 teaspoon dried thyme
> 1/2 teaspoon dried sage
> Freshly ground pepper to taste

Chop the goose liver and set aside. Wash the goose inside and out and pat dry with paper towels. Salt lightly inside and out.

Cook the potatoes until tender in boiling salted water, 10 to 12 minutes. Drain and let cool.

In a large skillet, melt the butter over medium heat. Add the onions and sauté until translucent, 3 to 5 minutes. Add the goose liver and sauté for 5 minutes. Put the potatoes through a ricer or mash with a potato masher. Combine the onions and liver mixture. Add the thyme, sage, salt to taste, and pepper and blend thoroughly. Let cool.

Preheat the oven to 325°F. Stuff the goose loosely with the stuffing and truss with cotton string. Place on a rack in a roasting pan, breast-side up. Prick the legs and wing joints all over with a fork to release the fat. Cook, basting with the pan juices, until the skin is crisp and a thermometer inserted into the thickest part of the breast registers 170°F, 2 to 2½ hours. Let rest for 15 minutes before carving. Remove and discard the trussing string. Remove the stuffing and transfer to a serving dish.

Game Hens with Savory Stuffing and Mead Applesauce

Serves 4

≷≷ Cornish game hens are an elegant choice for special-occasion meals. I've updated my mother's applesauce by sweetening it with mead, the traditional Irish honey wine. For a more colorful version with a slightly tart flavor, add cranberries.

4 Cornish game hens

Salt to taste, plus $1/2$ teaspoon

Freshly ground pepper to taste, plus $1/2$ teaspoon

8 slices white bread, crusts removed

$1/4$ cup minced fresh parsley

$1/2$ teaspoon poultry seasoning

12 tablespoons ($1^1/2$ sticks) plus 2 tablespoons butter

1 cup finely chopped onions

Mead Applesauce

6 Granny Smith apples, cored and quartered

2 tablespoons mead, preferably Bunratty Meade (see Resources, page 277)

2 tablespoons water

2 tablespoons sugar

2 tablespoons butter

1 tablespoon fresh lemon juice

Remove the giblets from the hens and reserve the livers. Wash the hens inside and out and pat dry with paper towels. Season inside and out with salt and pepper to taste.

Preheat the oven to 350°F. Cut the bread into cubes. Place on a baking sheet and toast in the oven until lightly browned, 10 to 15 minutes, stirring once or twice. In a large bowl, combine the toasted bread cubes with the parsley, 1/2 teaspoon salt, 1/2 teaspoon pepper, and the poultry seasoning.

In a medium skillet, melt the 3/4 cup butter over medium heat. Add the onions and cook until translucent, 3 to 5 minutes, then add the reserved livers and cook an additional 5 minutes. Remove the livers, chop finely, then add to the bread mixture.

Loosely pack the stuffing into the birds and truss them with cotton string. Increase the oven temperature to 375°F. Place the birds in an ovenproof baking dish, breast-side up. Melt the 2 tablespoons butter and brush over the birds. Bake until the skin begins to crisp and the juices run clear when the leg joint is pierced with a fork, 1 1/2 hours. Transfer the hens to a warm platter. Remove and discard the trussing string.

To make the applesauce: In a large saucepan over medium heat, combine the apples, mead, and water and cook until the apples begin to break down and become pulpy, 10 to 15 minutes. Remove the skins with a fork and discard. Add the sugar, butter, and lemon juice, and with a wire whisk, beat until smooth.

Cranberry-Mead Applesauce: Combine 1/2 cup fresh or frozen cranberries with the apples. Delete the butter and lemon juice. Process in a blender if you prefer a smoother consistency. Makes 2 1/2 cups.

Game Hens in Mead with Raisin-Rice Stuffing

Serves 4

〰〰 These game hens are basted with a rich blend of marmalade and mead, and the brown rice stuffing is studded with raisins and almonds. When basted with the pan juices, the skin becomes crispy-sweet, so pair the hens with a green vegetable like spinach or green beans for a contrast in flavor.

4 Cornish game hens

Salt and freshly ground pepper to taste

2 tablespoons butter

I onion, chopped

2 celery stalks, chopped

4 cups cooked brown rice

3/4 teaspoon minced fresh thyme or 1/4 teaspoon dried

3/4 teaspoon minced fresh tarragon or 1/4 teaspoon dried

1 1/2 teaspoons minced fresh sage or 1/2 teaspoon dried

3 tablespoons minced fresh parsley

1/2 cup golden raisins

1/4 cup chopped almonds

2/3 cup mead, preferably Bunratty Meade (see Resources, page 277)

1/3 cup orange marmalade

1/4 cup all-purpose flour

2 cups orange juice

Fresh watercress sprigs for garnish

Wash the hens and pat dry with paper towels. Season inside and out with salt and pepper.

Preheat the oven to 350°F. In a large skillet, melt the butter over medium heat. Add the onion and celery and sauté until the onion is translucent, 3 to 5 minutes. Stir in the cooked rice, thyme, tarragon, sage, parsley, raisins, almonds, and 1/3 cup of the mead. Stuff the hens loosely with the stuffing and truss them with cotton string. Place the hens in a roasting pan, breast-side up, and bake until the skin is crisp and the juices run clear when the leg joint is pierced with a knife, 1 1/2 hours.

Meanwhile, combine the remaining 1/3 cup mead and the marmalade in a small saucepan. Cook until the marmalade dissolves. Baste the hens twice during cooking with the marmalade mixture.

Transfer the hens to a warm platter. Remove and discard the trussing string. Place the roasting pan over low heat. Gradually stir the flour and orange juice into the pan juices, stirring to scrape up the browned bits from the bottom of the pan. Cook until the sauce thickens, 3 to 5 minutes. Add salt and pepper to taste. Strain the sauce into a gravy boat. Serve 1 hen per person, garnished with fresh watercress.

Wild Duck with Root Vegetables

⇔⇔ When weekend shooting parties were a regular event in turn-of-the-century Ireland, wild birds like grouse, snipe, mallard, and pheasant were shot in season, bagged, and brought to the kitchen to be prepared for the evening meal. Today, many of these wild birds can be purchased from specialty foods purveyors.

Serves 4

I cup water

I pound carrots, peeled and sliced

I pound parsnips, peeled and sliced

2 tablespoons olive oil

Salt and freshly ground pepper to taste

2 ducks, preferably wild, about 3 pounds each

2 apples, cored and quartered

I cup cranberry juice

1/2 cup dry red wine

1/4 cup sugar

I teaspoon whole cloves

2 pears, peeled, cored, and sliced

I onion, chopped

8 tablespoons (I stick) butter

Bring the water to boil in a medium saucepan. Add the carrots and parsnips. Cover, reduce heat to low, and simmer until the vegetables are nearly tender, about 15 minutes. With a slotted spoon, transfer the vegetables to a roasting pan, reserving the pan of cooking liquid. Toss the vegetables with the oil, salt, and pepper. Set aside.

Remove the giblets and neck from the ducks, rinse them in cold water, and transfer them to the reserved cooking liquid. Cover and cook over low heat for 35 minutes. Wash the ducks inside and out and pat dry with paper towels. Season inside and out with salt and pepper to taste.

Preheat the oven to 400°F. Insert 4 apple quarters into the neck and body cavities of each duck. Tie the legs together with cotton string. With a fork, prick the ducks all over to let the fat drain. Place the ducks on a rack in a roasting pan, breast-side down, and bake for 15 minutes. Place the pan of root vegetables in the oven. Turn the ducks over and bake for 15 minutes. Remove the ducks and vegetables from the oven. Remove the trussing string and discard.

Meanwhile, in a large saucepan, combine the cranberry juice, wine, sugar, and cloves and bring to a boil. Add the pears and onion, reduce heat to low, cover, and cook until the pears are tender, about 10 minutes. With a slotted spoon, transfer the pear mixture to a plate. Strain the poaching liquid and reserve 3/4 cup.

Drain the juices from the ducks and discard the apples. Arrange the ducks in the center of a platter and surround with the vegetables and poached pears. Keep warm. Pour the giblet stock into the roasting pan and bring to a boil. Strain, discard the fat, and reserve 3/4 cup of stock. In a medium saucepan, combine the reserved stock with the reserved poaching liquid and cook over medium heat until reduced by half. Stir in the butter and cook until the butter melts. Pour the sauce into a gravy boat and serve alongside the ducks.

Roast Duck with Apple Stuffing

Serves 4

≋ Even though many modern cooks consider duck—whether wild or farm-raised—to be restaurant fare rather than home cooking, it's gaining in popularity in Ireland and elsewhere. Duck is, after all, more flavorful than chicken, and recent studies indicate that a boneless, skinless duckling breast is lower in calories and fat than the same-size portion of boneless,

→

skinless chicken. A whole duck, paired here with an apple stuffing, is simple to prepare at home, yet impressive enough to make you feel as if you're dining out.

    1 duck, about 4 pounds
    Salt and freshly ground pepper to taste
    2 tablespoons butter
    1 onion, chopped
    3 celery stalks, chopped
    1 Granny Smith apple, peeled, cored, and chopped
    1/4 teaspoon ground cinnamon
    1 1/2 cups dried bread crumbs
    1/2 cup apple cider

Wash the duck inside and out and pat dry with paper towels. Season inside and out with salt and pepper.

Preheat the oven to 400°F. In a large skillet, melt the butter over medium heat. Add the onion, celery, and apple and sauté until the onion begins to soften, about 3 minutes. Remove from heat and stir in the cinnamon, salt, pepper, bread crumbs, and cider. Stuff the duck loosely with the stuffing. Truss with cotton string. With a fork, prick the duck all over to let the fat drain. Place on a rack in a roasting pan, breast-side down. Bake for 30 minutes, then turn and cook breast-side up for 1 hour. Reduce the oven temperature to 325°F and bake until the skin is crisp, 30 to 40 minutes more (a total cooking time of 2 hours to 2 hours 10 minutes). Baste 2 to 3 times with the pan juices during cooking. Transfer to a platter and let rest for 20 minutes. Remove and discard the trussing string, carve, and serve.

Breast of Duck with Cider and Poitín Sauce

Serves 4

≋ Boneless duck breast is a natural partner to a flavorful sauce. This cider and poitín sauce was served by Cathal Reynolds, chef-proprietor of Cre na Cille (Tuam, County Galway), with breasts of guinea fowl for his entry in the Irish Food Board's Chef of the Year competition in 1996, but it works equally well with duck. Serve this dish with Pureed Parsnips (page 16) or Turnip and Carrot Puree (page 21), and new potatoes boiled in their jackets.

> 4 tablespoons butter
>
> 2 boneless duck breasts, halved
>
> Salt and freshly ground pepper to taste
>
> 3 tablespoons Bunratty poitín (see Resources, page 277) or Irish whiskey
>
> 2/3 cup cider
>
> 1 tablespoon minced fresh tarragon or 1 teaspoon dried
>
> 2/3 cup heavy (whipping) cream
>
> Fresh watercress sprigs for garnish

In a large skillet, melt the butter over medium heat. Season the breasts with salt and pepper and cook skin-side down for 12 minutes. Drain the fat and cook meat-side down for 1 minute longer. Add the poitín or whiskey to the pan and let warm. Avert your face and light with a long-handled match. When the flames subside, transfer the breasts to a plate and keep warm. Add the cider and tarragon to the pan and cook until slightly reduced, about 5 minutes. Stir in the cream and cook, stirring often, until reduced to a sauce consistency, about 5 minutes. Cut each breast into 4 to 5 slices. Divide the sauce among 4 plates, arrange the breast pieces on top, and garnish with watercress.

Quail with Chestnut Stuffing
and Burgundy Sauce

Serves 4

⨯⨯ Like duck, quail meat is rich in color and has a delicate yet distinctive game flavor. At Moyglare Manor, a delightful Georgian manor house situated in Maynooth, County Kildare, chef Jim Cullinane frequently features game on his autumn menus. Here he pairs braces (2 birds per person) of the small birds with a full-flavored Burgundy sauce and a rich chestnut stuffing.

8 quail

1 pound chestnuts

1 tablespoon plus 2 teaspoons vegetable oil

2 cups homemade chicken stock or canned low-salt chicken broth

4 tablespoons unsalted butter

2 shallots, minced

1 cup dried bread crumbs

1 tablespoon minced fresh parsley

Salt and freshly ground pepper to taste

Burgundy Sauce

4 slices bacon, diced

1 small onion, chopped

1 small carrot, peeled and chopped

1¼ cups Burgundy wine

1¼ cups homemade chicken stock or canned low-salt chicken broth

1 tablespoon tomato puree

1 bay leaf

1 tablespoon all-purpose flour

1 tablespoon butter

Salt and freshly ground pepper to taste

Wash the birds inside and out and pat dry with paper towels. Set aside.

Preheat the oven to 425°F. Cut slits into the flat side of each chestnut. In a saucepan over medium heat, heat 2 teaspoons of the oil, add the chestnuts, and cook briskly, stirring constantly, to warm the chestnuts and loosen the skin from the shells, 3 to 5 minutes. Drain and let cool to the touch. Remove the shells and inner skins.

Using the same pan, combine the stock or broth and the chestnuts and cook over medium heat until the chestnuts are tender, 20 minutes. Drain (reserve the liquid) and mash. In a large skillet, melt the butter over medium heat. Add the shallots and sauté until translucent, about 3 minutes. Add the bread crumbs, chestnuts, parsley, salt, pepper, and enough of the reserved liquid to moisten the stuffing. Loosely stuff the birds and truss with cotton string.

In a large skillet, heat the remaining 1 tablespoon oil over medium heat. Brown each bird quickly on all sides. Transfer to a roasting pan and bake for 15 minutes.

To make the sauce: In a small skillet, cook the bacon over medium heat until lightly colored, 3 to 5 minutes. Add the onion and carrot and sauté until translucent, 5 minutes. Add the wine, turn heat to high, and cook for 2 to 3 minutes to reduce. Add the stock or broth, tomato puree, and bay leaf. Reduce heat to simmer and cook for 5 minutes. Whisk in the butter and flour and cook until the sauce thickens, 1 to 2 minutes. Strain the sauce and discard vegetables. Transfer the quail to a platter. Remove and discard the trussing string.

Place the roasting pan over low heat. Gradually stir in the Burgundy sauce, stirring to scrape up all the browned bits from the bottom of the pan. Cook until the sauce is well blended, 3 to 5 minutes. Add salt and pepper and strain the sauce into a gravy boat. Arrange 2 quail on each of 4 warmed plates and spoon the sauce over the top.

Medieval Castle Banquets

⬦⬦

Bunratty, Knappogue, and Dunguaire castles were once noble homes of Irish lords, a rank that was the zenith of medieval achievement and power. These castles, much like the medieval and Renaissance courts throughout Europe, were the hub around which the lives of Irish peasants, artisans, poets, and musicians revolved.

Visitors today can experience a taste of what dining in such surroundings must have been like. Since 1963, when Bunratty was the first of the three castles to be restored, medieval banquets (known collectively as Shannon Heritage Banquets) have been held nightly, offering original entertainment, legendary Irish hospitality, and fine food and drink in fairytale settings.

At Bunratty Castle, located on the main Ennis-Limerick Road in County Clare, visitors are the guests of the Earl of Thomond, once the master of the superbly restored fifteenth-century castle. During the thirty-five years since the famous banquets began, Bunratty's accomplished musicians have gained worldwide recognition and have performed for countless visitors and many distinguished heads of state.

The twice-nightly banquets begin with a formal greeting by the earl and his court, a welcoming glass of honey-rich mead (produced in the Bunratty Winery at the rear of the castle), and an aristocratic feast accompanied with fine wines. The current bill of fare consists of four courses, or *removes,* in keeping with the language of the court: a first course of leek and potato soup; courses of prime pork ribs with honey-whiskey sauce (see page 52), and chicken with apple and mead sauce; and dessert of syllabub (see page 275), with entertainment in between each. At Bunratty they describe the banquet as "food from the rich earth, music made in heaven."

At Knappogue Castle, in Quin, County Clare, the entertainment takes the form of a tribute in song, story, and dance to the women of Ireland: its imperious queens, inspirational saints, and occasional sinners. The music and poetry celebrate the gentle aspects of Ireland's past and the influential role of the women of Celtic Ireland.

The castle, a legacy of the McNamara clan, who built it in 1467, has held medieval banquets since 1967. Its four-course menu features smoked Irish salmon with cucumber and dill salad, carrot and mint soup, breast of chicken with Guinness and whole-grain mustard sauce, and praline soufflé. The castle banquets are offered nightly from May to October.

The medieval banquet at Dunguaire Castle, in Kinvara, County Galway, offers "food to please the palate and entertainment to lift the soul." The castle itself, built by the Hynes clan in 1520, is an inspirational place, occupying a site on the shore of Galway Bay that was a seventh-century stronghold of the kings of Connaught.

The players at Dunguaire celebrate some of Ireland's greatest writers—Synge, Yeats, Shaw, and O'Casey among them—and draw on Irish history, myth, and legend for their inspirations. While the banquet meal of smoked Irish salmon with brown bread, leek and potato soup, chicken with whole-grain mustard and cream sauce, and apple pie and cream is served, artists entertain with the profound, humorous, irreverent, and incisive words of some of Ireland's literary giants.

For further details on the castle banquets, see Resources, page 277.

Casserole of Guinea Fowl
with Grapes and Madeira

Serves 6

〜〜 Guinea hens are known around the world by many names: in France they're called pintades, in Italy they're known as *faraone*, and in England and Ireland they're called guinea fowl. Dermot and Kay McEvilly, proprietors of Cashel House Hotel (Connemara, County Galway), rely on farm-raised birds for this stewlike casserole, which includes two varieties of wine and green grapes.

> 2 guinea fowl
>
> 4 tablespoons butter
>
> 2 tablespoons olive oil
>
> 3 slices bacon, diced
>
> 2 shallots, minced
>
> 2 garlic cloves, minced
>
> 1/4 cup Madeira wine
>
> 3 tablespoons all-purpose flour
>
> 2 cups homemade chicken stock or canned low-salt chicken broth
>
> 1 1/4 cups dry white wine
>
> 8 white mushrooms, sliced
>
> 2 cups seedless green grapes

Wash the guinea fowl inside and out and pat dry with paper towels. Cut each bird into 6 serving pieces and remove the skin.

In a Dutch oven or heavy flameproof casserole over medium heat, melt the butter with the oil. Add the fowl pieces in batches and cook until lightly browned, 5 to 8 minutes. Reduce the heat, add the bacon, shallots, and garlic, and sauté until the vegetables are tender, 3 to 5 minutes. Add the Madeira, let warm, avert your face, and light with a long-handled match. Combine the flour with the stock or broth and wine and, when the flames subside, stir into the casserole. Cover and cook over low heat for 1 hour. Add the mushrooms and grapes and cook 30 minutes longer.

Braised Dromoland Pheasant
with Bacon and Kale

Serves 4

   The luxurious baronial castle of Dromoland (Newmarket-on-Fergus, County Clare) was originally the home of the O'Briens, barons of Inchiquin and direct descendants of the Irish high king Brian Boru. Today Dromoland Castle is one of the country's most sumptuous hotels, with many of its four hundred acres reserved for seasonal shooting and hunting. Pheasants are in season in Ireland from October to February, but generally don't appear on menus until late November, when they've taken on more fat. Throughout the fall and winter, the Dromoland dining room features game shot on the property, including this dish from executive head chef David A. McCann. Serve this with boiled or mashed potatoes.

2 hen pheasants
2¹/₂ pounds kale, cut into strips
2 tablespoons vegetable oil
6 slices bacon, diced
16 small white onions
2 cups homemade chicken stock or canned low-salt chicken broth
**Bouquet garni: 2 fresh parsley sprigs, 1 thyme sprig, 1 bay leaf,
   and 1 chervil sprig, tied together in a cheesecloth bag**

Wash the birds inside and out and pat dry with paper towels.

Blanch the kale in boiling salted water for 2 minutes, drain and plunge into cold water, then drain again.

In a large skillet, heat the oil. Add the pheasants and cook until lightly browned on all sides, about 10 minutes. Transfer the pheasants to a plate. Add the bacon and onions and cook until tender, 3 to 5 minutes. Add the kale. Place the pheasants on the bed of kale and onions. Add the chicken stock or broth and bouquet garni, cover, and cook over low heat until

→

tender and the juices run clear when the leg joint is pricked with a fork, 1½ hours.

Transfer the pheasants to a plate and let rest for 5 minutes. Remove the breasts and legs from the pheasants. Drain the kale mixture (reserve the liquid) and transfer to the center of a serving platter. Place the breasts and legs on top of the vegetables. Pour a little of the reserved cooking liquid around the plate and serve.

Medallions of Venison with Fricassee of Spinach

Serves 4

〰〰 *Venison* refers to the flesh of all types of deer, the most common being the red and roe. In Ireland, only the gentry had access to the estates where most deer were found, so venison was not common country fare. But times have changed, and venison is now being farm-raised in Ireland, Scotland, New Zealand, and several areas of the United States. Irish chefs love it because it's lean and low in fat and cholesterol, and patrons love it because it lacks both the chewiness and gaminess of wild deer. For some, venison still bears the cachet of estate, country house, and castle, so this recipe from Markree Castle (Collooney, County Sligo) seems apropos. Charles and Mary Cooper are the chef-proprietors of the castle hotel, which has been in the Cooper family since 1640. Serve this dish with wild rice and baby carrots.

Marinade

2 carrots, peeled and sliced

1 celery stalk, sliced

1 shallot, chopped

3/4 cup dry red wine

2 fresh tarragon sprigs or 1 tablespoon dried tarragon

2 fresh parsley sprigs

2 bay leaves

6 black peppercorns

1/3 cup olive oil

1 loin of venison, 2 to 2 1/2 pounds

3 ounces dried porcini mushrooms

10 ounces fresh spinach, stemmed

Salt and freshly ground pepper to taste

2 tablespoons butter

2 tablespoons canola oil

1 teaspoon minced garlic

1 tablespoon minced shallots

3/4 cup dry white wine

2 tablespoons demi-glace

1/4 cup brandy

1 1/4 cups heavy (whipping) cream

Fresh watercress sprigs for garnish

To make the marinade: In a large bowl, combine the carrots, celery, shallot, red wine, tarragon, parsley, bay leaves, peppercorns, and olive oil and let sit for 30 minutes. Add the venison, cover, and refrigerate for 4 to 5 hours. If using wild venison, marinate overnight.

In a small bowl, soak the wild mushrooms in warm water for 1 hour. Cook the spinach in boiling water for 1 minute, then drain and plunge into cold water and drain again. Chop coarsely and set aside. Pat with paper towels to dry.   →

Let the venison come to room temperature. Cut the loin into 8 medallions and place them between 2 sheets of plastic wrap. With the flat side of a meat mallet, pound gently to flatten slightly. Season the medallions with salt and pepper.

In a large skillet, melt the butter with the oil over medium heat and sauté the garlic and shallots until translucent, 2 minutes. Add the medallions and cook on both sides until the meat is browned on the outside and pink on the inside (slightly underdone), 3 to 5 minutes. Transfer the meat to a platter and keep warm. Squeeze the mushrooms dry. Add the wine, demiglace, brandy, and mushrooms to the skillet. Simmer until the liquid is syrupy, then add the cream and spinach and cook until the sauce is reduced, 5 minutes. Place 2 medallions of venison on each plate and spoon the spinach mixture over the meat. Garnish with the watercress.

Roast Venison with Cumberland Sauce

Serves 8

⪦⪧ Most cooks agree that the secret to tender venison is marinating it first and taking care not to overcook it. Cumberland sauce—a rich blend of port, orange, lemon, and red currant jelly—is a favorite accompaniment to roast venison, and is delicious with other game meats, potted game, and country pâtés. Double the sauce recipe to use again later. Serve this dish with Parsnip Cakes (page 17).

I venison roast, 4 to 4 1/2 pounds

2 tablespoons olive oil

2 garlic cloves, minced

1/2 teaspoon dried rosemary

1/4 teaspoon dried thyme

Salt and freshly ground pepper to taste

Cumberland Sauce

1 orange

1 lemon

1 cup red currant jelly

1/4 cup port wine

1 tablespoon cornstarch mixed with 2 tablespoons water

The day before cooking, place the roast in a large bowl and pierce it all over with a fork. In a small bowl, combine the oil, garlic, rosemary, thyme, salt, and pepper. Pour over the meat and turn to coat all sides. Cover and refrigerate overnight.

Meanwhile, make the sauce: Remove the zest from the orange and lemon. Cut the zest into fine shreds. Add to a small saucepan of boiling water. Reduce heat to a simmer and cook for 5 minutes. Drain the zest, then plunge it into cold water. Drain again and set aside.

Juice the orange and the lemon into a small saucepan over medium heat. Combine the juice and jelly and cook over medium heat until the jelly melts. Add the zest and port and boil rapidly until the sauce thickens, 5 to 8 minutes. Whisk in the cornstarch mixture and cook for 2 to 3 minutes to thicken. Transfer the sauce to a bowl or jar, cover, and refrigerate overnight.

Preheat the oven to 350°F. Place the venison in a roasting pan and bake until a meat thermometer inserted into the center of the roast registers 130°F, about 2 hours. (Venison should be medium rare, so be careful not to overcook it.) To serve, transfer the meat to a serving platter, spoon the Cumberland sauce around it, and pass the remaining sauce.

Venison Goulash

≶≶ This simple yet elegant stew is a favorite at Crookedwood House (Mullingar, County Westmeath), where chef-proprietor Noel Kenny makes it in winter with wild game, and in other seasons with farm-raised venison. The stew can be cooked on top of the stove or in the oven and is delicious with potatoes boiled in their jackets.

Serves 6

3 tablespoons vegetable oil

1 1/2 pounds loin of venison, cubed

1 onion, chopped

2 teaspoons juniper berries

3 cups homemade game or beef stock or canned low-salt beef broth

1 1/4 cups dry red wine

Salt and freshly ground pepper to taste

8 ounces oyster mushrooms

2/3 cup sour cream

In a large skillet, heat 2 tablespoons of oil over medium heat. Add the venison pieces in batches and cook until lightly browned on all sides, 5 to 8 minutes. Using a slotted spoon, transfer the meat to a Dutch oven or heavy flameproof casserole. Add the onion to the skillet and cook until translucent, 3 minutes. Transfer to the pan with the meat. Add the juniper berries, stock or broth, wine, salt, and pepper and cook, covered, on the stove over low heat (or in a preheated 300°F oven) until tender, about 2 1/2 hours.

Just before serving, heat the remaining 1 tablespoon oil in a small skillet over medium heat. Add the mushrooms and cook for 3 minutes. Add to the casserole and stir in the sour cream. Taste and adjust seasonings.

Wild Rabbit and Cider Stew

Serves 4

During the Middle Ages, cider was a popular beverage in Ireland, particularly in rural areas where water supplies were often unreliable, and naturally fermented (hard) apple cider was one of the most favored of liquids for game stews, especially rabbit. Brian and Anne Cronin, proprietors of the Blue Haven Hotel and Restaurant in the seaside town of Kinsale (County Cork), specialize in seafood in their maritime-themed restaurant, but they frequently include traditional country dishes like this homey stew, served with apple-potato cakes and a fresh green salad.

I rabbit, cut into serving pieces

2 tablespoons all-purpose flour

2 slices bacon, diced

I onion, diced

I carrot, peeled and diced

I teaspoon dried thyme

I bay leaf

2 tablespoons minced fresh parsley

2 tomatoes, chopped

Salt and freshly ground pepper to taste

I tablespoon sugar

I cup hard cider

I cup water

Wash and dry the rabbit pieces with paper towels and dust with the flour. In a large skillet, cook the bacon over medium heat until it begins to crisp, 3 to 5 minutes. Using a slotted spoon, transfer the bacon to paper towels to drain. →

Preheat the oven to 350°F. Cook the rabbit pieces in the bacon fat over medium heat until lightly browned, about 5 minutes. Add the onion, carrot, thyme, bay leaf, parsley, tomatoes, salt, and pepper and cook for 15 minutes. Add the sugar, cider, and water and bring to a boil. Transfer the stew to a Dutch oven or ovenproof casserole and bake until the rabbit is tender, 1 to 1½ hours.

Variation: Substitute Guinness or Murphy's stout for the cider. If you like the flavor of beef in stout, you'll love rabbit cooked in it.

Rabbit Pie with Soda Bread Crust

Serves 4 to 6

Old-fashioned Irish country fare can be found far from the Irish countryside in such places as Brookline Village, Massachusetts, where Cork native Matt Murphy and his Tipperary-born wife, Siobhan Carew, operate Matt Murphy's (14 Harvard Street), the only Irish pub in the Boston area included in the *Zagat's Survey*. Murphy's hearty farmhouse cooking has become the trademark of the pub, although Murphy likes to give his dishes a distinctly modern touch. Instead of the usual potato or pastry crust for this game pie, for example, he covers it with dough from his homemade soda bread. Serve it with a green salad.

1 tablespoon minced fresh tarragon

1 tablespoon minced fresh thyme

1 garlic clove, minced

1/4 cup olive oil

1/4 cup dry white wine

Salt and freshly ground pepper to taste

1 rabbit, cut up

8 cups homemade chicken stock or canned low-salt chicken broth

2 carrots, peeled and diced

3 celery stalks, diced

2 shallots, minced

1/3 cup all-purpose flour

1/3 cup butter

1/2 cup sherry

Soda Bread Crust

2 cups all-purpose flour

1 tablespoon salt

2 teaspoons baking soda

2 tablespoons minced fresh chives

1/2 cup (1 stick) melted butter

1/2 cup milk

Preheat oven to 425°F. In a medium bowl, combine the herbs, garlic, olive oil, wine, and salt and pepper to taste. Dredge the pieces of rabbit in the herb mixture and transfer to a baking sheet. Bake until the rabbit pieces are golden brown, 30 minutes.

Transfer the meat to a Dutch oven or large pot. Add the chicken stock or broth, carrots, celery, and shallots and bring to a boil over medium heat. Cover and simmer until the meat is tender and almost falling off the bone, about 1 hour. Transfer the meat to a plate to cool. When cool enough to

→

handle, take the meat off the bones. Strain the vegetables, reserving both the stock or broth and the vegetables.

In a medium saucepan over medium heat, combine the flour and butter. Add the reserved stock or broth in batches, whisking constantly until the sauce begins to thicken. When all the stock or broth has been added, add the meat and reserved vegetables and bring slowly to a boil. Stir in the sherry. Transfer to an 8-cup (10- or 11-inch diameter) ovenroof casserole dish.

To make the soda bread crust: Preheat the oven to 400°F. Sift the flour, salt, and baking soda together into a large bowl. Add the chives and melted butter. Stir with a wooden spoon until the flour and butter are combined, then add the milk. Mix until a soft dough forms. Roll out onto a floured board to fit the top of the casserole. Place on casserole, cut 4 to 6 slits in the dough, and bake until the top is golden brown, about 20 minutes.

Moses Checkley's Duck Liver Pâté

Named for the nineteenth-century proprietor of Moses Checkley's Eating House at No. 78 Fleet Street, this smooth liver pâté is a popular first course at the Oliver St. John Gogarty Restaurant (58/59 Fleet Street, Dublin). It's an adaptation of an original recipe from 1857.

Serves 4 as a first course

2 tablespoons butter

4 ounces duck livers

I tablespoon chopped onion

I garlic clove, minced

3 tablespoons minced fresh parsley

$1/2$ tablespoon dried thyme

2 ounces fresh pork fat

2 ounces fresh pork, cubed

$1/4$ cup Irish whiskey

I teaspoon Dijon mustard

3 to 4 drops Tabasco sauce

I cup heavy (whipping) cream, plus more as needed

Salt and freshly ground pepper to taste

Lettuce leaves and buttered toast for serving

Cumberland Sauce (page 201)

In a medium skillet, melt the butter over medium heat and sauté the livers, onion, garlic, parsley, and thyme until the livers are lightly browned, about 5 minutes. Remove from heat, mash the livers with a fork, and return to the pan over low heat. Add the pork fat, pork, whiskey, mustard, Tabasco, 1 cup cream, salt, and pepper, and simmer for 30 minutes. Remove from heat and let cool for 5 minutes. Transfer to a blender or food processor and process until smooth, adding more cream if necessary. Butter a 2-cup earthenware dish or mold and pour in the pâté. Refrigerate until firm, about 2 hours.

To serve, turn the pâté out onto a plate. Cut into 4 slices and serve on lettuce leaves with hot buttered toast and Cumberland Sauce alongside.

Warm Woodland Salad
with Champagne Vinaigrette

⩙ This salad from Kay O'Flynn, chef-proprietor at Rathsallagh House (Dunlavin, County Wicklow), makes a lovely first course or luncheon dish.

Champagne Vinaigrette

1 tablespoon champagne vinegar

3 tablespoons extra-virgin olive oil

1 tablespoon walnut oil

1 tablespoon minced garlic

1 teaspoon Dijon mustard

Salt and freshly ground pepper to taste

4 pigeon or pheasant breasts, halved, or
   1 pound duck or chicken livers

Salt and freshly ground pepper to taste

2 tablespoons vegetable oil

2 slices bacon, chopped

2 tablespoons minced fresh chives

2 tablespoons chopped scallion

8 white mushrooms, sliced

10 ounces mixed salad greens

1 cup croutons (page 27)

To make the vinaigrette: In a small bowl or screw-top jar, combine all the ingredients. Whisk or shake to blend.

Preheat the oven to 425°F. Sprinkle the breasts with salt and pepper.

In a large skillet over medium heat, heat the oil and cook the breasts until lightly browned, 3 to 5 minutes per side. Transfer the breasts to a roasting pan and bake in the oven for about 5 minutes. Remove and keep warm. (If using livers, sauté for a total of 5 minutes.)

In the same skillet, cook the bacon over medium heat until crisp, 5 to 8 minutes. With a slotted spoon, transfer the bacon to paper towels to drain. Reduce the heat, add the chives, scallions, and mushrooms to the pan, and cook until softened, 2 to 3 minutes. With a slotted spoon, transfer the vegetables to paper towels to drain. In a small saucepan, warm the vinaigrette over low heat for 2 to 3 minutes.

Arrange the greens on 4 salad plates. Divide the bacon and vegetables over the greens. Slice the breasts and arrange on top of the salad. Pour the warm vinaigrette over the meat and garnish with the croutons.

Wild Boar Sausages with Braised Red Cabbage on Cornmeal Pancakes

Serves 8 as a first course

When chef Patrick McLarnon of Ardtara Country House (Upperlands, County Londonderry) and chef John Halligan of the Rihga Royal Hotel (151 West 54th Street, New York) teamed up for a Saint Patrick's Day dinner at New York's James Beard House, they showcased not only their individual talents but Irish cooking. McLarnon created this unusual first course of sausage made from Northern Ireland farm-raised wild boar, which he serves with old-fashioned buttermilk pancakes and tangy red cabbage braised with apples, red wine, and red currant jelly.

1 small head red cabbage, cored and shredded

1 onion, chopped

1 cup dry red wine

1/2 cup red currant jelly

1/4 cup white wine vinegar

1 Granny Smith apple, peeled, cored, and sliced

Salt and freshly ground pepper to taste

8 wild boar sausages (see Resources, page 277)

Cornmeal Pancakes

1 cup all-purpose flour

1/4 cup cornmeal

1 teaspoon baking powder

1 teaspoon cream of tartar

2 tablespoons superfine sugar

1 egg

3/4 cup buttermilk

1 tablespoon vegetable oil

In a large saucepan, combine the cabbage, onion, wine, jelly, vinegar, apple, salt, and pepper. Add enough water to barely cover. Cover and cook until the cabbage is tender, 20 to 25 minutes.

In a large skillet, cook the sausages over medium heat until the juices run clear, 10 to 15 minutes. Set aside and keep warm.

To make the pancakes: Sift the flour, cornmeal, baking powder, cream of tartar, and sugar together in a bowl. Make a well in the center, add the egg and milk and, with a wire whisk, beat to a smooth batter.

In a large skillet or griddle over medium heat, heat the oil. Drop the pancake batter by tablespoonfuls onto the pan and cook on both sides until golden brown, 2 to 4 minutes per side.

To serve, place 1 pancake on each plate, top with some of the red cabbage, and place a sausage on top.

Part 7 From the Hearth

Breads and cakes are the Irishwoman's true forte;

she loves both making them and eating them…they are probably

the most traditional foods which still exist in Ireland.

THEODORA FITZGIBBON, *IRISH TRADITIONAL FOOD*

Two places in Ireland where visitors can still see old-fashioned hearth cooking are the Ulster-American Folk Park, County Tyrone, Northern Ireland, and Bunratty Folk Park, County Clare. Here you'll find two of the best evocations of what life in old Ireland was really like—from thatching and shearing to farming and weaving—and women in period costumes demonstrate how hearth baking was carried out before gas, electric, and microwave ovens existed.

There's a certain degree of romance to bygone days, when black iron skillets, griddles, and "haren" (hardening) irons were used for baking, but most of us are content to prepare old-style dishes with modern tools. With so many traditional Irish recipes available, it's easy to recapture old-fashioned cooking, whatever kind of oven you use.

My mother was a scratch cook who had a "lace curtain" attitude toward baked goods that were "store-bought" as opposed to homemade: the latter she considered to be the wholesome and accepted way of doing things, the former, unthinkable. It's not that we didn't eat our fair share of Twinkies and Devil Dogs, but when it came to serious breads and cakes, fruit bars and turnovers, homemade was good, "store-bought" was not.

Like many Irish cooks, my mother didn't often use yeast in baking, relying instead on buttermilk and soda to make her bread rise. All my aunts and cousins had their own version of what our family called "old-country cake" (raisin soda bread), and the obligatory black iron skillet in which to bake it. Studded with plumped-up raisins, laced with caraway seeds, and brushed lavishly with milk to produce a shiny crust, we'd eat it straight from the oven with gobs of butter.

In the days before the word *working* so often preceded *mother,* we had shortbread cookies, gingersnaps, or jam-filled oatmeal bars waiting on the kitchen table for us after school, and like an Irish kitchen where the hearth was not only the place for cooking but the heart of the home, our kitchen was always "open to callers" who might need a little hospitality. Having people over for tea was a delightful affair in my mother's kitchen, and in addition to the drink itself, many homemade sweets were served.

The reality of baking today is that even the most dedicated cooks—those who cringe at "store-bought" as my mother did—don't always have the time to bake their own bread. For when you do have time, the following are recipes for a wealth of Irish baked goods, from brown soda bread or oatmeal scones to whiskey cake and Guinness pudding.

Irish Soda Bread

Makes I loaf

≋ It's safe to say that every Irish cook has a recipe for soda bread that's been personalized either by name, ingredients, or method of baking. In the 1997 cooking contest sponsored by the Fitzpatrick Manhattan Hotel (687 Lexington Avenue), about one quarter of all the recipes submitted were for soda bread—including Aunt Eileen's, Grandma O'Hara's, Auntie Maura's, Donna's, and Terry's—and not one was the same! Two or three suggested plumping up the raisins in water or whiskey for expansion; another one or two insisted kneading was essential; one added sour cream, another soured eggnog, to the buttermilk; half were shaped into a round and cooked on a baking sheet, the others were baked in a loaf pan. This one, which uses corn oil, is my favorite.

4 cups all-purpose flour

1/4 cup sugar

I teaspoon baking soda

2 teaspoons baking powder

I teaspoon salt

2 large eggs

1 1/4 cups buttermilk

1/4 cup corn oil

2 teaspoons caraway seeds

I cup golden raisins

I tablespoon milk

Preheat the oven to 350°F. Lightly grease a baking sheet or line it with parchment paper.

In a large bowl, stir the flour, sugar, baking soda, baking powder, and salt together. In a separate bowl, beat the eggs, buttermilk, and oil together. Make a well in the center of the dry ingredients and pour in the buttermilk mixture. Add the caraway seeds and raisins. Stir until a soft dough has formed. →

Shape the dough into a large ball on a lightly floured board (flour your hands if necessary for easier handling). With a sharp knife, make a cross on the top. Place on the prepared pan. Brush the top with the milk. Bake in the center of the oven until golden brown, 30 to 40 minutes.

White Soda Bread

Makes I loaf

⇆⇆ Patrick McLarnon, chef at Ardtara Country House Hotel (Upperlands, County Londonderry) bakes this ultra-easy white bread daily for guests. Nearly obligatory in the breakfast bread basket, it also makes a wonderful crust for meat and game pies when rolled out to a 1/4-inch thickness.

  4 cups all-purpose flour

  I teaspoon baking soda

  I teaspoon cream of tartar

  I teaspoon salt

  1/4 cup superfine sugar

  2 cups buttermilk

Preheat the oven to 425°F. Lightly grease a 9-inch round cake pan or a 9-by-5-inch loaf pan.

Sift the flour, baking soda, cream of tartar, and salt together into a large bowl. Stir in the sugar. Make a well in the center, add the buttermilk, and with a fork, work the milk into the flour until a soft dough is formed. Turn into the prepared pan and bake for 10 minutes. Reduce the heat to 400°F and bake until the bread is golden brown and firm to the touch, about 45 minutes. Let cool slightly before slicing.

Mills Inn Brown Soda Bread

Makes 1 loaf

As with raisin soda bread, every Irish cook has a favorite brown bread recipe. This recipe, from Donal Scannel's Mills Inn (Ballyvourney, County Cork), is made with the traditional combination of brown and white flours. It's my personal favorite for sentimental reasons: my great-grandfather Daniel Crowley was born in Ballyvourney in 1821.

> 2 cups coarse whole-wheat flour or 1 cup each wheat bran
>   and old-fashioned oatmeal
>
> 2 cups all-purpose flour
>
> 1/2 teaspoon salt
>
> 1 teaspoon baking soda
>
> 1/2 teaspoon cream of tartar
>
> 1/4 cup sugar
>
> 4 tablespoons cold butter
>
> 2 cups buttermilk

Preheat the oven to 400°F. Lightly grease a 9-inch round cake pan.

In a large bowl, stir the flours or wheat bran and oatmeal, salt, baking soda, cream of tartar, and sugar together. With a pastry cutter, 2 knives, or your fingers, cut or work the butter into the dry ingredients to the texture of coarse crumbs. Make a well in the center and add the buttermilk. With a wooden spoon, mix until a soft dough is formed.

Turn the dough out onto a floured board and knead lightly, just enough to form a large ball. (Flour your hands if necessary for easier handling.) Flatten slightly. With a sharp knife, make a cross on the top. Place the dough in the prepared pan and bake until the bread is lightly browned and sounds hollow when tapped, 35 to 40 minutes.

Brown Bread Ice Cream

⧓

These thoroughly modern recipes for ice cream are a way clever chefs have found to utilize leftover brown soda bread, which doesn't keep very well. Now, rather than throw away unused slices, you can freeze them to have on hand for this distinctively Irish dessert. The first, from Eamonn O'Reilly, chef-proprietor at One Pico (12 Upper Camden Street, Dublin) requires an ice-cream maker; the second, from executive chef Patrick Brady of Dublin's Westbury Hotel, uses prepared ice cream. Both rely on Baileys Irish Cream for additional creaminess and flavor.

Eamonn O'Reilly's
Brown Bread Ice Cream

2 cups brown soda bread crumbs

6 egg yolks

3/4 cup superfine sugar

2 cups heavy (whipping) cream

1 cup milk

1 teaspoon vanilla extract

1/2 cup Baileys Irish Cream

Preheat the oven to 375°F. Spread the bread crumbs onto a baking sheet and bake until lightly browned, 10 to 15 minutes.

In a large bowl, whisk the egg yolks and sugar together until smooth. In a medium saucepan, combine the cream, milk, and vanilla extract over medium heat and heat until bubbles form around the edges of the pan. Whisk into the egg yolks and let cool. Pour through a fine-meshed sieve. Stir in the bread crumbs and Baileys. Freeze in an ice-cream maker according to manufacturer's instructions. Makes about 2 pints.

Patrick Brady's
Brown Bread Ice Cream

1 1/2 cups brown soda bread crumbs

1/2 cup firmly packed brown sugar

1 cup almonds, crushed

1 quart vanilla ice cream, softened

1 cup Baileys Irish Cream

Preheat the oven to 400°F. In a small bowl, combine the bread crumbs, brown sugar, and almonds. Spread out on a baking sheet and toast until golden brown, 10 to 15 minutes, stirring twice. Remove from the oven and let cool. Crush into small pieces with a rolling pin. In a large bowl, combine the bread crumb mixture, ice cream, and Baileys and mix well. Pour into individual parfait glasses or a plastic container and freeze until firm. Makes 1 1/2 quarts; serves 8 to 10.

Lifeforce Mill Brown Bread

Makes I loaf

〰️ Visitors to the Lifeforce Mill, one of County Cavan's newest attractions, not only get a tour of the mill but a unique opportunity to bake a loaf of bread made from the mill's own stone-ground whole-wheat flour, then collect it hot out of the oven when they depart. Milling on the site can be traced back to medieval times, when a flour mill was part of a fourteenth-century Franciscan monastery, and the current mill building is more than one hundred years old. In 1995 the restored property opened as a tourist attraction and resumed operation as a mill. In addition to stone-ground whole-wheat flour, Lifeforce also produces pinhead oats and oatlets, both of which are combined in this recipe from the mill.

I¹/₂ cups all-purpose flour

I teaspoon baking soda

¹/₄ cup steel-cut oats, preferably Lifeforce or McCann's brand (see Resources, page 277)

¹/₂ cup oatmeal, preferably Lifeforce or McCann's brand quick-cooking (see Resources, page 277)

I cup whole-wheat flour

I teaspoon salt

I¹/₂ cups buttermilk

Preheat the oven to 400°F. Grease a 9-by-5-inch loaf pan.

In a large bowl, sift together the all-purpose flour and baking soda. Add the oats, oatmeal, whole-wheat flour, and salt, and stir to combine. Make a well in the center and add the buttermilk. Stir until a soft dough is formed. Turn into the prepared pan and bake until lightly browned, 40 to 45 minutes.

Guinness and Malt Wheaten Bread

Makes 1 loaf

⇕⇕ When traveling around Ireland, my husband and I always rate the brown bread we're served, starting with the first basket brought at breakfast, straight through to the tray brought to accompany dinner. At a hotel dining room in Belfast a few years ago, we thought we had found one of the all-time bests. But not only did we discover that it hadn't been made by some clever pastry chef in the hotel kitchen, it wasn't even made by the local bakery down the road. This delicious bread was "store-bought," wrapped in cellophane and closed with a twist tie! We learned that the bread was originally made in a small bakery in Groomsport, County Down, and became so popular that Margaret Waterworth, chef-proprietor of Adelboden Country Lodge and Kitchen, now sells it commercially. She shared the recipe with me.

> 2 cups coarse whole-wheat flour, or 1 cup each wheat bran
>   and quick-cooking oatmeal, preferably McCann's brand
>   (see Resources, page 277)
>
> 2 cups fine whole-wheat flour, plus more for sprinkling
>
> 1/2 cup sugar
>
> 1 teaspoon baking soda
>
> 1 teaspoon salt
>
> 8 tablespoons (1 stick) butter
>
> 1 teaspoon malt extract (see Note)
>
> 1 1/4 cups buttermilk
>
> 1 1/4 cups Guinness stout

Note:

Malt extract, also called barley malt, is available in natural foods stores.

Preheat the oven to 375°F. Generously grease a 9-by-5-inch loaf pan and sprinkle it with whole-wheat flour.

→

In a large bowl, mix the whole-wheat flours or wheat bran and oatmeal, sugar, baking soda, and salt together. With a pastry blender, 2 knives, or your fingers, cut or work in the butter to the consistency of coarse bread crumbs. Make a well in the center, add the malt, buttermilk, and Guinness, and, with a wooden spoon, mix to a porridge consistency. Do not overbeat.

Pour into the prepared pan and sprinkle some fine whole-wheat flour on top. Bake for 30 minutes. Turn the oven temperature down to 325°F and bake about 30 minutes more, until the bread is browned and springs back when gently pressed. Turn the oven off, open the door, and let the bread sit for 30 minutes. Unmold onto a wire rack to cool completely before slicing.

Bread and Butter Pudding with Whiskey Sauce

Serves 6 to 8

≶ Traditional bread pudding has always been a favorite of thrifty housewives looking for ways to use up leftover bread. Lately, it's become a stylish dessert in Irish restaurants and country houses as well, as this recipe from Cashel House Hotel (Connemara, County Galway) indicates. Proprietor Dermot McEvilly says it's a favorite with his guests, particularly when topped with a spoonful or two of whiskey sauce. A drizzling of Baileys Irish Cream works well, too.

1/4 cup golden raisins

1/2 cup hot water

4 tablespoons butter at room temperature

10 slices white bread

1 cup milk

1 cup heavy (whipping) cream

2 teaspoons vanilla extract

3/4 cup superfine sugar

1/8 teaspoon ground nutmeg

1/2 teaspoon ground cinnamon

3 eggs, beaten

Whiskey Sauce

1 cup milk

2 tablespoons sugar

2 egg yolks

2 tablespoons Irish whiskey

Preheat the oven to 350°F. Grease an 8-inch round or square baking dish. In a small bowl, combine the raisins and water and soak for 10 minutes.

Butter the bread, remove the crusts, and cut each slice in half diagonally. Arrange half of the bread, buttered side up, in the prepared pan. Drain the raisins and sprinkle them over the bread.

In a small saucepan, combine the milk, cream, vanilla extract, sugar, nutmeg, and cinnamon. Cook over medium heat until the mixture just begins to boil, 5 to 7 minutes. Remove from heat and whisk in the eggs. Arrange the remaining pieces of bread over the raisins. Pour the custard over the bread and let soak for 10 minutes.　　　　　　　　　　　→

Cover with aluminum foil and place the dish in a baking pan. Add hot water to the baking pan to reach two thirds up the sides of the pudding dish and bake until the custard is set, 50 to 55 minutes. Let cool for a few minutes in the baking pan before removing.

To make the sauce: In a small saucepan, heat the milk over medium heat until it just begins to boil. Remove from heat. In a small bowl, whisk together the sugar and egg yolks until light and fluffy. Whisk the yolk mixture into the milk. Simmer over low heat, stirring constantly, until the sauce thickens, about 10 minutes. Stir in the whiskey. To serve, spoon the warm pudding onto plates and spoon the warm sauce over.

Bunratty Park Fruit Scones

Bunratty Folk Park, situated behind the castle in the village of Bunratty (County Clare), is a charming re-creation of life in nineteenth-century Ireland, including a village street, farmhouses, a water mill, a blacksmith forge, and a display of nineteenth-century agricultural machinery. The folk park not only preserves the spirit of the past, it also preserves hearty and wholesome traditional recipes for which the Irish are famous, like this one for fruit scones.

Makes 18 scones

4 cups all-purpose flour

2 teaspoons baking powder

Pinch of salt

$^1/_2$ teaspoon baking soda

$^1/_4$ cup sugar

4 tablespoons cold butter

$^3/_4$ cup raisins

2 eggs, beaten

2 cups buttermilk

$^1/_4$ cup heavy (whipping) cream

Butter and jam for serving

Lightly whipped cream for serving (optional)

Preheat the oven to 400°F. Lightly grease a baking sheet.

In a large bowl, combine the flour, baking powder, salt, baking soda, and sugar. With a pastry blender, 2 knives, or your fingers, cut or work the butter into the flour mixture until it resembles coarse crumbs. Add the raisins. Gradually stir in the eggs and buttermilk and mix until a soft dough forms. Turn the dough onto a lightly floured surface and roll into a 1-inch-thick round. With a 2-inch biscuit cutter, cut the scones into rounds and place on the prepared pan. Brush the tops with the cream. Bake until golden brown, about 20 minutes. Serve warm, with butter, jam, and whipped cream if you like.

Variation: Add 2 teaspoons mixed spice (page 234) to the recipe, and replace the raisins with $^1/_3$ cup raisins and $^1/_3$ cup mixed candied peel.

A Taste of Ulster

⬦⬦

Visitors to Northern Ireland (County Ulster) hoping to find the best traditional and modern recipes using Ulster produce should look for the Taste of Ulster logo.

Northern Ireland establishments that are members of this organization carefully select and feature Ulster dishes on their menus daily, offering freshwater fish, seafood, shellfish, lamb, beef, vegetables, and the famous Armagh apples. Home-cured hams and bacon, fresh and smoked salmon, herring, and brown trout are all specialties that no visitor to Ulster should miss. Recipes from Ulster chefs are found throughout this book.

Ulster Farmhouse Scones

Makes 18 scones

〰〰 One of the most delightful stops on a tour of the Ulster American Folk Park (County Tyrone) is the Mellon Homestead, the cottage where Pittsburgh financier Thomas Mellon was born in February 1813. Originally located in nearby Camphill, the cottage is now the centerpiece of the folk park. The premises are typical of the small farmsteads that so many Irish people left behind as they sought a new life in America. The aroma of turf fires and baking bread contributes to the special atmosphere of bygone days, and if you're lucky enough to catch a cooking demonstration at the Mellon house, you can sample genuine Ulster farmhouse baking, like these potato scones.

> 2 cups all-purpose flour
>
> 3 teaspoons baking powder
>
> I teaspoon salt
>
> 4 tablespoons cold butter
>
> 1/2 cup mashed potatoes
>
> I Golden Delicious apple, peeled, cored, and grated
>
> I tablespoon superfine sugar
>
> 1/4 cup milk
>
> I egg, beaten
>
> Butter and apple jelly for serving
>
> Lightly whipped cream for serving (optional)

Preheat the oven to 350°F. Lightly grease a baking sheet.

In a large bowl, sift the flour, baking powder, and salt together. With a pastry blender, 2 knives, or your fingers, cut or work the butter into the flour mixture until it resembles coarse crumbs. Add the mashed potatoes to the flour. Stir in the apple, sugar, and milk and mix well until a soft dough is formed.

→

Turn the dough onto a lightly floured board and roll out into a 1-inch-thick round. With a 2-inch biscuit cutter, cut the scones into rounds and place on the prepared baking sheet. Brush the tops with the beaten egg. Bake until golden brown, about 15 minutes. Serve warm, with butter, apple jelly, and lightly whipped cream if you like.

McCann's Steel-Cut Oat Scones

≷≷ For centuries, the gentle rains and cool climate of Ireland have made its rolling hills and green pastures home to the finest milling grains in the world. Of these, steel-cut oats are the most famous. The rich, nutritious, golden grain with the robust flavor has made Ireland renowned for its long-cooking oatmeal, and since 1800, when John McCann founded his famous mills on the edge of the Nanny River, McCann's Irish oatmeal has won awards throughout the world. While it's perhaps best known as a hot breakfast cereal, the nutty taste and texture of steel-cut oats are delicious in baking too, as in the recipes that follow.

Makes 12 scones

1 cup steel-cut oats, preferably McCann's brand
  (see Resources, page 277), toasted (see Note)

1¼ cups buttermilk

1 cup whole-wheat flour

½ cup all-purpose flour

2 tablespoons firmly packed light brown sugar

2 teaspoons baking powder

1 teaspoon baking soda

¼ teaspoon ground cinnamon

½ cup mixed candied peel or raisins

4 tablespoons cold butter

2 tablespoons heavy (whipping) cream

Butter and jam for serving

Note:

To toast steel-cut oats, preheat the oven to 300°F. Spread the oats in a baking pan and toast for 20 to 25 minutes or until lightly browned, stirring once or twice. Store in an airtight container in a cool place.

Preheat the oven to 350°F. Generously grease a 9-inch pie plate.

In a small bowl, stir the oats and buttermilk together. Let stand for 25 minutes.

In a large bowl, combine the flours, 1 tablespoon of the brown sugar, the baking powder, baking soda, cinnamon, and peel or raisins. Add the butter and, with a pastry blender, 2 knives, or your fingers, cut or work in the butter until it resembles coarse crumbs. Stir in the oats and buttermilk until just blended. Do not overmix.

Pat the dough into the prepared plate, molding it gently to fit. With a floured kitchen knife, score through the dough almost to the bottom, making 12 wedges. In a small bowl, combine the cream and remaining 1 tablespoon brown sugar. With a pastry brush, coat the top of the dough. Bake until golden brown, 15 to 20 minutes. Remove from the oven and immediately cut through the wedges. Serve warm, with butter and jam.

Oatmeal Bars

Makes 2 dozen bars

⤉ These hearty oatmeal bars are drizzled with chocolate for a nice contrast in flavors.

2 cups steel-cut oats, preferably McCann's brand
(see Resources, page 277), toasted (see page 229)

2 eggs

1¼ cups nonfat milk

1 cup (2 sticks) unsalted butter at room temperature

1 cup firmly packed dark brown sugar

1½ cups all-purpose flour

1 teaspoon baking powder

½ teaspoon baking soda

½ teaspoon ground cinnamon

1 cup raisins

2 squares (2 ounces) semisweet chocolate, chopped

Preheat the oven to 350°F. Generously grease a 9-by-12-inch baking pan.

In a blender or food processor, combine the oats, eggs, and milk. Process for 1 minute, then let rest for 30 minutes.

In a large bowl, cream the butter and sugar until light and fluffy. Add the oat mixture and stir to blend. Sift in the flour, baking powder, baking soda, cinnamon, and raisins and stir again to blend. Pour into the prepared pan and bake until lightly browned and firm to the touch, about 30 minutes. Remove from the oven and let cool in the pan on a wire rack.

While the bars are cooling, melt the chocolate in a double boiler over barely simmering water. Drizzle over the top of the bars. Let the chocolate set before cutting into 1-by-3-inch pieces.

A Trio of Tea Cookies

≶ These traditional homespun cookies are perfect partners with tea.

Oatmeal Cookies

Makes 4 dozen cookies

1¼ cups (2½ sticks) butter at room temperature

½ cup firmly packed light brown sugar

½ cup granulated sugar

1 egg

1 teaspoon vanilla extract

1½ cups all-purpose flour

1 teaspoon baking soda

1 teaspoon salt

1 teaspoon ground cinnamon

3 cups quick-cooking oatmeal, preferably McCann's brand
(see Resources, page 277)

3/4 cup raisins

½ cup chopped walnuts

Preheat the oven to 375°F. In a small bowl, cream the butter and sugars together until light and fluffy. Beat in the egg and vanilla. Sift the flour, baking soda, salt, and cinnamon together and, with a wooden spoon, stir to combine. Add the oatmeal, raisins, and walnuts and mix well.

Drop rounded teaspoonfuls of batter 1 inch apart onto an ungreased baking sheet and bake until golden brown, 12 to 15 minutes. Let the cookies cool on the pan for 1 minute before transferring them to wire racks to cool completely. Serve with Irish breakfast tea.

Variation: For a smoother cookie, omit the raisins and walnuts. Turn the dough out onto a floured board and roll out to an ⅛-inch thickness. Cut into rounds with a biscuit cutter and bake as above.

Shortcake Cookies

12 tablespoons (1¹/2 sticks) butter at room temperature
¹/4 cup superfine sugar
1¹/2 cups all-purpose flour

Makes 2 dozen cookies

Preheat the oven to 300°F. Generously grease a baking sheet.

In a small bowl, cream the butter and sugar together until light and fluffy. Sift in the flour and, with a wooden spoon, blend well. Form the dough into a ball. On a board that has been lightly sprinkled with superfine sugar, roll the dough out to an ¹/8-inch thickness. With a biscuit cutter, cut into rounds.

Place on the prepared baking sheet and bake until golden brown, 25 to 30 minutes. Transfer to a wire rack to cool. Serve immediately, or store in an airtight container.

Gingersnaps

4 tablespoons butter at room temperature
¹/2 cup firmly packed dark brown sugar
3 tablespoons molasses
1 egg
1³/4 cups all-purpose flour
2¹/4 teaspoons baking powder
2 teaspoons salt
1 teaspoon baking soda
1¹/2 teaspoons ground ginger

Makes 4 dozen cookies

In a medium bowl, cream the butter and sugar together until light and fluffy. Beat in the molasses and egg. Sift in the flour, baking powder, salt, baking soda, and ginger and beat well. Cover and refrigerate for 1 hour.

Preheat the oven to 350°F. Generously grease a baking sheet.

Roll tablespoonfuls of dough into balls with your hands. Place 2 inches apart on the prepared pan and, with a spatula or the bottom of a small tumbler that has been dipped in water, flatten each cookie. Bake until crisp, about 20 minutes. Transfer the cookies to wire racks to cool. Store in an airtight container.

Three Irish Tea Cakes

"Having tea" can mean anything from a light supper at the kitchen table to a formal affair complete with silver service and Irish linen. Any one of these cakes and a few small sandwiches are all you need.

Raisin Tea Cake

Serves 8

Mary Tuohy, a Cappagh, County Tyrone, native who now lives in Redbank, New Jersey, has been making this raisin tea cake for so long that she can almost do it from memory. She says, "I can't remember where the recipe came from, but we used to bake it over an open turf fire back home. It came to me on a piece of dilapidated paper, which I still have." It's a very moist cake, she says, nearly foolproof. "You can't go wrong with it."

→

Mixed Spice

1 tablespoon coriander seeds

1 two-inch cinnamon stick, crushed

1 teaspoon whole cloves

1 teaspoon allspice berries

1 tablespoon ground nutmeg

2 teaspoons ground ginger

2 1/4 cups water

3 cups raisins

8 tablespoons (1 stick) cold butter, cut into small pieces

1 cup sugar

3 cups all-purpose flour

2 teaspoons baking soda

1 teaspoon salt

1 egg, beaten

The day before baking, make the mixed spice: In a spice grinder, combine the coriander seeds, cinnamon, cloves, and allspice. Grind until powdery. Pour into an airtight container. Add nutmeg and ginger and mix well. Measure out 1 level tablespoon and store the remainder in a cool place for later use.

Combine the mixed spice with the water, raisins, butter, and sugar in a medium saucepan. Bring to a boil, then reduce heat and simmer for 20 minutes. Remove from heat and let cool completely. Cover and refrigerate overnight.

The next day, let the raisin mixture sit at room temperature for 1 hour. Preheat the oven to 350°F. Generously grease a 9-inch round cake pan.

Sift the flour, baking soda, and salt together into a large bowl. Stir in the raisin mixture and blend well. Stir in the egg. Pour into the prepared pan. Place on the center rack of the oven with a pan of water. Bake until the cake is lightly browned and a skewer inserted into the center comes out clean, about 1^1/4 hours.

Lemon-Whiskey Cake

Serves 6

This is a no-frosting-required cake, lightly flavored with whiskey and lemon. For a decorative touch, place a paper doily on top and sift some confectioners' sugar over it.

Zest of 1 lemon

^{1}/4 cup Irish whiskey

12 tablespoons (1^1/2 sticks) butter at room temperature

^{3}/4 cup superfine sugar

3 eggs, beaten

2 cups all-purpose flour

Pinch of salt

^{3}/4 cup almonds, ground

The day before baking, cut the lemon zest into julienne and combine in a small bowl with the whiskey. Let soak overnight.

The next day, preheat the oven to 350°F. Generously grease a 9-inch round cake pan.

In a medium bowl, cream the butter and sugar together until light and fluffy. Whisk in the eggs. Sift in the flour and salt and stir to blend. Fold in the almonds. Strain the whiskey, discarding the zest, and stir the whiskey into the batter. Pour into the prepared pan and bake until the cake is golden brown and a skewer inserted into the center comes out clean, about 1 hour.

Irish Oatmeal Cake with Nut Topping

This oatmeal cake with a nut topping will add a festive spirit to any tea party, although the recipe was originally created for McCann's oatmeal as a Saint Patrick's Day dessert.

Serves 8

I cup quick-cooking oatmeal, preferably McCann's brand (see Resources, page 277)

1¹/2 cups boiling water

8 tablespoons (I stick) unsalted butter at room temperature

I cup firmly packed light brown sugar

I cup granulated sugar

2 tablespoons Irish whiskey

2 eggs

1¹/2 cups all-purpose flour

I teaspoon ground cinnamon

I teaspoon baking soda

Nut Topping

6 tablespoons (³/4 stick) unsalted butter at room temperature

¹/2 cup firmly packed light brown sugar

¹/4 cup heavy (whipping) cream

I tablespoon Irish whiskey

I cup chopped nuts

¹/2 cup shredded coconut

Preheat the oven to 350°F. Grease and flour a 9-inch round or square cake pan.

In a large bowl, combine the oatmeal and water and let stand for 20 minutes.

In a small bowl, cream the butter and sugars together until light and fluffy. Add the whiskey and eggs and beat until well blended. Stir in the oatmeal.

In a medium bowl, combine the flour, cinnamon, and baking soda. Add to the oatmeal mixture and stir to combine. Pour the batter into the prepared pan and bake until the cake is golden and a skewer inserted into the center comes out clean, about 30 minutes.

Meanwhile, make the topping: In a small bowl, cream the butter and sugar together until light and fluffy. Blend in the cream and whiskey. Stir in the nuts and coconut. Cover and set aside until the cake is done.

Remove the cake from the oven. Spread the nut topping over the hot cake. Broil until the topping is bubbling and the coconut is toasted, about 5 minutes. Transfer to a wire rack and let cool for at least 15 minutes before cutting.

Barmbrack

The word *Halloween* owes its origin to the ancient Celtic harvest festival called Samhain (pronounced "sowen"), which occurred on the eve of the Celtic New Year, November 1, a time when departed souls supposedly walked the earth. With the arrival of Christianity in Ireland, November 1 became known as All Souls' Day, a time to remember the dead. Several foods are traditionally eaten on All Hallows' Eve, especially colcannon (see page 7) and barmbrack. Bracks (from the Irish *breac*, meaning "speckled") are cakes studded with dried fruits and raisins, which create a speckled effect when sliced. Those that are made with yeast are called "barmbracks," and those that use baking powder and fruit soaked in tea or cider are called "tea bracks" or "cider bracks."

According to tradition, hidden in the Halloween barmbrack were tokens to foretell the future: a ring for the bride-to-be, a thimble for the one who would never marry, a coin for the one who would be wealthy, and a small piece of cloth indicating the one who would be poor. Fortune-telling aside, barmbrack is delicious any time of the year, and is best when served warm with butter.

4 cups all-purpose flour

1/2 teaspoon ground cinnamon

1/2 teaspoon Mixed Spice (page 234)

1/4 teaspoon ground nutmeg

Pinch of salt

4 tablespoons cold butter

1 package (2 teaspoons) active dried yeast

1/2 cup superfine sugar

1 1/4 cups milk

1 egg, beaten

1 cup golden raisins

1/2 cup dried currants

1/4 cup mixed candied peel

1 egg yolk beaten with 2 tablespoons water

Sift the flour, cinnamon, mixed spice, nutmeg, and salt together into a medium bowl. With a pastry blender, 2 knives, or your fingers, cut or work the butter into the flour until it resembles coarse crumbs. In a medium bowl, combine the yeast with 1 teaspoon of the sugar. In a small saucepan, warm the milk until bubbles form around the edges of the pan, then add 1 teaspoon to the yeast mixture.

Pour the remaining milk and the egg into the yeast mixture. Combine with the dry ingredients and add the remaining sugar. Blend well with a wooden spoon or knead with your hands in the bowl until the batter is stiff but elastic.

Fold in the raisins, currants, and mixed peel. Cover the bowl with a damp cloth or plastic wrap and let sit in a warm place until doubled in size, about 1 hour. On a lightly floured board, knead for 2 to 3 minutes. Divide the dough in half and form into 2 balls. Place each in a greased 9-by-5-inch loaf pan and let rise in a warm place for 30 minutes.

Preheat the oven to 350°F. Brush the top of the loaves with the egg yolk mixture to glaze. Bake until the bread is golden and a skewer inserted into the center comes out clean, about 1 hour. Turn out onto wire racks and let cool completely before cutting.

Cider Brack

〰️ Soaking the fruit overnight in hard cider adds not only flavor but a nice texture to this cake.

Serves 10 to 12

1 cup dark raisins

1 cup golden raisins

3/4 cup firmly packed brown sugar

1 cup plus 2 tablespoons hard apple cider,
    preferably Bulmer's brand (see Glossary, page 276)

1/2 cup candied mixed peel

Grated zest of 1 orange

8 tablespoons (1 stick) butter, melted

2 eggs, beaten

2 cups all-purpose flour

2 teaspoons Mixed Spice (page 234)

1/2 teaspoon ground cinnamon

Pinch of salt

1 tablespoon granulated sugar

The day before baking, combine the raisins, brown sugar, and 1 cup of cider in a medium saucepan. Bring to a boil, then reduce heat to low and simmer for 5 minutes, stirring once or twice. Let cool, cover, and refrigerate overnight.

The next day, let the raisin mixture sit at room temperature for 1 hour. Preheat the oven to 350°F. Grease a 9-inch round pan and line the bottom with a round of parchment paper.

Add the mixed peel, orange zest, melted butter, and eggs to the raisin mixture and stir to blend. Sift the flour, mixed spice, cinnamon, and salt together into the raisin mixture and stir to blend. Pour into the prepared pan. Bake until the cake is firm to the touch and a skewer inserted into the center comes out clean, 1 to 1½ hours. Remove the cake from the oven, leaving the oven on.

In a small saucepan over medium heat, combine the 2 tablespoons cider with the granulated sugar and cook over medium heat until the sugar is dissolved. Brush the cider glaze over the top of the cake and return the cake to the oven until the top is shiny, about 3 minutes. Let the cake cool in the pan for 20 minutes. Unmold and remove the parchment paper. Slice and serve spread with butter.

Irish Christmas Cake

Serves 10 to 12

≋ Christmas is the most important holiday in the Irish calendar. Everything seems to come to a halt for most of December, with celebrations that range from parties and fancy dress balls to races and reveling on Saint Stephen's Day, December 26. The centerpiece at every event is the spicy fruitcake known as *cáca Nollag*. Boston-based Shaun Folan, who emigrated from Inverin (Connemara, County Galway) in 1993, bakes and sells *cáca Nollag* in shops throughout Boston's Irish neighborhoods. Before adding the marzipan and icing, Folan recommends transferring the cake to a plate several inches larger in diameter than the cake to allow for frosting and decorating. Note that this cake is made several weeks before serving. The marzipan is added the day before the cake is frosted and served. →

2 1/4 cups dried currants

2 cups golden raisins

I cup dark raisins

1/4 cup candied cherries

1/4 cup candied mixed peel

2/3 cup chopped almonds

Grated zest and juice of I lemon

1 1/2 teaspoons Mixed Spice (page 234)

1/2 teaspoon ground nutmeg

I cup Irish whiskey

I cup (2 sticks) butter at room temperature

I cup firmly packed light brown sugar

5 eggs

2 cups all-purpose flour, sifted

Marzipan

2 1/4 cups whole blanched almonds

1 1/4 cups superfine sugar

2 eggs

Drop of vanilla extract

1/2 teaspoon fresh lemon juice

1/4 cup Irish whiskey

2 egg whites, beaten until frothy, for brushing

Royal Icing

2 egg whites

4 cups confectioners' sugar, sifted

2 tablespoons fresh lemon juice

Holly sprigs for decoration

The day before baking (and several weeks before serving), combine all the fruit, peel, zest and juice, spices, and nuts in a large bowl with 1/2 cup of the whiskey. Let soak overnight.

The next day, preheat the oven to 275°F. Grease a 9-inch round cake pan and line the bottom with a round of parchment paper.

In a large bowl, cream the butter and sugar together until light and fluffy. Add the eggs, one at a time, beating each in thoroughly and adding some of the sifted flour with each egg. Fold in the remaining flour and mix in the soaked fruit by halves.

Pour into the prepared pan and bake until the cake is firm to the touch and a skewer inserted into the center comes out clean, about 2 hours. Let cool in the pan for 30 minutes. Prick the top of the cake with a skewer in several places and pour the remaining 1/2 cup whiskey over the top. Wrap in plastic wrap, then aluminum foil, and store in a cool, dark place for several weeks to allow the cake to mature. The cake can be unwrapped occasionally and more whiskey added, if desired.

The day before serving, make the marzipan: In a blender or food processor, process the almonds to the consistency of fine crumbs. Transfer to a large bowl and mix in the sugar. Add the eggs, vanilla, lemon juice, and whiskey and stir until a smooth paste is formed.

Line a pastry board with waxed paper and lightly dust it with some sugar. Roll the paste out to about 10 inches in diameter. Unwrap the cake and brush the top of the cake with the egg whites. Gently lift the marzipan onto the top of the cake and roll again. With a sharp knife, trim the edges so the marzipan fits the top of the cake like a disc. Cover the cake with plastic wrap and refrigerate overnight. →

The next day, make the icing: In a large mixing bowl, beat the egg whites. Gradually beat in the sugar and lemon juice and continue beating until the icing is stiff enough to spread.

Using a flexible spatula, spread the icing over the top and sides of the cake. Decorate with sprigs of holly.

Irish Whiskey Cake

≋ Despite the status of Irish Christmas cake as a seasonal icon, there are people who prefer a lighter fruitcake. This recipe from the makers of Jameson Irish whiskey flavors both the cake and the frosting with a small dose of spirits.

Serves 12

   I cup golden raisins
   1 1/2 cups cold water
   8 tablespoons (I stick) butter at room temperature
   1/2 cup granulated sugar
   I egg
   1 1/2 cups all-purpose flour
   2 teaspoons baking powder
   I teaspoon baking soda
   3/4 teaspoon ground cloves
   3/4 teaspoon ground nutmeg
   Dash of ground allspice
   1/2 teaspoon salt
   I cup chopped walnuts
   1/4 cup Irish whiskey, preferably Jameson brand
   Irish Whiskey Icing (recipe follows)
   Walnut halves for garnish (optional)

Preheat the oven to 350°F. Grease two 9-inch-round cake pans and line the bottom with rounds of waxed paper.

In small saucepan, combine the raisins and water and bring to a boil. Simmer, uncovered, for 20 minutes. Drain, reserving the liquid. Let cool.

In a large bowl, cream the butter and sugar together until light and fluffy. Add the egg and beat until blended. Sift in the flour, baking powder, baking soda, spices, and salt. Stir in 3/4 cup of the reserved liquid, the raisins, walnuts, and whiskey. Pour into the prepared pans. Bake until the layers are golden brown and a skewer inserted into the center comes out clean, 30 to 35 minutes. Let cool in the pans on wire racks before icing. With a flexible rubber spatula, spread the icing between the layers and on the top and sides of the cake. Garnish with walnut halves, if desired.

Irish Whiskey Icing

**Makes enough for one
2-layer 9-inch cake**

4 tablespoons butter at room temperature

3 1/2 cups confectioners' sugar, sifted

1 egg

1/4 cup Irish whiskey

In a small bowl, cream the butter and sugar together until light and fluffy. Add the egg and whiskey and beat again until smooth.

Guinness Cake

Serves 10 to 12

〰 Another variation on the traditional Christmas cake is this popular dessert made with stout. It's best made several weeks in advance of Christmas, a practice I favor since it's one less thing to do during the hectic season.

I cup (2 sticks) butter at room temperature
I cup firmly packed light brown sugar
4 eggs, lightly beaten
2 1/2 cups all-purpose flour
2 teaspoons Mixed Spice (page 234)
2 cups dark raisins
2 cups golden raisins
1/2 cup candied mixed peel
I cup walnuts, chopped
3/4 cup Guinness stout

Preheat the oven to 325°F. Generously grease a 9-inch springform pan and line the bottom with a round of parchment paper.

In a large bowl, cream the butter and sugar together until light and fluffy. Gradually beat in the eggs. Sift in the flour and mixed spice. Add the raisins, mixed peel, and walnuts. Stir in 1/2 cup of the Guinness and mix to a soft consistency.

Pour into the prepared pan and bake for 1 hour, then lower the temperature to 300°F and cook until a skewer inserted into the center comes out clean, about 1½ hours (a total of 2½ hours). Let cool in the pan on a wire rack.

Unmold from the pan, prick the top of the cake with a skewer in several places, and spoon the remaining ¼ cup Guinness over. Wrap in plastic wrap, then aluminum foil, and store in a cool, dark place for at least 1 week before eating, or up to 2 months.

Part 8

From the Orchards
and the Fields

Apple trees are lovely in their architecture,

their winter beauty so aspiring in their lines,

so incredibly wonderful in the thousand leaflets that

bud out from each dark limb when spring summons them.

Over all our great orchard lands at the moment,

could one float above them high enough to see it all,

one could find a new whiteness spread beneath that is not snow

but fruit tree blossom.

COLIN JOHNSTON ROBB, *BLOSSOMTIME IN IRELAND'S APPLE GARDEN*

In Ireland, the fences and hedgerows of natural vegetation that bear wild fruits, nuts, and berries were originally left to serve as boundaries when land was cleared and property lines were drawn between neighbors. Hedgerows still grow willy-nilly along country lanes, county roads, and dual carriageways. Thankfully so, for wild sloes, brambles, and gooseberries are still ripe for picking to make up into jams, jellies, puddings, pies, and tarts.

Like all the foods from the Irish table, desserts (the Irish call them "sweets") were prepared from the ingredients on hand, and when fruits were in season, good cooks always took the best advantage. My first-generation Irish-American mother was no exception, and nothing could beat her strawberry-and raspberry-filled summer pudding, her apple-oatmeal crumble in fall, or the elaborate custard-covered, jam-filled, fruit-laden, whiskey-soaked dessert known as trifle, which she reserved for special occasions like Christmas or Easter. "Putting up" fruit jams and jellies in Mason jars and sealing them with paraffin was a task she also carried out with great enthusiasm, and one we knew would translate into a year's worth of sweets.

They say that strawberries from the fields of Wexford are the sweetest and apples from the orchards of Armagh and Tipperary are the juiciest, but quality fruits and berries grow throughout Ireland and many other places. So while the sight of hedgerows may be as distant as the memories of your grandfather's farm, and your favorite apples may come from Washington, Oregon, or Pennsylvania and be named Granny Smith or Golden Delicious instead of Bramley's Seedlings or Cox's Orange Pippin, an apple cake, a strawberry fool, or a batch of rhubarb jam is definitely within your reach.

Irish Apple Cake

Serves 10 to 12

≳≳ Food historian and cookbook author Theodora FitzGibbon once said, "All Irish people have a very sweet tooth," and if you grew up in an Irish household you know this to be true. In the earliest times, the sweet was a simple concoction of fruit and honey; later, cooks found that fruit and berries were equally delicious baked in pies, puddings, and cakes. Apples are the basis of many traditional and contemporary Irish desserts.

4 tablespoons butter at room temperature

I cup granulated sugar

I egg, beaten

4 Granny Smith apples, cored, peeled, and diced (2 cups)

1/4 cup chopped walnuts

I teaspoon vanilla extract

1/2 teaspoon baking powder

1/2 teaspoon baking soda

1/2 teaspoon salt

1/2 teaspoon ground cinnamon

1/2 teaspoon ground nutmeg

I cup all-purpose flour

Whipped cream or vanilla ice cream for serving

Preheat the oven to 350°F. Generously grease an 8-inch square cake pan.

In a large bowl, cream the butter and sugar together until light and fluffy. Add the egg, apples, nuts, and vanilla and stir well. Sift in the dry ingredients and mix well. Pour the batter into the prepared pan and bake until the cake is lightly browned and a skewer inserted into the center comes out clean, about 45 minutes.

Let cool in the pan for 5 minutes, then unmold and serve warm or at room temperature with whipped cream or vanilla ice cream.

Potato-Apple Cake

〰〰 Some recipes for this old-fashioned cake, also called "pratie apple," call for it to be cooked on a griddle. It is delicious served straight from the oven, with a cup of tea.

Serves 4 to 6

4 baking potatoes, peeled and cut into 2-inch pieces

2 tablespoons butter

1 tablespoon granulated sugar

1/4 teaspoon ground ginger

3/4 cup all-purpose flour, sifted

4 Granny Smith apples, peeled, cored, and sliced

2 tablespoons butter

1/2 cup firmly packed light brown sugar

Whipped cream for serving, or confectioners' sugar
      for dusting (optional)

Preheat the oven to 425°F. Lightly grease an 8-inch pie plate.

Cook the potatoes in boiling salted water until tender, 12 to 15 minutes. Drain and mash. Add the butter, sugar, and ginger and mix well. Stir in the flour to make a soft dough. On a lightly floured board, form the dough into a ball and divide it in half. Roll half into an 8-inch-diameter circle and fit it into the prepared pie plate. Arrange the apple slices by overlapping them in 2 concentric circles over the dough. Moisten the edges of the dough with cold water.

Roll out the remaining dough into an 8-inch circle and place it on top of the apples. Press the edges together and flute them to make a standing edge. With a sharp knife, make 4 or 5 slits in the top to let steam escape. Bake until browned, 25 to 30 minutes.

Remove from the oven and cut a 2-inch circle in the top pastry to make a lid. Remove this carefully, add the butter and brown sugar, and replace the lid. Return to the oven and bake until the butter and sugar have melted, about 5 minutes. Slice and serve immediately, with whipped cream or a dusting of confectioners' sugar, if you like.

Upside-down Apple and Soda Bread Tart

Serves 6 to 8

Chef Derry Clarke (L'Ecrivain, Dublin) gives a traditional Irish soda bread a new identity by using it as the base for a caramelized upside-down apple tart.

1/4 cup raisins
1/4 cup Bunratty poitín (see Resources, page 277) or Irish whiskey
2 cups cake flour
1 tablespoon baking powder
1/4 cup granulated sugar
8 tablespoons (1 stick) cold butter or margarine, plus 4 tablespoons
1/2 cup buttermilk
1 cup superfine sugar
1 tablespoon ground cardamom
2 Granny Smith apples, cored and sliced horizontally (about 16 slices)
Lightly whipped cream or ice cream for serving

In a small bowl, combine the raisins and poitín or whiskey and soak for 30 minutes.

→

Preheat the oven to 400°F. In a large bowl, sift the cake flour, baking powder, and granulated sugar together. With a pastry cutter, 2 knives, or your fingers, cut or work in the 8 tablespoons butter until it resembles coarse crumbs. Drain the raisins, reserving the poitín or whiskey. Stir the raisins into the flour, then stir in the buttermilk to make a dough. On a lightly floured surface, knead for 20 seconds. Roll or pat the dough into a 12-inch-diameter circle.

In a large skillet, combine the sugar, reserved soaking poitín or whiskey, the 4 tablespoons butter, and the cardamom. Cook over medium-low heat until the butter melts and the sugar caramelizes. Add the apple slices in batches and cook for 2 to 3 minutes (they should still be crunchy). With a slotted spoon, transfer the apples to a plate. Cook the caramel over low heat until it thickens.

Spread the caramel in a 12-inch quiche pan. Arrange the apple slices by overlapping them in 2 concentric circles over the caramel and cover with the dough. Bake until the crust is golden brown, about 15 minutes. Let cool for 10 minutes, place a serving plate on top, and invert. Slice and serve warm with whipped cream or ice cream.

Oatmeal-Apple Crumble with Whiskey Cream Sauce

Serves 4

≋ Who hasn't enjoyed an apple crisp, cobbler, crumble, or brown Betty, some of the simplest of all fruit desserts to prepare? When Donegal native Joe Friel, executive banquet chef at New York's Plaza Hotel, makes an apple crumble, he gives it an Irish accent by using Irish oatmeal and serves it with a sauce flavored with Irish whiskey.

6 Granny Smith apples, peeled and cored

1 cup granulated sugar

1 cup all-purpose flour

1 cup (2 sticks) butter, cut into pieces

3 tablespoons quick-cooking oatmeal, preferably McCann's brand (see Resources, page 277)

1/2 teaspoon ground ginger

1/2 teaspoon ground cinnamon

Irish Whiskey Cream Sauce

1 cup heavy (whipping) cream

2 tablespoons honey

2 tablespoons Irish whiskey

Preheat the oven to 375°F. Butter an 8-inch square baking dish.

Slice each apple into 6 wedges and arrange the wedges on the bottom of the prepared dish.

In a large bowl, stir the sugar and the flour together. With a pastry cutter, 2 knives, or your fingers, cut or work in the butter to the texture of coarse crumbs. Stir in the oatmeal, ginger, and cinnamon. Spread evenly over the apples and bake until the apples are tender and the topping is browned, about 40 minutes.

To make the sauce: In a deep bowl, beat the cream until stiff peaks form. Dissolve the honey in the whiskey. Fold the honey mixture into the whipped cream. To serve, spoon the apple crumble among 4 plates and spoon some cream sauce over the top.

Old-fashioned Baked Apples with Mincemeat

〜〜 A baked apple is one of the most popular desserts in Ireland. You can alter the filling to suit the season, or cover the apples with frozen pastry to make apple puffs (apple dumplings).

Serves 4

> 4 McIntosh apples, cored
> 1/2 cup prepared mincemeat
> 2 tablespoons butter
> 1 cup apple cider

Preheat the oven to 375°F. Pare 1/4 inch of apple peels from the upper half of each apple to prevent splitting. Place each apple upright in an 8-inch baking dish. Fill the apple cavities with mincemeat and dot with butter. Pour the apple cider around the apples and bake, basting with the pan juices several times during cooking, until the apples are tender, 30 to 40 minutes.

Baked Apples with Raisin-Nut Filling: In a small bowl, combine 1/4 cup packed light brown sugar, 1 teaspoon ground cinnamon, 1/4 teaspoon ground nutmeg, 1/4 cup slivered almonds, and 1/4 cup golden raisins. Fill the cavities of the apples in the above recipe with this mixture. Combine 3/4 cup water, 1/4 cup Irish Mist liqueur, 1 tablespoon fresh lemon juice, and 1/4 teaspoon grated orange zest and pour around the apples. Bake as above.

Apple Puffs: Roll out 1 sheet of puff pastry to about 1/8 inch thick and cut into 4 squares. Place 1 stuffed apple on each square of pastry. Dampen the edges of each square and bring the opposite corners together on top of the apples to make a pouch. Press the edges of the sides and top together firmly to seal. Prick the pastry once or twice at the top. Place on a baking sheet and bake in a preheated 400°F oven until the pastry is lightly browned, 25 to 30 minutes. Serve warm, with whipped cream or any of the whiskey cream sauces in this chapter, if desired.

Armagh Apples with Cooley Mountain Sauce

Serves 2

≋ This unusual dessert is a delicious variation on the traditional recipe for baked apples. It's based on two Irish varieties of apples from County Armagh, though your own local red and green apples will do. Terry McCoy, chef-proprietor of the Red Bank Restaurant (Skerries, County Dublin), uses local whiskey from the Cooley Mountains in County Louth, but any Irish whiskey will do nicely.

Cooley Mountain Sauce

3 egg yolks

1/4 cup superfine sugar

1/3 cup Irish whiskey

2 McIntosh apples

2 Granny Smith apples, peeled, quartered, cored and cut into 8 slices

2 tablespoons butter, plus 1 teaspoon if needed

1/2-inch cinnamon stick

6 whole cloves

2 tablespoons sugar

2 teaspoons honey

1 tablespoon heavy (whipping) cream, if needed

To make the sauce: In a double boiler over simmering water, whisk the egg yolks, sugar, and whiskey together until thick and creamy. Remove from the heat and keep warm.

Poach the whole McIntosh apples in gently boiling water to cover until the apples are tender, about 6 minutes. With a slotted spoon, transfer the apples to a wire rack and let cool to the touch. Cut a 1/4-inch slice from the top of each poached apple. Carefully scoop out the flesh, leaving a 1/4-inch-thick shell. Discard the core and reserve the shells. Chop the flesh and transfer to a small bowl. →

In a medium skillet, melt the 2 tablespoons butter over medium heat. Add the cinnamon stick, cloves, sugar, honey, and apple slices. Cook the apples until they begin to soften, about 2 minutes. Remove the cinnamon stick, discard the cloves, and with a slotted spoon transfer the apple slices to a plate. Cook the pan juices until slightly thickened and combine with the chopped apple flesh. If there is not enough juice, add the 1 teaspoon butter and 1 tablespoon cream.

Spoon 1 or 2 tablespoons of the chopped apple flesh back into each shell and stand the apple slices in it. Place each apple in the center of a warm serving plate, pour the sauce from the pan around the edge, and spoon some of the whiskey sauce over the top.

Eve's Puddings with Whipped Whiskey Cream

〰〰 At Caragh Lodge, a Victorian fishing lodge nestled on the shore of Caragh Lake, County Kerry, chef-proprietor Mary Gaunt will gladly cook her guests' catch of the day (usually trout, for which the lake is famous), but she has a deft hand with desserts as well. These old-fashioned apple puddings have a spongelike consistency, and are served warm with a sprinkle of almonds, a dusting of sugar, and a dollop of whiskey cream.

Serves 8

3 Granny Smith apples, peeled, cored, and chopped

1/4 cup fresh lemon juice

8 tablespoons butter at room temperature

1/2 cup plus 1 tablespoon sugar

1 egg

1 cup all-purpose flour

1 1/2 teaspoons baking powder

1/2 teaspoon salt

2 tablespoons milk

1 tablespoon slivered almonds, toasted (see Note)

1/2 cup confectioners' sugar

Whipped Whiskey Cream

1¹/₄ cups heavy (whipping) cream
2 tablespoons Irish whiskey

Preheat the oven to 375°F. Butter eight 6-ounce ramekins.

Sprinkle the apples with the lemon juice to prevent discoloring. In a medium bowl, cream 6 tablespoons of the butter with the ¹/₂ cup sugar until light and fluffy. Beat in the egg, then stir in the flour, baking powder, and salt. Add the milk and blend to a smooth batter.

Divide the apples among the prepared ramekins. Sprinkle a little of the 1 tablespoon sugar over the top of each, dot with the remaining 2 tablespoons butter, and spoon in the pudding mixture. Place the ramekins on a baking sheet and cook until the puddings are lightly browned, about 20 minutes.

Let cool slightly, then run a knife around the edge of each pudding to loosen.

To make the whiskey cream: In a deep bowl, beat the cream until stiff peaks form. Fold in the whiskey.

To serve, unmold the puddings onto plates, sprinkle with the almonds, and dust with confectioners' sugar. Place a spoonful of whiskey cream alongside each pudding.

Note:

To toast almond slivers, preheat the oven to 250°F. Spread the almonds in a baking pan and toast for 5 to 10 minutes or until lightly browned, stirring once or twice.

Apple and Whiskey Crème Brûlée

Makes 6 servings

〰 Charles and Mary Cooper, chef-proprietors of Markree Castle, County Sligo's oldest inhabited castle, enjoy experimentation and innovation in their cooking. Here they add finely diced apples and Irish whiskey to classic crème brûlée (also known as Cambridge cream, for its popularity at the English university) for a distinctive Irish version.

2 Granny Smith apples, peeled, cored, and diced

1/2 cup fresh lemon juice

2 tablespoons butter

6 tablespoons superfine sugar

2 tablespoons Irish whiskey

5 egg yolks

1/2 teaspoon vanilla extract

I cup heavy (whipping) cream

I cup milk

3 tablespoons granulated brown sugar

I tablespoon confectioners' sugar

Preheat the oven to 350°F. Butter six 6-ounce ramekins.

Sprinkle the apples with the lemon juice to prevent discoloring. In a medium skillet over medium heat, melt the butter. Add the apples, 2 tablespoons of the superfine sugar and cook until the apples begin to soften, 2 to 3 minutes. Reduce heat to simmer, stir in the whiskey, and cook for 2 to 3 minutes more. Divide the mixture among the prepared ramekins.

In a medium bowl, whisk the eggs, remaining 4 tablespoons sugar, and vanilla together. Add the milk and cream and whisk until well blended. Pour over the apples. Set the ramekins in a large baking pan and add hot water to come halfway up the sides of the ramekins. Bake until the custard is set, about 35 minutes. Remove from the oven and let cool in the baking pan for 15 minutes. Remove from the water bath, cover with plastic wrap, and refrigerate until serving time.

To serve, preheat the broiler. Sprinkle the top of each custard with 1 table-spoon of the brown sugar and place under the broiler until caramelized, 3 to 5 minutes. Dust with confectioners' sugar.

Toasted Oatmeal and Bushmills Crème Brûlée with Rhubarb Compote

Serves 6   ≈≈   This version of crème brûlée also takes on an Irish touch with the addition of toasted oatmeal and the ubiquitous Irish spirit. Patrick McLarnon, chef at one of Northern Ireland's most delightful country houses, Ardtara (Upperlands, County Londonderry), keeps it a fixture on the menu although he changes the fruit compote seasonally and experiments with the method of cooking. Here he uses a small ramekin which is a perfect size given the richness of the crème.

2 tablespoons steel-cut oats, preferably McCann's brand (see Resources, page 277)

2 tablespoons Bushmills Irish whiskey

5 egg yolks

1/2 cup superfine sugar

2 cups heavy (whipping) cream

Rhubarb Compote

1 1/2 cups water

1 1/2 cups granulated sugar

1 pound rhubarb, cut into 1-inch pieces

6 tablespoons confectioners' sugar   →

Preheat the oven to 375°F. Butter six 6-ounce ramekins.

Place the oats into a shallow ovenproof dish and toast in the oven until they start to brown and smell nutty, about 10 minutes. Remove from oven and pour on the whiskey, which will evaporate from the heat of the pan. Reduce heat to 325°F.

In a small bowl, whisk the egg yolks and sugar together until the sugar is dissolved. Add the cream and oats and stir to blend. Spoon the mixture into the prepared ramekins. Set the ramekins in a large baking pan and add hot water to come halfway up the sides of the ramekins. Bake until the custard is set, about 45 minutes. Remove from the oven and let cool in the baking pan for 15 minutes. Remove the ramekins from the baking pan, cover with plastic wrap, and refrigerate until serving time.

To make the compote: In a small saucepan, combine the water and sugar and bring to a boil over medium heat. Boil for 2 minutes, reduce heat, add the rhubarb, and cook until tender, about 10 minutes.

To serve, preheat the broiler. Dust each custard with 1 tablespoon confectioners' sugar and place under the broiler until caramelized. Serve with a spoonful of rhubarb compote on the side.

Variation: If rhubarb is not available, use the method above to stew your favorite seasonal fruit, or use sliced fresh fruit.

Apple Fool

⇔ One of the loveliest ways to use seasonal fruits and berries is in what the Irish call fruit fools. The word *fool* refers to the simplicity of this dessert, classically a combination of only pureed fruit and whipped cream. A fruit fool is really quite a clever dessert, however, as it can be made ahead of time and looks spectacular served in Irish crystal stemware.

I pound Granny Smith apples, peeled, cored, and sliced

Grated zest of 1/2 lemon

1/2 teaspoon ground cloves

2 tablespoons water

1/3 cup superfine sugar

2 eggs, separated

1/2 cup sour cream

In a small saucepan, combine the apples, lemon zest, cloves, and water. Cover and simmer until the apples are soft, about 10 minutes. Transfer to a blender or food processor and puree until smooth. Return to the saucepan and stir in the sugar. Add the egg yolks and stir over low heat for 5 minutes. Remove from the heat and let cool for 10 minutes. Stir in the sour cream and refrigerate for 1 hour.

In a large bowl, beat the egg whites until stiff, glossy peaks form. Fold into the cold apple puree. To serve, divide the mixture into 4 stem glasses.

Blackberry and Almond Fool

≋ The blend of blackberries and almonds creates a delightful fruit fool, and the almond flavor is highlighted by the amaretti crumbled over the top. Unlike most recipes for fruit fools, here the blackberries are left whole and simply topped with an almond-flavored cream.

Serves 4

1/2 cup heavy (whipping) cream

1/2 cup sour cream

2 tablespoons sugar

3 drops almond extract

1 pint fresh blackberries

4 Amaretti Sablés (page 273)

In a deep bowl, beat the cream until stiff peaks form. Fold in the sour cream, sugar, and almond extract until blended.

Reserve some of the berries for garnish. Divide the remaining berries among 4 stem glasses and top with the almond cream. Crumble 1 cookie over each serving and garnish with reserved berries.

Strawberry and Baileys Fool

Serves 6

Without a doubt, one of the prettiest fruit fools is made with strawberries. In this version, David Foley, head chef at the Hibernian Hotel (Eastmoreland Place, Dublin) uses Baileys Irish Cream. He also layers his fool, alternating the deep-colored pureed fruit with the paler whipped strawberry cream.

> 2 cups strawberries, hulled
> 2 cups heavy (whipping) cream
> 1/2 cup Baileys Irish Cream
> Confectioners' sugar for dusting

Refrigerate 6 stem glasses. Reserve 6 of the strawberries. In a blender or food processor, puree the remaining strawberries until smooth. In a large, deep bowl, beat the cream until stiff peaks form. Add half the strawberry puree and the Baileys and fold in until blended.

Divide 1/4 of the strawberry cream mixture among the glasses. Top with a layer of the fruit puree and continue to alternate layers of cream and fruit. Slice 1 strawberry over the top of each glass and dust with confectioners' sugar.

Rhubarb Tart

〰〰 Rhubarb grows easily in Ireland and has always been a staple of country gardens. Like gooseberries, rhubarb is a spring fruit that many look on as a harbinger of summer. In this tart, created by Warren Massey, chef-proprietor of Popjoy's (Terenure, County Dublin), puff pastry serves as the base, and the tartness of the fruit is balanced with a sweet whiskey cream sauce.

Serves 4

> 1 sheet frozen puff pastry, thawed
>
> 1 pound rhubarb, thinly sliced
>
> 4 tablespoons butter
>
> 1¼ cups superfine sugar
>
> 1 cup heavy (whipping) cream
>
> 1 teaspoon Irish whiskey

Preheat the oven to 350°F. On a lightly floured board, roll out the pastry. Using a 4-inch-diameter plate as a guide, cut the dough into 4 rounds. Using your fingers, pleat the pastry around the edges to form a small dish with a ¼-inch rim. Carefully arrange the sliced rhubarb in 2 concentric circles on top of each tart, making sure there are no gaps. Brush the tarts with melted butter and sprinkle with ¾ cup of the sugar. Bake until the rhubarb is tender and caramelized, 25 to 30 minutes.

Meanwhile, in a deep bowl, beat the cream with the remaining ½ cup sugar and whiskey until soft peaks form. To serve, place each tart on a warm plate and top with a dollop of whiskey cream.

Glazed Strawberry and Lemon Curd Tart

Serves 4

⟩⟩ This ultra-easy fruit tart takes less than half an hour to prepare, requires only a quick toasting of oatmeal, and uses prepared lemon curd for the creamy filling. Toasted oatmeal is combined with crushed biscuits for the crust, and other fresh fruits can be substituted for or added to the strawberries, if desired. To order real Irish ingredients, see Resources, page 277.

Lemon Curd

2 eggs

2 egg yolks

1/4 teaspoon salt

1/2 cup sugar

1/2 cup lemon juice

Zest of 1 lemon

6 tablespoons cold butter, cut into pieces

Beat eggs, yolks, salt, and sugar in a small saucepan until smooth and light colored. Add lemon juice, zest, and butter and cook over medium heat, stirring constantly, until butter melts, about 5 minutes. Reduce heat to medium-low and continue cooking until curd is thick enough to coat the back of a spoon, about 5 minutes. Curd should be thick like hollandaise sauce. Makes about 1 1/4 cups.

1 1/2 cups crushed digestive biscuits, such as Jacobs or Bolands brands, crushed

1/2 cup steel-cut oats, preferably McCann's brand, toasted (see page 229)

4 tablespoons unsalted butter, melted

1/2 cup sour cream

1/2 cup prepared lemon curd, such as Morley's, or homemade (recipe at left)

1/2 cup strawberry preserves, preferably Irish

2 cups fresh strawberries, hulled and sliced

Whipped Whiskey Cream (page 259)

Preheat the oven to 300°F. In a medium bowl, combine the biscuits, oats, and melted butter. Press into the bottom and halfway up the sides of a 9-inch springform pan. Refrigerate for 15 minutes.

In a small bowl, combine the sour cream and lemon curd. With a rubber spatula, spread the sour cream mixture over the oat layer all the way to the edges. Refrigerate for 15 minutes. Meanwhile, in a small saucepan over low heat, melt the preserves.

Overlap the strawberries in 2 concentric circles on top of the filling and spoon the melted preserves over the fruit. Refrigerate at least 1 hour. To serve, cut into 4 wedges. Serve a dollop of whiskey cream alongside each wedge.

Summary Pudding

≋ This deliciously simple dessert is popular both in England and Ireland. As its name indicates, summer berries are the main ingredient. After the fruit and bread have mingled overnight, the result is a colorful and unusual dessert that looks almost too pretty to eat.

Serves 4 to 6

> **6 cups mixed ripe berries, such as raspberries, strawberries, blackberries, or blueberries**
> **3/4 cup sugar**
> **24 slices white sandwich bread, crusts removed**
> **Whipped cream for serving**

In a large saucepan, combine the berries and sugar. Cook over medium heat until the berries begin to break down and the sugar is dissolved, about 5 minutes. Remove from the heat and let cool for 10 minutes.

Line a 4-cup soufflé dish, mixing bowl, or charlotte mold with plastic wrap. Cut 16 slices of bread in half to form two triangles each. Cut the remaining slices in half to form 2 rectangles each. Piece half of the triangles together in the bottom of the mold to cover it completely. Place the rectangles around the side of the mold, overlapping each one. Spoon the berries into the mold. Arrange the remaining bread triangles over the top and cover with plastic wrap. Set mold on a plate to catch any juices that spill out. Lay another plate on top and place a 2-pound weight or a can of food on it to ensure that the bread absorbs all the juices. Refrigerate overnight.

To unmold, remove the plastic wrap from the top. Invert the mold onto a clean serving plate. Remove plastic wrap from the rest of the pudding. Cut into wedges and serve with whipped cream.

Steamed Summer Fruit Sponge Puddings

Serves 4

⇔ These steamed puddings, which combine sponge cake with the bounty of summer fruits, were created by John Heggtveit, executive chef at Cork's sumptuous Hayfield Manor Hotel (Perrott Avenue, College Road). This innovative Norwegian-born chef uses a professional steamer to make his lighter-than-air fruit puddings, but the same effect can be achieved by cooking the puddings in a water bath covered with plastic wrap.

> 8 tablespoons (1 stick) butter at room temperature
>
> 1/2 cup sugar
>
> 2 eggs
>
> 1 cup all-purpose flour
>
> 1 1/2 teaspoons baking powder
>
> 1 tablespoon milk
>
> 1/2 to 3/4 cup mixed berries, such as strawberries, raspberries, or blueberries
>
> Whipped cream or vanilla ice cream for serving

Preheat the oven to 225°F. Butter four 6-ounce ramekins.

In a medium bowl, cream the butter and sugar together until light and fluffy. Beat in the eggs one at a time. Sift in the flour and baking powder and stir to blend. Stir in the milk to make a smooth batter.

Fill each ramekin half full with batter. Divide the fruit among the ramekins and cover with the remaining batter. Place the ramekins in a large baking pan and add hot water to come halfway up the sides of the ramekins. Cover the baking pan with plastic wrap and bake until the sponge is set and lightly browned, about 1 hour. Serve with a spoonful of whipped cream or ice cream.

Tipperary Fruit Compote

Serves 8

〰 A bowl of fresh fruit takes on an Irish air when it's laced with Irish Mist liqueur. Any fruit—from kiwi to melon and grapes to pineapple—can be used in this compote.

6 cups bite-sized pieces of fresh fruit
^{1}/3 cup Irish Mist liqueur
3 tablespoons fresh lemon juice

Misty Sauce

2 eggs, separated
^{1}/2 cup sugar
2 tablespoons Irish Mist liqueur

Arrange fruit in a clear glass bowl. Combine the Irish Mist and lemon juice and drizzle over the fruit. Stir gently to combine. Refrigerate for at least 1 hour and up to 4 hours.

To make the sauce: In a medium bowl, beat the egg whites until soft peaks form. Gradually beat in ^{1}/4 cup of the sugar and continue beating until stiff, glossy peaks form. In a small bowl, beat the egg yolks with the remaining ^{1}/4 cup sugar and the Irish Mist. Fold the egg yolk mixture into the egg white mixture. Cover and refrigerate for 1 hour. To serve, spoon the sauce over the fruit, or divide among stemmed glasses.

Irish Heritage Trifle

⇟⇟ Sometimes called "tipsy cake" or "tipsy parson," trifle is a delightful combination of liquor-soaked ladyfingers or cake and fruit. Here, the spirits are Ireland's newest liqueur, Celtic Crossing. Serve this in a deep glass bowl—preferably Irish crystal such as Waterford, Cavan, or Tipperary crystal—for a dramatic effect.

Custard Sauce

2 cups milk

3 eggs or 6 yolks, beaten

1/4 cup sugar

1/8 teaspoon salt

1 12-ounce homemade or bakery sponge cake or 18 ladyfingers, split

2/3 cup raspberry or strawberry preserves

3 cups fresh berries or a mixture of berries, sliced pears, and sliced peaches, plus more for garnish

1/2 cup Celtic Crossing liqueur or Irish whiskey

Whipped cream for serving

To make the sauce: In a medium saucepan over medium heat, warm the milk until bubbles form around the edges of the pan. Reduce the heat to low, stir in the eggs, sugar, and salt, and cook, stirring frequently, until thickened into a custard that coats the back of a spoon, 6 to 8 minutes. Remove from heat and let cool.

Cut the sponge cake into 1/2-inch-thick slices. Spread the cake or ladyfingers with the preserves. Place half in the bottom of a glass bowl. (If using ladyfingers, stand some upright around the sides of the bowl.) Add half the fruit, sprinkle with the spirits, and repeat with the remaining cake or ladyfingers and fruit. Cover with the custard sauce and refrigerate for at least 1 hour and up to 4 hours. To serve, spoon onto serving plates, top with whipped cream, and garnish with a berry or slice of fruit.

Pavlova

⋟⋞ The national dessert of New Zealand, Pavlova shows up frequently on Irish menus as well. Though elegant in appearance, it's surprisingly simple to make and can be filled with either fruit, as it is here, or chocolate cream.

Serves 10

- 1 teaspoon cornstarch
- 1/8 teaspoon salt
- 1 cup granulated sugar
- 4 egg whites
- 1 teaspoon distilled white vinegar
- 1 1/2 teaspoons vanilla extract
- 1 cup heavy (whipping) cream
- 2 cups sliced mixed fruit or mixed fruit and berries, plus more for garnish

Preheat the oven to 250°F. Line a baking sheet with a 12-inch square of parchment paper.

In a small bowl, combine the cornstarch, salt, and all but 2 tablespoons of the sugar; mix well. In a large bowl, beat the egg whites with the vinegar and 1 teaspoon of the vanilla until frothy. Gradually beat in the sugar mixture and continue beating until stiff, glossy peaks form.

Pile the meringue onto the prepared baking sheet and spread to form a 9-inch round, heaping up the edges a little to form a rim. Bake until the meringue is dry and firm, about 1 1/4 hours.

Turn the Pavlova carefully upside down on a wire rack. Let cool for 5 minutes, then gently peel off the paper.

In a deep bowl, beat the cream with the reserved 2 tablespoons sugar and the remaining $1/2$ teaspoon vanilla until stiff peaks form. Spoon the whipped cream into the center of the Pavlova and top with the sliced fruit and berries. To serve, slice and garnish with more fruit.

Strawberry and Peach Sablés

Serves 8

〰 The French word *sable* means "sand," giving an appropriate name to these delicate almond-flavored biscuits that are sandy in texture and color. Eamonn O'Reilly, chef-proprietor of One Pico (12 Upper Camden Street, Dublin), combines them with whipped cream and fruit for a delicious triple-decker fruit-filled dessert.

Amaretti Sablés

$1/2$ cup superfine sugar

I cup butter at room temperature

2 cups all-purpose flour

I egg

I tablespoon heavy (whipping) cream

12 amaretti cookies, crushed

2 cups heavy (whipping) cream

2 tablespoons superfine sugar

2 to 3 fresh peaches, peeled, pitted, and sliced

2 cups fresh strawberries, hulled and sliced, plus a few for garnish

Confectioners' sugar for dusting

4 mint sprigs for garnish

Preheat the oven to 350°F. Line a baking sheet with parchment paper. →

To make the sablés: In a large bowl, combine the sugar and butter and beat until well blended. Add the flour, egg, and cream and mix until the mixture resembles pastry dough. Add the crushed cookies and blend again. Shape the dough into a ball, cover with plastic wrap, and refrigerate for 1 hour.

On a lightly floured board, roll the pastry out to a 1/4-inch thickness. With a 2-inch biscuit cutter, cut the dough into 24 rounds. Place on the prepared pan and bake until lightly browned, 10 to 12 minutes. Transfer to a wire rack to cool.

In a large, deep bowl, beat the 2 cups of cream with the 2 tablespoons sugar until stiff peaks form.

To assemble, spread a cookie with a layer of whipped cream, then top with peach slices. Add a second cookie, spread it with whipped cream, and top with strawberry slices. Top with a third cookie. Dust with confectioners' sugar. Repeat with the remaining cookies and fruit. Garnish with a sprig of mint and a few strawberry slices.

Lemon Syllabub

Serves 6

⟳ Syllabub has been made since dairying was first practiced in Ireland. The original version was a drink made by milking a cow directly into a bowl containing some old milk, which caused the liquid to froth. By the eighteenth century, syllabub had evolved into a dessert made with a combination of wine, lemon juice, and cream, sometimes frothed with egg white. Serve this in Irish crystal for an elegant touch.

Grated zest of 1 lemon

3 tablespoons fresh lemon juice

1/2 cup sweet white wine such as Gewürztraminer or Riesling

1 1/4 cups heavy (whipping) cream

1/4 cup superfine sugar

Fresh berries for garnish

Amaretti Sablés (page 273) or Oatmeal Cookies (page 231) (optional)

In a small bowl, combine the lemon zest, juice, and wine. Cover and let stand at room temperature for at least 3 hours.

In a deep bowl, beat the cream with the sugar until stiff peaks form. Gently fold in the lemon mixture. Spoon into 6 stemmed glasses and refrigerate for at least 2 hours or up to 4 hours. Garnish with berries and serve with cookies, if you like.

Glossary

Ale: A fermented alcoholic beverage brewed from malt and hops. Two popular Irish brands are Harp's Lager, brewed by Guinness in Dundalk, County Louth, and widely available outside of Ireland, and Smithwick's, also brewed by Guinness at St. Francis Brewery, Kilkenny, which is not available for export.

Baileys Irish Cream: An alcoholic beverage made from double cream, Irish whiskey, neutral spirits, and natural flavors.

Bangers: Sausages traditionally made of pork and bread crumbs.

Black Pudding: A sausage made of pork blood, ground pork, oatmeal, onion, spices, and water, traditionally served as part of an Irish breakfast. See also White Pudding.

Bouquet Garni: A combination of herbs, usually fresh parsley, thyme, bay leaf, and chervil, tied together in a cheesecloth bag and used during cooking to flavor a dish.

Boxty: A traditional Irish potato pancake made with cooked mashed potatoes and grated raw potatoes.

Brack: A cake studded with dried fruits and raisins, traditionally eaten on All Hallows' Eve.

Celtic Crossing Liqueur: An alcoholic beverage made from fine aged malt whiskeys and cognac. It was created in 1996 to commemorate the 150-year anniversary of the Irish Famine, to honor those who emigrated to America, and to celebrate their achievements.

Champ: A mixture of mashed potatoes and scallions that is served with melted butter. Also called poundies.

Cider: A beverage pressed from apples, often fermented. Bulmers, Strongbow, and Linden Village are three popular alcoholic ciders available in Ireland in bottles and cans. There are several American brands that can be substituted in cooking.

Coddle: A pork and potato casserole.

Colcannon: A mashed-potato dish flavored with kale or cabbage, traditionally eaten on All Hallows' Eve.

Corned Beef: Beef cured in a seasoned brine. The word "corned" refers to the salt used in the brine.

Demi-glace: A meat glaze extract, created by boiling down a meat stock to a syrupy consistency; also called glace de viande.

Dulse: An edible red seaweed, mainly used in soups and condiments.

Fadge: A potato pancake traditional in Northern Ireland, served as part of an Irish breakfast called an Ulster "fry."

Fool: A simple dessert made of pureed fruit and whipped cream.

Irish Bacon: Meat cut from the loin of a pig, which is then cured (salted) rather than smoked. Irish bacon can be a thick slab or loin (boiling bacon), a joint, or sliced into "rashers," which are served as part of an Irish breakfast.

Irish Mist: An alcoholic beverage made from distilled spirits, honey, and herbs.

Mâche: A leafy salad green with a tangy, nutlike flavor. Also called corn salad, field salad, or lamb's lettuce.

Mead: An alcoholic beverage made from white wine, honey, and herbs. Originally mead was the drink of the ancient Gauls and Anglo-Saxons and made from fermented honey and water.

Pinhead oats and oatlets: Pinhead (steel-cut) oats are whole grain groats (the inner portion of the oat kernel) that have been cut into two or three pieces. Minimal processing helps pinhead oats retain their distinctive taste and nutritional value. They are golden in color and resemble rice particles. Oatlets are rolled, flaked oats that have been steamed, rolled, re-steamed, and toasted.

Poitín: An alcoholic beverage distilled from barley, sugar, and water. Originally made in pot stills over a peat fire, it was banned in Ireland in 1661 and only recently legalized.

Porter: A dark brown, strong-flavored beer made from roasted barley, hops, yeast, and water.

Rabbit: A dish featuring cheese melted with wine, ale, or milk.

Rashers: Thin slices of bacon. Traditionally served as part of an Irish breakfast.

Stout: A strong, dark beer made with hops and dark-roasted barley. Guinness and Murphy's are the most popular Irish brands.

Whiskey: Irish whiskey undergoes a triple distillation process and a three-year maturing period that make its taste different from that of Scotch whisky. The oldest Irish whiskey brands are those of the Irish Distillers Group: Jameson, Bushmills, Paddy, and Powers. The newest brands are Locke's, Tyrconnell, and Kilbeggan, from the re-opened Cooley/John Locke's Distillery, Kilbeggan, County Westmeath. Most brands are widely available.

White Pudding: A sausage made with ground pork, oatmeal, onion, spices, and water, traditionally served as part of an Irish breakfast. See also Black Pudding.

Resources

Use this guide to find food and beverages from Ireland and hard-to-find ingredients called for in some recipes.

To find a shop in your area that carries Irish products, contact the Irish Trade Board, 345 Park Avenue, New York, NY 10154; phone 212-371-3600, fax 212-371-6398; or the Irish Food Board, 12 West 37th Street, 4th Floor, New York, NY 10018; phone 212-268-5617, fax 212-268-8450.

Cheese

To find out where you can buy Kerrygold Irish Swiss, Blarney, Oak Smoked Blarney, and Vintage Cheddar Cheeses in your area, contact The Irish Dairy Board, 825 Green Bay Road, Suite 200, Wilmette, IL 60091; phone 847-256-8289, fax 847-256-8299.

To find out where you can buy Tipperary Irish Cheddar in your area, or to order it by mail, contact Dairygold U.S.A. Inc., 140E Commerce Way, Totowa, NJ 07512; phone 800-386-7577 or 973-890-5155, fax 973-890-5156.

To find out where you can buy Irish farmhouse cheeses in your area, contact Crystal Food Import Corporation, P.O. Box 460, 245 Summer Street, East Boston, MA 02128; phone 800-225-3574 or 617-569-7500, fax 617-561-0397.

Cookies, Biscuits, and Crackers

To find out where you can buy Bolands, Jacobs, Braycot, or Bewleys cookies, crackers, and shortbreads in your area, or where to order them by mail, contact Bewley Irish Imports, 1130 Greenhill Road, West Chester, PA 19380; phone 610-696-2682, fax 610-344-7618; Irish Food Distributors, 500 Saw Mill River Road, Yonkers, NY 10701; phone 914-376-3322, fax 914-376-3396; DPI Skandia Foods Corporation, 615 East Brook Drive, Arlington Heights, IL 60005; phone 708-364-9704, fax 708-364-9702; or Ireland's Own, 48–14 54th Avenue, Maspeth, NY 11378; phone 718-472-1915, fax 718-472-1204.

Condiments

Honey

To find out where you can buy Mileeven's Honey products in your area, or to order them by mail, contact DPI Skandia Foods Corporation, 615 East Brook Drive, Arlington Heights, IL 60005; phone 708-364-9704, fax 708-364-9702; or Ireland's Own, 48–14 54th Avenue, Maspeth, NY 11378; phone 718-472-1915, fax 718-472-1204.

Jam, Jelly, Marmalade, Preserves, Lemon Curd, and Chutney

To find out where you can buy Alexander's Irish Liquor Preserves and Marmalades in your area, or to order them by mail, contact

Bewley Irish Imports, 1130 Greenhill Road, West Chester, PA 19380; phone 610-696-2682, fax 610-344-7618; or DPI Skandia Foods Corporation, 615 East Brook Drive, Arlington Heights, IL 60005; phone 708-364-9704, fax 708-364-9702.

To find out where you can buy Chivers Jams, Marmalades, and Fruitfield Marmalades, or to order them by mail, contact Irish Food Distributors, 500 Saw Mill River Road, Yonkers, NY 10701; phone 914-376-3322, fax 914-376-3396; DPI Skandia Foods Corporation, 615 East Brook Drive, Arlington Heights, IL 60005; phone 708-364-9704, fax 708-364-9702; or Ireland's Own, 48–14 54th Avenue, Maspeth, NY 11378; phone 718-472-1915, fax 718-472-1204.

To find out where you can buy Harrison's Jams, or to order them by mail, contact DPI Skandia Foods Corporation, 615 East Brook Drive, Arlington Heights, IL 60005; phone 708-364-9704, fax 708-364-9702.

To find out where you can buy The Real Irish Food Company Preserves and Chutneys in your area, or to order them by mail, contact Irish Food Distributors, 500 Saw Mill River Road, Yonkers, NY 10701; phone 914-376-3322, fax 914-376-3396.

To find out where you can buy Shamrock Preserves and Marmalades and Morley's Lemon Curd in your area, or to order them by mail, contact Shamrock Foods, 35 Somerset Avenue, Winthrop, MA 02152; phone 617-846-3012, fax 617-846-4616.

Mustard

To find out where you can buy Lakeshore Wholegrain Mustard in your area, or to order it by mail, contact Bewley Irish Imports, 1130 Greenhill Road, West Chester, PA 19380; phone 610-696-2682, fax 610-344-7618; DPI Skandia Foods Corporation, 615 East Brook Drive, Arlington Heights, IL 60005; phone 708-364-9704, fax 708-364-9702.

Demi-glace

Demi-glace can be ordered through Williams-Sonoma, P. O. Box 7456, San Francisco, CA 94120-7456; phone 800-541-2233, fax 415-421-5153.

Fowl

Duck

To find out where you can buy duck or duck parts in your area, or to order whole ducklings, whole boneless ducklings, boned or partially boned duckling breasts by mail, contact Culver Duck Farms, Inc. 12215 C.R. 10, P.O. Box 910, Middlebury, IN 46540; phone 800-825-9225 or 219-825-9537, fax 219-825-2613.

Goose, Guinea Fowl, Pheasant, and Quail

To order fresh farm-raised goose, guinea fowl, pheasant, and quail by mail, contact D'Artagnan, 399–419 Saint Paul Avenue, Jersey City, NJ 07306; phone 800-DARTAGN or 973-792-0748; fax 973-792-6113.

Meat

Lamb

To order farm-raised, free-range lamb legs, chops, racks, shanks, stew meat, or custom-cut parts, contact Jamison Farm, 171 Jamison Land, Latrobe, PA 15650; phone 800-237-5262; fax 724-837-2287.

Pork

To find out where you can buy Irish pork products, including bacon, ham, sausages, and black and white pudding in your area, or to order them by mail, contact Dairygold U.S.A. Inc., 140E Commerce Way, Totowa, NJ 07512; phone 800-386-7577 or 973-890-5155; fax 973-890-5156.

Rabbit

To order fresh farm-raised rabbit by mail, contact D'Artagnan, 399–419 Saint Paul Avenue, Jersey City, NJ 07306; phone 800-DARTAGN or 973-792-0748; fax 973-792-6113.

Venison

For Cervena farm-raised venison from New Zealand, contact D'Artagnan, 399–419 Saint Paul Avenue, Jersey City, NJ 07306; phone 800-DARTAGN or 201-792-0748; fax 201-792-6113. D'Artagnan also sells Scottish wild venison, hunted on estates and processed by facilities supervised by the European Economic Community Inspectors (like the USDA).

For New York state farm-raised venison, contact Millbrook Venison Products, RR2, Box 133, Verbank Road, Millbrook, NY 12545; phone 800-774-DEER or 917-677-8457.

For Texas farm-raised fallow and axis venison, contact Broken Arrow Ranch, 104 Junction Highway, Ingram, TX 78025; phone 800-962-4263.

Wild Boar Sausage

To order wild boar sausages by mail, contact D'Artagnan, 399-419 Saint Paul Avenue, Jersey City, NJ 07306; phone 800-DARTAGN or 973-792-0748; fax 973-792-6113.

Mushrooms

Wild and exotic mushrooms, including crimini, shiitake, oyster, portabella, and enoki, can be ordered by mail from Phillips Exotic Mushrooms and Accessories, 909 East Baltimore Pike, Kennett Square, PA 19348; phone 800-AH-FUNGI or 610-388-6082; fax 610-388-3985.

Oatmeal

To find out where you can buy McCann's Irish Oatmeal in your area, contact Paul Germann & Associates Inc., 39 Winding Trail, Mahwah, NJ 07430; phone 201-934-6953; fax 201-934-0486.

Lifeforce Stoneground Wholemeal Flour, Porridge Oatlets, and Pinhead Oats are available at the Lifeforce Mill, The Mill Rock, Cavan Town, County Cavan, Ireland; phone 011-353-49-62722; fax 011-353-49-62923.

Salmon, Smoked

To order authentic oak-smoked wild Irish salmon by mail, contact Specialty Foods of Ireland, 494 Saw Mill River Road, Yonkers, NY 10701; phone 888-894-7474.

Spirits

Mead

To find out where you can buy authentic Irish mead (bottled as Bunratty Meade) in your area, contact Camelot Importing Co., Inc. P.O. Box 146, 3130 Bordertown Road, Old Bridge, NJ 08857; phone 800-4-CAMELOT or 908-727-3020; fax 908-727-0201.

Poitín

To find out where you can buy authentic Irish poitín bottled by the Bunratty Winery, call Camelot Importing Co., Inc., P.O. Box 146, 3130 Bordertown Road, Old Bridge, NJ 08857; phone 800-4-CAMELOT or 908-727-3020; fax 908-727-0201.

Resources for Sites

Use this guide as a reference for places in Ireland mentioned in the text.

Bunratty Folk Park

For information on Bunratty Folk Park, contact the Irish Tourist Board, 345 Park Avenue, New York, NY 10154; phone 800-223-6470 or 212-418-0800.

Castle Banquets

For information on the medieval castle banquets at Bunratty, Knappogue, and Dunguaire, contact the Irish Tourist Board, 345 Park Avenue, New York, NY 10154; phone 800-223-6470 or 212-418-0800; or CIE Tours International, 100 Hanover Avenue, P.O. Box 501, Cedar Knolls, NJ 07927; phone 800-248-6832.

Cobh, "The Queenstown Story"

For information on "The Queenstown Story" at the Emigration Museum and Heritage Center at Cobh, contact the Irish Tourist Board, 345 Park Avenue, New York, NY 10154; phone 800-223-6470 or 212-418-0800.

Strokestown Park

For information on the Famine Museum at Strokestown Park, contact the Irish Tourist Board, 345 Park Avenue, New York, NY 10154; phone 800-223-6470 or 212-418-0800.

Taste of Ulster

For information on A Taste of Ulster food initiative, contact the Northern Ireland Tourist Board, 551 Fifth Avenue, Suite 701, New York, NY; phone 800-NITB-1994, fax 212-922-0099; or the Northern Ireland Tourist Board, St. Anne's Court, 59 North Street, Belfast BT1 1NB, phone 011-44-1232-231221.

Ulster American Folk Park

For information on the Ulster American Folk Park, contact the Northern Ireland Tourist Board, 551 Fifth Avenue, Suite 701, New York, NY; phone 800-NITB-1994, fax 212-922-0099.

Index

Credits

Theodora FitzGibbon quote, page 1, used with permission of David Higham Associates.

Lyrics from the song "Solid Ground" by Dougie MacLean, page 5, used with permission of Dunkeid Records. The lyrics were inspired by Chief Seattle's speech and letter to President Washington.

Carrot Soup, page 30, and cheese making quote, page 71, reprinted with permission of *Bon Appétit*. *Bon Appétit* is a registered trademark of Advance Magazine Publishers Inc., published through its division The Condé Nast Publications Inc. Copyright © 1997 by The Condé Nast Publications Inc. Reprinted with permission.

Recipes for Honey-Glazed Bacon with Apple-Whiskey Sauce, page 42; Glazed Bacon with Red Currant Sauce, page 45; Spiced Pork Roast with Apple-Thyme Cream Sauce, page 50; Black Pudding and Bacon Salad, page 55; Roast Breast of Chicken with Cabbage and Bacon, page 58; Fillet of Baby Beef Stuffed with Spinach and Ham, page 67; Knaves of Beef Stuffed with Wild Mushrooms, page 68; Irish Farmhouse Cheese Parcels with Root Vegetable Salad, page 80; Cheddar, Bacon, and Oatmeal Soufflé, page 92; Pasta Baked with Cheese and Stout, page 95; "Grilled" Lamb Chops and Tomatoes with a Garlic Crust, page 114; Rack of Lamb, page 126; Roasted Salmon Wrapped in Bacon, page 140; Smoked Salmon on Oatmeal Pancakes with Cucumber-Dill Sauce, page 144; Gratin of Oysters on Creamed Leeks with Guinness Hollandaise, page 161; Smoked Haddock and Potato Soup, page 170, Mussel Soup with Oatmeal-Herb Crust, page 171; Breast of Duck with Cider and Poitín Sauce, page 191, Venison Goulash, page 202; McCann's Steel-Cut Oat Scones, page 228; Oatmeal Cookies, page 231; Irish Oatmeal Cake with Nut Topping, page 236; Barmbrack, page 238; Upside-Down Apple and Soda Bread Tart, page 253; Oatmeal-Apple Crumble with Whiskey Cream Sauce, page 254; Armagh Apples with Cooley Mountain Sauce, page 257; Rhubarb Tart, page 266; and Glazed Strawberry and Lemon Curd Tart, page 267, were used with permission of the Irish Food Board (Bord Bia).

"It All Began with Brisket," page 89, used with permission of Veronica Steele.

Cheddar Colcannon Torte, page 94, and Baked Cheddar and Scallion Soup, page 100, used with permission of B.B.C. Enterprise and *Gourmet Ireland*.

Theodora FitzGibbon quote, page 213, used with permission of Gill & Macmillan.

Table of Equivalents

The exact equivalents in the following tables have been rounded for convenience.

U.S.	Metric
1/4 teaspoon	1.25 milliliters
1/2 teaspoon	2.5 milliliters
1 teaspoon	5 milliliters
1 tablespoon (3 teaspoons)	15 milliliters
1 fluid ounce (2 tablespoons)	30 milliliters
1/4 cup	60 milliliters
1/3 cup	80 milliliters
1 cup	240 milliliters
1 pint (2 cups)	480 milliliters
1 quart (4 cups, 32 ounces)	960 milliliters
1 gallon (4 quarts)	3.84 liters
1 ounce (by weight)	28 grams
1 pound	454 grams
2.2 pounds	1 kilogram

U.S.	Metric
1/8 inch	3 millimeters
1/4 inch	6 millimeters
1/2 inch	12 millimeters
1 inch	2.5 centimeters

Fahrenheit	Celsius	Gas
250	120	1/2
275	140	1
300	150	2
325	160	3
350	180	4
375	190	5
400	200	6
425	220	7
450	230	8
475	240	9
500	260	10